Sex and Politicians
Affairs
Of State
By
Kerry Segrave

Branden Publishing Company
Boston

Library of Congress Cataloging-in-Publication Data

Segrave, Kerry, 1944-
  Sex and politicians : affairs of state / by Kerry Segrave.
    p. cm.
  Includes bibliographical references and index.
  ISBN 0-8283-1938-3 : $17.95
  1. Heads of state--Sexual behavior--Case studies.
  2. Statesmen--Sexual behavior--Case studies.
  3. Politicians--Sexual behavior--Case studies.
  4. Biography--20th century. I. Title.
D412.6.S42 1990
909.82'092--dc20
[B]   90-36039

Branden Publishing Company
17 Station Street
Box 843 Brookline Village
Boston, MA

CONTENTS

SEX AND POLITICIANS

The man who has ruled Zaire since 1965 is Joseph Mobutu. At least that's what he was named at birth. Unhappy with this remnant of colonialism he changed it to Mobutu Sese Seko Koko Ngbendu Wa Za Banga. The last part of his name means "the cock who jumps on anything that moves" - which could apply to a lot of the of men profiled in this book.(1)

Mobutu is not in this book although judging by his name he probably should be. However, there seems to be no material readily available on the sexual aspects of his life. Which is true for a lot of modern day leaders. Men such as Egypt's Gamel Nasser, who was rumored to have been a womanizer, or various Japanese leaders who have been subject to the same rumors. All too many biographers don't bother to unearth such material or, if they do, don't include it in their books, perhaps considering it unimportant.

It's a premise of this book that such behavior - womanizing - is important, that it throws a light on character as few other traits can. It is a premise of this book that men who carry womanizing to a neurotic and pathological extent, particularly such as those in the first two sections, *Lady Killers* and *Goats* are not fit for high office nor for any elected office for that matter and should be shunned by voters. It is no accident that the most extreme womanizers such as Adolf Hitler, Idi Amin, JFK, Raphael Trujillo, to name a few have been among the worst and most destructive leaders in modern times. This book is limited to men who have headed a country sometime from 1945 onward, plus a dozen men who were not leaders but major political players in the USA, Canada, or the UK, over the same period. Material on some is brief and sketchy. It is NOT a premise of this book that men who are monogamous, faithful to their wives, are good leaders because of that. If you know that a man is faithful you have no indicator, based solely on that fact by which to judge leadership ability. He may or may not be a good leader. If you know a man is a compulsive womanizer then you know everything that you need to know. He will be a destructive and inadequate leader. Compulsive womanizing is but an outward manifestation of a constellation of negative traits. Womanizing is not the same as adultery although some writers, when sexual fidelity is mentioned, like to lump together such men as FDR and JFK. They are totally different. FDR was, strictly speaking, an adulterer, while JFK was a compulsive womanizer - too defective to have been a leader.

For many decades there was an unspoken "gentlemen's agreement" that things such as marital infidelity and alcohol abuse were not mentioned by the media. Said Raymond Strother, consultant to Gary Hart, "There used to be a gentlemen's agreement about reporting such things. But it isn't just gentlemen reporting anymore. Women writers are forcing higher standards of conduct from candidates. They're more critical of personal things." There is some truth to that.(2)

Womanizing by men such as JFK, RFK, and LBJ did not become general public knowledge until after they were dead. FDR's affair took about thirty years to surface after his death. In all cases the behavior was well known to large numbers of members of the media who routinely covered these people. Yet the code of silence held. The rationale seemed to be of the "boys will be boys" variety and that a man's private life was indeed private. Deeper, and more cogent reasons were that the media members were overwhelmingly male, from reporters to editors to publishers. Many in the media probably womanized and drank as much as the politicians did. And there was no tattling. Also, many in the media likely held women in the same contempt as did the politicians. It was only female objectifying-- a non-issue. Why report it.

Strother seems to feel that things have changed, at least in North America. Maybe they have, time will tell if it's a permanent shift. Hart was shot down over it, rightly so. And early in 1989 John Tower was denied a cabinet post in the Bush administration for his womanizing, and much other questionable behavior. Other reasons might be a more aggressive brand of journalism in general fostered by the Vietnam War and Watergate, a more cynical and demanding populace disappointed in leaders after those same events.

Sometimes the behavior of the womanizer has been so gross that it had to be reported or someone involved - other than the politician - went public and forced it on the media. Either way the event became a headline story. Some examples are: Ted Kennedy and Chappaquiddick, Wilbur Mills and a car load of fighting drunks in the middle of the night, or Wayne Hays's friend saying she was paid for something other than work. In all cases the media code of silence was broken. The media has dealt with this with a tremendous outpouring of an "it doesn't matter" sentiment when the womanizer has been exposed. *The Times* (London) editorialized that "History suggests that (personal conduct) is also not relevant: a person's capacity to hold high office cannot be measured by his distance from the angels."(3) Anthony Lewis writing an op-ed piece in *The New York Times* said, "Judging by history, the correlation between Puritan sexual behavior and wise political leadership is zero. Lloyd George, Franklin Roosevelt and John F. Kennedy all made great contributions to democracy to name just a few... who might never have held high office if put to the test of blue-nosed moralism.(4) Jonathan Alter wrote, in *Newsweek*, "sexual morality has had little bearing on whether men turn out to be good presidents.(5)" The same sentiment has come from a somewhat unexpected source-- a woman. Geraldine Ferraro, the 1984 Democratic vice-presidential candidate said, "Private morality... is not a determining factor in whether a person can properly carry on the business of our country... I don't equate allegations of sexual promiscuity with lack of integrity."(6) Since womanizing doesn't matter, since it has no effect, why does the media go out of its way to suppress it and not report it?

The other major defense for not reporting womanizing revolves around the issue of privacy. A man's private life must remain sacred. The *New Republic* wondered: "Aren't politicians entitled to some privacy? Aren't some matters - sexual habits - ... irrelevant to their official duties? Isn't there a danger ... of trivializing the political discourse, of driving interesting people from public life and leaving us to be ruled by antiseptic nerds?"(7) Fred Hechinger went even farther writing that, "The current moralistic melange of politics and sexual spying has unhappy overtones of similar abuse by totalitarianism plotters. From the Nazis' purges to Moscow's bugged bedrooms, that mixture has been bad news for personal liberties."(8)

Another writer, feeling the media went too far in reporting on Gary Hart felt the press had not found the right balance in handling the candidates' private lives. In other words, a call to pull back. However, *The New York Times* editorialized, also in the wake of the Hart affair, that the public needed to know as much as possible about the candidate "beyond the proper, debatable bounds of privacy." They noted that voters elect a person and while the person's policies can change, his character won't. Feminist writer Suzannah Lessard has gone the farthest in advocating that privacy should he sacrificed in the case of presidential candidates because of the nature of the presidency. The office has enormous significance and she argues, a presidential candidate is asking the voters for a much greater mandate because of the personal power accruing to that office and the ways he can use it.(9)

Yet Lessard backs off by agreeing with the privacy principle and wanting it excepted for only presidential candidates. A pathological womanizer is not acceptable as a president nor should he be a Senator, or Congressman, or in any other office. Anyone seeking public office of any type should be liable to full public scrutiny. Everything of interest in the person's background should be aired. Those who want to grab the perks of elected public office must be prepared to sacrifice. Those who want a truly private life can stay in the private sector. Reporters feel the press is doing its job and screwing around should only be reported if it affects the man's public work. However, by pretending that no amount of contempt for women would ever affect public work these newsmen have created their own Catch-22.

When the public has been asked for its opinion on the subject the answers have often been contradictory. Given that the subject is sex and politicians that is not surprising. In a poll taken about four weeks after the Hart scandal first broke 51 percent of those polled believed the press should report on the extramarital affairs of presidential candidates. Seventy-one percent of respondents felt their president should be held to a higher standard of morality than other Americans as he was a moral symbol for the nation. Yet 47 percent of those people felt marital infidelity had nothing to do with a person's qualifications for President. One third regarded adultery as unpardonable and disqualified a person for the job. Fifty-two percent of respondents said they would prefer a "morally straight - like a Sunday school teacher - person" but 52 percent preferred a president who "has a charismatic, exciting personality and fools around a little bit in his sexual life" to one who is "completely faithful to his wife but has a rather dull personality." This is an example of a forced poll in which respondents are given a choice of a faithful but dull person to a charismatic womanizer. Why not a choice between a charismatic faithful person and a dull womanizer?

Asked whether a candidate with loose personal morals is more likely to carry that behavior into public office 52 percent replied they thought he would. A candidate with a single publicized fling in his past would lose 23 percent of the voters while a candidate rumored to have occasional sexual flings would lose 38 percent of the voters. Another poll asked its respondents if a candidate's sex life was relevant to his suitability for public office. Sixty-three percent said no and 37 percent said yes. Yet when these same people were asked if their decision to support a presidential candidate would be influenced by reports of sexual misconduct 55 percent said yes while 45 percent said no. A poll in Canada found one in three respondents said a politician's private life was a concern at the ballot box.(10)

Almost twenty years after Chappaquiddick, 15 percent of respondents in a poll felt Ted Kennedy shouldn't have been in the car with Mary Jo; 33 percent criticized him for delaying in reporting the accident and 46 percent were negative because he lied about his role in the affair. When people were asked to rate nine presidents - from FDR to Reagan - on how well they did on the job they were rated an follows; FDR, JFK, Truman, Ike, Reagan, Ford, Carter, LBJ, Nixon. When they were ranked morally it was: Truman, Carter, FDR, Ford, Reagan, Ike, LBJ, Nixon, JFK. Men thought Truman was the best President since FDR while women opted for JFK.

Surprisingly or not, womanizing, or one-time adultery is not practiced by the majority of the general population. A Kinsey survey in the late 1940s and early 1950s found, for married people, that 50 percent of males and 26 percent of females had affairs. A survey done by *Playboy* in 1982 reported figures of 48 percent for men and 38 percent for women. Other studies have indicated that "an overwhelming majority of Americans consider adultery to he wrong." And from these surveys, less than half engage in it.(11)

Does womanizing make a difference? Ask Gary Hart, John Profumo, Ted Kennedy, Andreas Papandreou, Juan Peron, Nelson Rockefeller, to name a few. Hart and Kennedy both lost shots at the presidency; Profumo was ousted from politics permanently; Papandreou lost an election and fell from power; Peron was helped out of office because of it; Rockefeller lost his chance for a shot at the presidency and it literally killed him. The idea that there is no such thing as bad publicity is also wrong, ask these same men. There may be no such thing as bad publicity in some areas of show business - but not in politics. Politicians are well aware that womanizing may very well do them no good with the voters, or citizens at large for any flaunting is normally done only before the inner circle. Even men with absolute dictatorial power such as Hitler and Mussolini went to great pains to keep their activities from the masses. Some, like Nkrumah and Hitler have gone so far as to try and create a public image of themselves as virtual celibates. Compulsive womanizing can have an effect in the sense that the leader spends all his time screwing and has that much less time to devote to legitimate affairs of state. Many of these men, like Bokassa and Trujillo, drain the treasury by having full time staff whose sole job is to supply women - to procure. Even JFK had aides who devoted some of their time to procuring.

And there are even more concrete effects. J. Edgar Hoover had tapes of JFK screwing a suspected German spy and Kennedy found his position compromised, as one writer noted, because "in wanting to keep a lid on his past Kennedy was willing to betray one of his key constituents - the blacks - a group who helped put him in the White House, and, in addition, inevitably also hampered his brother's forthcoming campaign against organized crime." Hoover saw to it that JFK and RFK didn't get too close to Martin Luther King. Hoover had a powerful hold on them - because of womanizing. As Attorney General RFK had to devote some of his time to damage control for

9--Sex and Politicians

his brother, and covering up his own dirt, time which could have been better spent if they weren't such arrogant womanizers.(12)

Some observers have tried to explain womanizing as being virtually genetic. Biologist Edward O. Wilson says the masculine role is that of being "aggressive, dominant and promiscuous." Psychologists have argued the main reason politicians become womanizers is that many are men of great drive and ambition which is "frequently associated with a high sex drive."(13) Yet obviously men are not all promiscuous. Half the male population, at least in North America, do not seem to engage in one-time adultery, let alone promiscuity. Among politicians many are monogamous and faithful. Of recent US presidents Truman, Nixon, Ford, Carter and Reagan are faithful, by all accounts. Ike and FDR each had one brief affair, while JFK and LBJ were womanizers. Even the so-called macho countries of the Mediterranean area don't produce all promiscuous men. Franco of Spain and Salazar of Portugal weren't. The French are great lovers but De Gaulle was faithful, it seems. Any man who becomes head of his country, or a high ranking political figure is, by definition, ambitious and possessed of drive. Yet they don't all womanize. Obviously it is just as often connected with low sex drive, measured in number of sex partners.

Womanizing is an individual trait found in some men and not in others. It is associated with misogyny, male chauvinism and with an exploitative view of women. It is a consistent and destructive characteristic. Almost invariably it is a trait which is established from early on. A man does not obtain power and then become a womanizer. Rather, the womanizer who obtains power simply has the opportunity to indulge it more frequently, and does. It is a sign of an unhealthy narcissism and the blatant womanizing by a politician is often evidence of a grandiose sense that the normal rules don't apply to them. Gary Hart is an example of that. By challenging journalists to catch him in the act he was displaying an arrogance that they wouldn't or couldn't and even if they did it would not matter for he was "above" it. He was also engaging in the childish and immature activity of wanting to display the "scalps" he had taken, to show everybody what a "real" man he was.

10--Affairs of State

So institutionalized has womanizing become that rarely does one find a sense of shame attached to it. Yet the Don Juan type is a man who uses women to gives himself a sense of power. He is incapable of making a commitment or forging a deep relationship with a woman. As psychologists have noted "Such a man holds women in contempt." Such behavior is immature and exploitative - not the traits one wants to find in a leader. Calling sexual behavior private is to ignore a major sign of a man's character. If a candidate was a member of a private club that excluded blacks or Jews that information would, and should be subject to public scrutiny. So ingrained is womanizing in our culture that it isn't considered to be a serious issue like bigotry against blacks or Jews. In some cultures womanizing has even been legalized - polygamy. The attitude that a man has for women privately can't he isolated from his attitude toward women in public life. With womanizing males in power there is no chance for any kind of equality between the sexes being achieved.(14)

Suzannah Lessard's article on Ted Kennedy illustrates many of the difficulties in discussing the topic of womanizing, the resistance to it and how ingrained the topic is, and how male biased it is. The *New Republic* commissioned the feminist writer to do the article and then refused to print it. The *Washington Post* was then offered the article but refused it because "its serious political arguments were based on assumptions that violate the convention"-- whatever that means. However, the *Post* did print bits of the article in its gossip column regarding the fuss over it at the *New Republic*. The article was published in the end by the *Washington Monthly*.(15)

The article itself was mild indeed. It's strongest position was simply that voters might want to think about a candidate's womanizing before voting. That it was not beneath a voter's dignity to take such a matter into account. With regard to the womanizing candidate Lessard weakly and timidly concluded about this trait that "It is not a reason to reject him out-of-hand. He may have enough to offer that one decides that it is worth the risk." As mild as this article was, it still had trouble getting published.(16)

A man who habitually and cynically uses women and discards them at his pleasure is not a man who represents the interest of any woman, or man. He will not be sensitive to, nor serious about issues raised

11--Sex and Politicians

by the women's movement. If he is willing to lie and cheat to his spouse, whom he presumably cares about, then what will he do to the average voter whom he doesn't know at all. If he is willing to humiliate, and or discard an older wife who perhaps helped him get where he is, for a much younger woman how will he treat other members of society? How will he respond to older women, or older people, or those with little power in society in general?

Philosopher Georges Bataille has said, regarding sexual intercourse "a taste for constant change is certainly neurotic." Years ago Abraham Maslow wrote that the sexual act is, or can he, "a dominance act... hasty copulations are most often best viewed as... dominance affairs." He added that an emotional need satisfied by extramarital affairs was "the desire to conquer, to collect scalps." Alfred Kinsey noted that "the closest parallel to the picture of sexual response is found in the known physiology of anger." There is a surprising degree of consensus that hostility and domination, as opposed to intimacy and physical pleasure, are central to sexual excitement. Robert Stoller wrote that "it is hostility - the desire, overt or hidden, to harm another person - that generates and enhances sexual excitement."(17)

Author Charles Stember adds that humiliating the sexual object is, for men, a vital part of the sex act, not an extra. Psychoanalytic theory argues that a certain amount of sadism is considered an essential element of male sexuality. Kate Millett used a phrase, describing something slightly different, that is appropriate for the womanizing politician as well - "hunter-fighter-fucker."(18)

This hostility is all too evident in the womanizing politician. It is no accident that the most gross womanizers in this book have also been the most evil, most destructive, and the most inept leaders. Those who fuck a lot fight a lot - they do little else. The faithful man may be just as bad but he may not be. The worst womanizers in the White House were JFK and LBJ. They are the worst not just in the modern era but the worst since day one. What it had taken the US almost two hundred years to build up was largely and swiftly dismantled by this pair in just eight short years.

The US that Nixon almost took over in January, 1961 was a far cry from the US he did inherit in January, 1969. It was JFK who was largely responsible for the beginnings of the Vietnam War - he sent soldiers and not "advisers." It was JFK who authorized the use of chemical warfare in that country - the first country to use such weapons since World War I. It was JFK who planned assassination attempts on Castro. It was JFK, who tried to stop Martin Luther King's march on Washington. It was JFK who did nothing for blacks and women, and so on. It was LBJ who dramatically escalated the war, unleashed massive bombings, whose "Great Society" was also limited to white men. And so on. These two laid the basis for massive inflation whose effects continue to be felt today. It was JFK and LBJ who knocked the US out of the position of undenied economic supremacy and moved it far down the list. It was these two who also undermined the social fabric of the nation through black riots, war protest riots, feminist protests, draft evading and so on. Nixon took over a country that had been run into a shambles, economically, morally, spiritually and culturally, or set well on the way towards it. Is it a coincidence or a result of their womanizing mentality? Leading the nation at the height of US power they symbolized what was wrong. Women wanted a fair hearing and adjustments to their grievances but they wouldn't get it from a pair of neurotic womanizers who loathed them all. A friend of JFK once said that he, JFK, "liked women." He didn't. He liked to fuck women but that's not the same thing. Nor would this pair be expected to listen to blacks. JFK sold them out because the FBI's Hoover had him compromised over sex tapes. As a super rich kid, JFK had no feel for, nor interest in, blacks and poverty. LBJ was just a vulgar low-life white trash from Texas. Minorities could forget him. But he mocked them with his "Great Society" gibberish and they took to the streets. However, both were very good at fucking - super cocksmen. And those that fuck a lot fight a lot. And so we got a nightmare - Vietnam.

Actress Shirley Maclaine once said, in defense of the Kennedy's womanizing, "I would rather have a President who does it to a woman than a President who does it to a country."(19) Unfortunately such men do it to both. Politicians are a corrupt enough lot at the best of times. We don't need the added corruption of a womanizer. There's a famous saying that "power corrupts and absolute power corrupts absolutely." It seems to have passed into the realm of truth. Perhaps because it is a nice little sexist adage which takes the blame or responsibility from the individual and places it on the thing - power. The saying is backwards. It should be: corrupt men corrupt power and absolutely corrupt men corrupt power absolutely.

The role of the women involved is harder to discern. There is no shortage of females ready and willing to be used by the womanizing politicians. Back when Robert Redford was the hottest screen heartthrob a survey claimed that "most women would rather go to bed with the President of the United States, whoever he might be, than with Robert Redford." The women attracted to such men of power appear to be legion in our society and, as Stember noted, "it seems to be a specifically female tendency to convert this to sexual interest." Psycho-analytic theory postulates that masochism is an essential component of female sexuality. Feminist Nancy Reeves attributes the drive to cultural forces and not biological ones but admits that "even some semi-liberated women demand to be treated as prey." Lessard sees a pathology on the part of these women - a sense of inadequacy. When she asked feminists about Ted Kennedy's womanizing, she found that some were bothered a lot by it but some were bothered not at all. Yet he stands as an enemy to every feminist.(20)

Females display this kind of willing victim behavior to politicians but also to other groups such as rock stars, and pro athletes. The argument that women are attracted because of the fame, wealth, status and power, which is otherwise denied them teeters, when one includes mass murderers. Apparently most of these men are flooded, in prison, with letters from women eager to have sex with them and/or to marry them. Men such as Ted Bundy and Richard Speck. While in jail Bundy married one such woman and even managed to father a child with her. The woman, a professional - social worker - lost her job because she spent so much time away from work in service to him. The compulsive womanizers in this book were that way when they were young - and unknowns. Yet they were still as active, as successful womanizers, and as contemptuous of females as when they much later got power. Men such as Sukarno and Mussolini. Is there a female pathology at work which is roughly equal, but opposite, to that of the womanizer?

14--Affairs of State

Not all the men profiled in this book are, in my opinion, womanizers. All those in the first three sections are, and some of the others. The material represents what is known about modern world leaders and their sex habits, at least for a small selection. Very likely it hardly scratches the surface.

LADY

KILLERS

The *Lady Killers* are set apart from other men in this book by one basic distinction: women who have been involved with these men have ended up suddenly, unexpectedly, prematurely and mysteriously dead. In other respects their sexual habits have varied from the neurotic and pathological such as Idi Amin and John Kennedy down to the totally bizarre world of Adolf Hitler. As a group they hold women in greater contempt and have more hatred for them than the *Goats*, which is no easy feat. Perhaps, though, that explains why they are *Lady Killers*. This group also harbors physical beaters, rapists, cowards, and the heavily moneyed who are able to orchestrate lip-service investigations and engineer massive cover-ups of their activities.

Four of these men have had serious charges of murder levelled against them yet none likely did murder the woman in question. Nevertheless, they are an extremely violent and vicious group. It's self evident for the first three men but applies to the Kennedys as well. The two younger Kennedys never had enough power to demonstrate that fully but some of it is evident in their cover-ups when a woman near them died. Robert staged a vicious vendetta against Jimmy Hoffa but also against figures such an Roy Cohn, the latter simply because he beat Bobby out of the job as Joe McCarthy's top legal aide during the height of that notorious era - it was a job Robert coveted highly. It was the JFK regime which initiated bizarre plots, failed ones, to murder Fidel Castro; it was JFK, who heated up Vietnam by changing American "advisers" into "soldiers". JFK has the distinction of authorizing the use of chemical/biological warfare agents in Vietnam - not just to defoliate but also to destroy food crops. That marked the first time a country had used chemical warfare since World War I. Even Hitler, who had a stockpile of new generation nerve gas on hand and ready (the Allies didn't in the mid 1940s), refused to allow it to be used. Hitler's sex life was so strange and repugnant to the women involved that some tried to commit suicide. The greatest mystery surrounds the death of his niece, whom he lived with. Rumors of murder persist but most feel it was a suicide although Hitler's behavior could have helped her toward that path.

Joseph Stalin was an accomplished wife beater and like Hitler, had the woman closest to him die by her own hand. Stories of murder continue here as well but the death is generally regarded as a suicide. Also like Hitler, Stalin's behavior undoubtedly helped propel her in that direction.

Idi Amin's sexual antics included what amounted to de facto rape although he had no shortage of willing volunteers. In keeping with the gross nature of his regime in general so was the death which involved him. One of his wives was found dismembered and stuffed into the trunk of a car.

Jack and Robert Kennedy both had affairs with Marilyn Monroe and indeed shared her for a time as their affairs seem to have overlapped. Charges of murder have been made against Robert over the actress's death but only from extreme factions. However, the Kennedy boys, in their cavalier treatment of her, may have contributed to undermining her mental balance which was precarious enough at the time. They certainly managed to control the investigation into her death.

Ted Kennedy has never been accused of murder in the death at Chappaquiddick and yet, by his acts of omission, he very likely did cause the woman to die. After drinking, womanizing and causing a death, he walked away free and clear after a patented Kennedy cover-up was executed. Beware the *Lady Killers*; they are dangerous to your health.

ADOLF HITLER

The sex life of Adolf Hitler is more bizarre than that of any other man in this book. What he enjoyed the most was to be kicked, whipped, pissed on and shit on. It is not even clear if he ever had "normal" intercourse in the sense of penis in the vagina. If he did it was likely an infrequent event. Many of the reports on his activities are contradictory. Whatever his sex life was it left the women involved unhappy and depressed. Many of them turned to suicide attempts - and some succeeded. Hitler was born on April 20, 1889, came to power in Germany in 1933 and ruled it until his death by suicide on April 30, 1945.

Of his early years there is very little information. As a young man in Vienna, during the period 1906-1910, he was said to idealize women and stared at them from a distance. Morality was a genuine concern with him in those years. However, one report claims he was listed as a sexual pervert by the Vienna police, although this could have been "more by association with perverts than by actual practice." While walking through Vienna's red-light district with a friend, Adolf expressed his disgust about prostitution all through their stroll. An observer noted that "Many women found Adolf sexually attractive, but these were precisely the women he despised." While he was looking for a room to rent in Vienna, accompanied by the same friend, he was confronted by an aging prospective landlady who opened her robe to him to reveal nothing underneath but panties. So embarrassed was Hitler by this display that he quickly fled the house. Years later fellow Nazi Ernst "Putzi" Hanfstaengl saw similar behavior when he and his wife watched Adolf squirm out of situations where females had literally invited the Nazi leader to go to bed with them.(1)

As late as 1918-1919, it was still reported that he showed no active interest in sex. Then in August, 1919, he went to a physician and told him he thought he had syphilis. The doctor checked him over and said he would give him a blood test although he didn't think he had the disease. To this Adolf said, "If I don't have syphilis why am I totally impotent?" The physician cured this and then, according to this report, Hitler began to form liaisons with women - having at least a dozen over the next few years. Rumors that Adolf had venereal disease would surface again and again over the years. Putzi thought he got it as a young man in Vienna. Other rumors were that he contracted syphilis during World War I and that it was never cured with the symptoms recurring in 1937 and again in 1942. Contrary to all the rumors there is no evidence that he ever had a venereal disease. There were also sometimes rumors that he was a homosexual. He wasn't.(2)

Putzi first met Hitler around 1922 and immediately thought, "He had no normal sex life." His wife agreed and added. "I tell you he is a neuter." Elaborating, Ernst said, "I had formed the firm conviction that he was impotent, the repressed, masturbating type... From the time I knew him, I do not suppose he had orthodox sexual relations with any woman."(3)

The first reliable account of a woman involved with Hitler puts the time around 1926 when Hitler was staying in the village of Berchtesgarden. Maria Reiter worked as a clerk in her mother's dress shop. They met while separately walking their dogs. She was 16; he was 37. The first date was arranged by an intermediary and was an invitation for Mimi, as Hitler called her, to attend one of his speeches. Stories about Adolf running around with a teenager did him no political good and he abruptly broke off with her in 1928. That same year she claimed she tried to hang herself but failed. Maria later married a hotelkeeper but crossed paths with Hitler again in late 1931 or early 1932. Rudolf Hess came to see her, as an intermediary, and tell her Hitler wanted her to visit him. Reiter packed her overnight bag, left her husband, and journeyed to Hitler to spend one night in his apartment. Of that night she recalled, "I let him do whatever he wanted with me." Adolf, she said, begged her to be his mistress but she refused, insisting on marriage. He wouldn't marry her so she went back home. In 1934 they spent another night together and again he refused to marry her. That was their last meeting. Maria divorced and then married an SS officer in 1936. When he died in the war, Hitler sent her one hundred roses.(4)

Around this same period Adolf was involved with another teenager, Jenny Hoffman. Her father, Heinrich, was a friend of Hitler and a member of the Nazi party. When Heinrich became aware of the relationship, after Jenny told him, he became angry and would have little to do with Adolf for a time. The rift was healed when the Nazi leader appointed Heinrich the official Party photographer as well as giving him exclusive rights to photos of the Fuhrer - which made Hoffman wealthy. Some associates believed their leader had committed some sort of sexual indiscretion and then bought Hoffman's silence with those rights.(5)

At the end of the 1920s Adolf began a liaison with Geli Raubal, the woman that seemed to mean the most to him in the end. In September, 1929 Hitler moved into a much larger apartment than he had previously inhabited. One reason was because of his growing staff and importance in German politics. Privately though, it was because Geli was moving in with him. Angela Maria Raubal - known as Geli - was the twenty-one year old daughter of Adolf's half-sister, also named Angela Raubal. Mother and daughter both moved into the apartment with Geli occupying the bedroom next to Hitler. Geli was described as beautiful, frivolous, and gay. She had no interest in politics and was interested only in having a good time. Of these two women Hitler said, "These women are so oddly primitive. A hairdresser, clothes, dancing, theaters can distract them from any serious activity. The only thing they're willing to read are magazines and novels."(6)

Adolf liked to escort Geli to social functions and he made no secret of his interest in her. The arrangement caused raised eyebrows among his party associates. He had insisted that his half-sister also move in with her daughter to forestall such criticism. Even though he claimed Geli as a relative the grumbling about them continued. Hitler arranged for his niece to take singing lessons - Geli had originally wanted to do just that but the idea was vetoed by Adolf - so he could say Geli had come to Munich to study music but couldn't afford her own apartment. None of this made any difference and by the beginning of 1931 it was common knowledge they were having an affair - at least among the Nazi Party elites. The public image of Germany's leader - put out by Goebbels - would he that of a puritan, a man with no interest in women. Most Germans would believe this right up to the end.(7)

The relationship between them didn't go smoothly. Extremely jealous of her, Hitler watched over her constantly, picked out her clothes and the company she could keep, and generally regulated her life. He was captivated by her and considered Geli "the complete embodiment of his ideal of womanhood." Despite the attention and surveillance from Hitler it was rumored that Geli managed to run around behind her uncle's back. Adolf once caught her in the arms of his driver and, in a fury, fired the man on the spot. On her part Geli was said to be hot tempered and jealous of any attention Adolf paid to other women. Not long before her death, Geli discovered Hitler was seeing another woman who would become important in his life, Eva Braun, when she discovered a letter from her thanking Adolf for taking her to the theater.(8)

As an artist Hitler claimed the right to draw her in the nude and produced a number of obscene drawings. Also rumored was that Adolf had whipped her with a bullhide whip. The Nazi leader also screened lewd films in his movie room. Whatever was going on in the relationship, Geli was not happy. She confided to a friend that was so because she couldn't bring herself "to do what he wants me to do." Another time she said, "My uncle is a monster. You would never believe the things he makes me do." Most people thought Geli was sweet, unaffected and charming. However, not Hanfstaengl, who called her "an empty-headed little slut, with the coarse bloom of a servant-girl, without either brains or character."(9)

The couple had a furious shouting match on September 18, 1931, with Hitler screaming in a fury. What caused the quarrel is not known but they had happened in the past and this one seemed not exceptional. Geli shot herself to death around midnight that same night. None of the servants in the house heard the shot. Her death remains largely a mystery. Rumors have persisted that Adolf killed her - perhaps over an affair she was having. There is no evidence to support such an allegation and it most likely is the suicide it appeared to be. Hitler showed a great deal of grief and despair at the time of Geli's death and carried a picture of her with him for the rest of his life. The room in which she killed herself was kept exactly as she left it. After her death he said, "It turns out that women play a larger role in a man's life than we are inclined to suppose when we are not deprived of their presence. It is true that I have overcome the urge to physically possess a woman. But the value I placed on the loving hand of a female being who was close to my heart, and how much the constant solicitude she shed on me meant to me - that I am learning only now, when they are lost to me."(10)

At least one author has said that the great despair over Geli's death was mainly an act on Adolf's part. Another report has it that despite the number of years they lived together their affair "likely was never consummated." Yet another claim is that the doctor who examined the body said Geli was a virgin.(11) After Geli had died, Hitler went to his doctor and explained that after he had fired his driver whom he had found his niece with his attitude toward her changed "and his demands became more frequent and 'varied.'" Adolf wanted to know if these demands could have caused Geli to kill herself. The doctor said "no." Likely this was a reference to his various sexual perversions.

Hanfstaengl had heard stories from women who had been with Hitler and when they were alone he was "both a sadist and a masochist." Ernst also claimed his suspicions were confirmed when he saw the nude drawings of Geli - which he thought could only have been drawn by a sadist. According to fellow Nazi Otto Strasser, Geli told him "Hitler made her undress... He would lie down on the floor. Then she would have to squat over his face where he could examine her at close range and this made him very excited. When the excitement reached its peak, he demanded that she urinate on him and that gave him sexual pleasure. Geli said the whole performance was extremely disgusting to her and... it gave her no gratification." Others gave similar accounts of the Fuhrer's perversions. He also liked to be shit on, kicked and whipped with the whip he often carried. Father Bernard Stempfle helped Hitler edit *Mein Kampf* in 1929 and said Adolf had written his niece a "shockingly compromising letter which explicitly mentioned his masochistic and coprophilic inclinations." As for "normal" intercourse his drive in that direction must have been weak or non-existent. Hitler often spoke of keeping pure "the flame of life." Hanfstaengl insisted he was impotent.(12)

By 1932 Eva Braun was established as his second, and last, live-in companion. She would stay with him till the end. However, he would have other involvements during, and before, their time together. One affair was with Winifred Wagner in 1932. She was bright and famous, the daughter-in-law of composer Richard Wagner. Associates hoped this potential match would work, but it didn't. Wagner was once asked by Hitler to whip him. On a couple of other occasions he treated her like a mother and asked her to punish him. Winifred visited Adolf's physician and said she was surprised and shocked by his approach to sex and that one side of him was "like that of a beast." Winifred decided she wanted no more to do with him.(13)

A German film director claimed he supplied starlets to Hitler for the night during the war. The foreign minister of Italy thought the Fuhrer had a brief affair with a twenty year old named Sigrid von Lappus. US military intelligence reported evidence Hitler had liaisons with two young Munich women, Frauleins Abel and Haue. A financial contributor to the Nazi Party found Hitler down on his knees making a declaration of love to his daughter - to the embarrassment of all concerned. A reported liaison with Suzi Liptauer led to her attempting suicide after just one encounter with Hitler. Inge Ley did commit suicide after an affair with the Nazi leader. A German actress, Renate Mueller, also committed suicide after liaising with Hitler. Another reported affair was with a naive British woman named Unity Walkyrie Mitford, who hoped for an alliance between Germany and Britain. When war was declared by Britain in 1939, she shot herself in the head, in Germany. Adolf had her treated by the best doctors and brought flowers to her in the hospital. One author concludes that Hitler was intimate with seven women by his count and of this number six turned to suicide bids with Geli, Ley and Mueller succeeding. The other three, Eva Braun, Reiter, and Liptauer failed in their attempts. Mitford's suicide attempt was considered a political act.(14)

When Renate Mueller once spent the night with Hitler, he first described to her in detail the medieval and Gestapo methods of torture. After they had undressed, the Fuhrer lay on the floor condemning himself as unworthy. He groveled and heaped accusations on himself. Making persistent demands to Renate that she kick him, the scene became intolerable to her. Nevertheless, she acceded and kicked him a few times. "This excited him greatly; he became more and more excited."(15)

Eva Braun was an eighteen year old clerk in Heinrich Hoffman's photography shop when Hitler first met her. They saw each other occasionally while Geli was still alive. In the early months of 1932, she became his live-in mistress. The photographer considered her "frivolous, vain, feather-brained, inconsequential" while one of Hitler's doctors thought her "cheap, arrogant and selfish." Eva was completely ignorant of politics willingly agreeing with any and all of her leader's ideas. The Fuhrer wanted her to remain invisible and take no part in politics. Rarely was she ever seen out in German society. Only the inner circle knew of her existence. Many in that inner circle thought their leader was asking for trouble and wouldn't survive a second scandal. Some considered him "a sexual deviate who indirectly caused Geli's death by his perverted demands on her coupled with his unfaithfulness." About the only thing Eva didn't do for Adolf was to gain weight "much to Hitler's disgust because he preferred voluptuous women." Tall, full-figured women were his favorites.(16)

Braun was said to be devoted to Hitler and he was her first and only lover. According to Nazi Albert Speer, "Hitler kept his Eva like a puppet in a doll's house. She was a part of the ambience like the canary cage, the rubber tree... and the kitchy wooden clocks." When dignitaries such as cabinet ministers came to call at Hitler's residence he made her stay in her room. To him Braun was socially acceptable only within limits. He had little consideration for her feelings and once said, in her presence, "A highly intelligent man should take a primitive and stupid woman." He shunned intelligent women.(17)

Eva tried suicide twice. On November 1, 1932, she shot herself in the neck. The reasons were that she was depressed because Adolf was spending a lot of time electioneering and had little left for her. Jealousy was also a motive as at least one rival for the Fuhrer's affections had sent her photos of the campaigning Hitler posing with women. The same reasons were at the root of her second attempt on May 29, 1935, when she again shot herself. That time she had heard rumors about Unity Mitford. Eva finally accepted the fact she could live with him only on his terms.(18)

Braun had long hoped to marry the Fuhrer but he always refused. He told Albert Speer that "Lots of women are attracted to me because I am unmarried." Speer added, "Hitler believed that he had a powerful sexual appeal to women. But he was also wary about this." Adolf always told Eva he couldn't marry her as he had to devote himself to the nation. To an aide he confided he would lose votes if he married. "So, I have a girl at my disposal in Munich." The Fuhrer elaborated on the subject of marriage by saying, "For me marriage would have been a disaster. There's a point at which misunderstanding is bound to raise between man and wife; it's when the husband cannot give his wife all the time she feels entitled to demand. I'd have had nothing of marriage but the sullen face of a neglected wife, or else I'd have skimped my duties... The bad side of marriage is that it creates rights. In that case, it's far better to have a mistress. The burden is lightened, and everything is placed on the level of a gift." To his secretary the Fuhrer said, "Eva is very nice, but, in my life, only Geli could have inspired in me genuine passion. I can never think of marrying Eva. The only woman I could have tied myself to for life would have been Geli."(19)

The record regarding the sex life of Eva and Adolf is confusing. Braun once told Speer that they had normal sex. Later she told him, "Hitler was less potent than she liked." Eva told her sister that her sex life with the Fuhrer was "completely normal." To a close friend she told a different story saying, "As far as his manhood is concerned, I get absolutely nothing from him." Talking about sex and "depraved" sexual practices were among his favorite topics. Often he asked young women to confide in him with detailed descriptions of their sexual experiences. At least one person besides Hanfstaengl concluded Hitler was impotent. During the war Dr. Walter Langer compiled psychological observations on the Fuhrer for the Americans. Langer agreed there was a strong masochistic stream in him and that his sexual relations with women were "apparently of an unusual nature and account for the suicide of his niece Geli Raubal and the two successive suicide attempts made by Eva Braun."(20)

Eva joined Hitler in his bunker on April 15, 1945. She had had ample time and opportunities to escape Germany and she joined the Fuhrer against his wishes. Braun's hopes were realized on April 29 in the bunker as the Allies closed in. The pair married that day. The next day Eva Braun and Adolf Hitler committed suicide together.

"It's a fact that women love real men," said Hitler. "It's their instinct that tells them they should seek the protection of a hero."(21)

JOSEPH STALIN

Joseph Stalin's reported sex life, like Hitler's, is full of confusing and contradictory accounts. What is clear is that he bestowed on his women the same contempt he displayed for his country. He was born Iosif Víssarionovich Djugashvili on December 21, 1979, taking the name Stalin - man of steel - around 1910. By 1928 power was substantially his in Russia and he ruled the country until his death on March 5, 1953.

Stalin met his first wife in Georgia when he roomed in the house of an elderly woman named Ekaterina Svanidze, who had an eighteen year old niece with the same name. The couple began by living together, but young Ekaterina complained to Stalin's mother that he had no intention of marrying her. Pressure was applied by both of these women and the couple finally were married in a religious ceremony. Various accounts give the date as anywhere from 1902 to 1907, with 1904 being the most probable. A son was born to them in 1908. Ekaterina died about 1910.(1)

The bride was a devout Christian who believed a woman's place was in the home and who submitted to Stalin's will. Of this marriage one observer commented, "His marriage was a happy one because his wife, who could not follow him in intellectual attainments, regarded him as a demigod, and because, being a Georgian woman, she was brought up in the sacrosanct tradition that a woman is born to serve... This truly Georgian woman watched over the welfare of her husband in fear and trembling."(2)

The brutality that was so much a part of the dictator's make-up was evident in 1908 when Ekaterina was pregnant. A man who rented them rooms recalled that Joseph "used to curse her in the most disgusting way. And kick her in the belly." Another observer commented that in his dealings with women, whether they were mother, daughter, or wives, "he was foulmouthed, disrespectful and capable of physical violence." When he was in the company of a group of Bolshevik females known to be highly "moral women" Stalin took great delight in humiliating them by singing obscene songs in front of them. On occasion he had abused his mother by calling her, in public, "you old whore." He did have tender feelings for his first wife. At her funeral he reportedly said, "She was the one creature who softened my strong heart. She is dead, and with her have died any feelings of tenderness I had for humanity."(3)

During the period around 1913, when Joseph was exiled to Siberia for four years, he lived with a peasant woman whose husband was away at war. The woman bore Stalin a son. A second account has it that this peasant woman was unmarried and had received a written promise of marriage from Joseph. By this account they had two children - the first was stillborn, the second survived. Years later this woman "had nothing good to say of him. She had brought up her son to dislike his father intensely."(4)

Back from Siberian exile Joseph began to see Nadezhda Alliluyeva. He had known her parents since 1900, one year before Nadezhda was born. Joseph boarded with the family in 1917. The daughter was only sixteen when the 38 year old roomer moved in. Soon a romantic attachment developed between them. She saw him as a hero of the liberating cause. The couple married in 1918 or 1919. Nadezhda was then working as Stalin's secretary. Whatever Joseph saw in his new wife it wasn't intellect he was looking for as he hated such woman, referring to them as "herrings with ideas." One account of their courtship has it that in due course Nadezhda announced that she was pregnant. Her father, Sergei, upheld the principle of free love as a true communist. However, when he and his wife heard the news, they reacted traditionally and demanded that Stalin marry their daughter. Nadezhda gave birth to a son in 1920, and again in 1926 to daughter Svetlana. Given the birth date and possible marriage dates this pregnancy story is unlikely, though possible.(5)

The marriage was under a strain from the beginning. One reason was Stalin's involvement in politics which left little time for his family. Nadezhda was also not as submissive as Ekaterina. She didn't appreciate that her husband insisted on using foul language when he entertained guests in her presence. Another problem was her husband's reported infidelities which were described by one observer as "passing affairs with government secretaries and the like." The couple had an angry scene around 1927 when Nadezhda threatened to commit suicide if Joseph didn't break off his dalliance with a Georgian singer. Stalin relented and shipped the singer off to a job in a far off city. Another rumored mistress of the Russian leader was a girl named Yolka Andreyevna who bore him a son.(6)

After joining the Communist Party in 1918 Nadezhda became a member of Lenin's staff in 1919 working as a secretary. Suddenly she found herself expelled from the party in 1921 and had to appeal directly to Lenin for a letter to get reinstated. It remains unknown who had her expelled but suspicion points squarely to Stalin, who had much influence at the time. He might have done this because he wanted his wife to quit work and stay home to be a traditional housewife. This all came not long after the birth of their first child and added to the strains on the marriage.

A similar crisis erupted in 1926 after Svetlana's birth. On that occasion Nadezhda packed up her two kids and left Stalin returning to live with her father in Leningrad. She intended to start an independent life but Stalin phoned her and persuaded her to return to him. As inducements he promised her to hire a governess for the kids and to allow her to pursue higher education. He kept his promises. Although they were living together again the marriage was apparently now a sexless one. Nadezhda slept in her own bedroom while Joseph slept "either in his office or in a little room with a telephone next to the dining room."(7)

29--Sex and Politicians

While Nadezhda knew little or nothing of the atrocities her husband was beginning to commit in Russia, she had her eyes opened when she went back to school, as her husband had promised. She enrolled, anonymously, for a course in industrial chemistry. Not knowing who she was her fellow students initiated her into the excesses of Stalin's regime for the first time. When she confronted her husband at home with these charges Nadezhda found herself abused in obscene terms and accused of "collecting Trotskyite rumors." Ordered arrested were those students who had enlightened his wife. Nadezhda decided to go to the Ukraine herself to see if some of the rumors were true - about a famine there caused by government confiscation of foodstuffs for other parts of the USSR. Stalin went into a rage and threatened to divorce her and exile her to Siberia. She went anyway. Stalin asked his doctor to "bring her to reason." After she returned Nadezhda told the doctor "Stalin had deceived the people of the U.S.S.R." and she was ashamed.(8)

Joseph and Nadezhda joined some other people at a friend's apartment on November 8, 1932, to celebrate the fifteenth anniversary of the October Revolution. At the party Stalin and his wife had a fight in public. One reason may have been an argument over a woman named Rosa Kaganovich whom Stalin was rumored to be seeing. A second reason may have been over remarks made by Nadezhda about Stalin's treatment of the peasantry. The Russian leader went into a rage and threw a lit cigarette down her dress or, in one account, the couple came to blows. Nadezhda fled the apartment and Joseph pursued her. The next morning, November 9, at about 4 AM Nadezhda was dead from a pistol shot.

Several stories about how she died have been advanced. One is that Nadezhda committed suicide. Certainly she was depressed and unhappy in her marriage. Also, she had a sister and a brother who were both incapacitated by psychiatric conditions. A second version is that when the couple arrived home Stalin came upon his wife with a pistol. The couple struggled over the weapon and it discharged, accidentally killing Nadezhda. Third is the version that Stalin killed his wife. When they got home Joseph started to beat his wife with his fists. Someone in the house broke up the scuffle. Nadezhda called her husband a murderer. Stalin pulled out his pistol - he always carried one - and shot her dead. Before her funeral, according to this version, Stalin gathered the members of the Politburo and confessed to the killing saying, "I lost my head, didn't want my wife to meddle with the leadership of the party." He asked to be relieved from all party duties and from his position as leader. One of the members, Vyacheslav Molotov, intervened and made an impassioned speech on Stalin's behalf listing his accomplishments - and saved him. Reportedly the Russian leader wept through the night of his wife's death. On the death certificate the cause of death was listed as "paralysis of the heart." Each of these stories has its adherents. However, most subscribe to the suicide or accidental shooting versions.(9)

Rosa Kaganovich has also given rise to many contradictory stories. Some accounts claim Stalin began to see her while Nadezhda was still alive. Others maintain they began their affair only after her death. Either Rosa remained Stalin's lover until she disappeared from sight or she married Stalin and was later divorced by him. A minority opinion - led by Svetlana - maintains that there was no such person as Rosa. What is not in dispute in that Kaganovich had brothers - two or three - who were all in high posts in Stalin's administration. They were Jews. Svetlana felt it was inconceivable that her father would have been involved with a Jewess as he was strongly anti-semitic. This, of course, misunderstands the nature of sexuality. Mussolini had a long relationship with a Jewess. History is rife with such examples. Slave owners in America often had sex with their black slaves, all the while despising blacks. Most of Stalin's biographers accept the existence of Rosa and some sort of liaison between her and Stalin. The brothers were ultimately purged from the regime and Rosa disappeared.(10)

Even when he was with Rosa, Stalin found time for other women, at his estate near Moscow and at his villa. After Nadezhda's death his chief aide and bodyguard, Nikolai Vlasik, presented his boss with a group of waitresses at his country home and he selected Valechka Istomina. She became his housekeeper and, by the time of Stalin's death, was accepted as his unofficial widow. Valechka was described as "corpulent, neat, served deftly at the table and never joined in any conversation. And she remained fiercely loyal to her master to his death and after."(11)

31--Sex and Politicians

One account has it that after Nadezhda's death Stalin "began an endless depraved and debauched life." One other dalliance of note was with Liza Kazanova, a friend of his late wife. When they began the affair Liza was engaged. Her intended, an officer in the Red Army, suddenly found himself transferred to China. On the way to his new posting he was sentenced to jail for 25 years for "counter-revolutionary activity." When the affair ended Liza, like Rosa, disappeared from sight. According to one rather bizarre account Stalin began to worry about his sexual potency sometime in the late 1930s. His comrade, Mikhail Kalinin, recommended a rejuvenating operation and so he underwent a monkey gland transplant. This all sounds, and probably is, far fetched but Russia did have, at the time, an experimental farm of monkeys whose glands were transplanted into humans. Only political prisoners were used for these experiments.(12)

Someone once confronted the Russian leader with the "glass of water" theory of sex - that one has sex when one needs it, as a thirsty man takes a drink - to which Stalin commented, "Who wants to drink dirty water." Chancing upon a publication devoted to sexual perversions Stalin asked an aide, "Do people really do this sort of thing?" While he once described sex as a healthy and natural occupation necessary to procreate children he added that "people ought to forego it during a national emergency such as the First Five Year Plan! A man's true emotional bond should be with his class and people, not with his woman."(13)

IDI
AMIN

One of Idi Amin's wives - as a Muslim he was allowed four at a time - died under mysterious circumstances. While he likely wasn't directly involved in her death, he has indeed had men killed. The husbands and boyfriends of women he has wanted. So extreme is his treatment of women that he is one of the very few men profiled in this book who has resorted to what amounts to rape. He also enjoyed beating women and discussing his sexual conquests.

Idi was born around 1925. On January 25, 1971, he was a Major-General in the Ugandan army and leader of a coup which seized power that day. Idi ruled Uganda until he was ousted in 1979. Initially he went into exile in Libya. He remains in exile today, somewhere in Africa. Essentially illiterate, Amin can't write and has only a very minimal ability to read.

As a young man, Idi joined the colonial army in Uganda in 1946, the British Army's King's African Rifles. The first report of a sexual escapade by Idi came when he was a sergeant, in the early 1950s. He was caught in bed with the wife of a colleague and then chased naked down the street. A British officer recalled, "In 1955 there was only one blot on his copybook. His records showed that he had had venereal disease which made him ineligible for a good conduct stripe."(1)

It was about the time of that report that Idi met his first wife. She was Malyamu Kibedi (Sarah), in her early twenties, who has been described as an intelligent and beautiful six footer. There was not initially a wedding as we think of one. Amin just paid the bride price and the union was then recognized. An official wedding of the couple took place in 1966. By then they had several children. That same year Amin took Kay Adroa as his second wife. Kay was a Christian, the daughter of a Protestant clergyman and a student at Uganda's Makerere University. This relationship was basically sexual. Kay became the junior wife or wife number two to Sarah. These two wives were said to have got on well together. Idi "arranged a roster, but Kay received the glut of his attention." More than once each of these women were beaten by Amin and more than once each had to be treated by her doctor at a hospital for injuries sustained. Over the years up to these marriages he had many affairs.(2)

Nora became wife number three in 1967. This was largely a marriage of political convenience as Nora had links with Uganda's leader of the day, Milton Obote, whom Amin would overthrow in 1971. To curry favor with Obote, Idi went to the leader's tribal area and selected a pretty girl. Idi told her relatives he had picked her and paid the dowry price. Nora had no say in the matter. In Idi's household Nora had lower status than the first two wives and did much of the work. Wife number four was Medina whom he wed in 1971 or 1972. During 1973 Amin's household held four wives and about twenty children, some of them from his mistresses. At any one time he had a harem of some thirty women scattered around Uganda that he could draw upon. All of them were followed by spies and none dared to go out with other men.(3)

In addition to these were scores of one night stands. One writer has said that Amin has had sex with "many hundreds and possibly thousands of women." They have ranged from twelve year old schoolgirls to white women in their forties. Known as a primitive man, he reportedly often beats his women and has a reputation as a "ferociously aggressive lover." Most of the women who graduate to mistress only last a couple of months. This writer states, "It is Amin's reputation, and his macabre reign of terror, that turns on many women. I have spoken to a number of attractive women who said they could not resist the underlying sexual attractiveness of the man." These sentiments are echoed by Henry Kyemba, a former minister in Amin's government, who said that Idi "regards his sexual energy as a sign of his power and authority. He never tries to hide his lust. His reputation for sexual performance is so startling that women often deliberately make themselves available, and his love affairs have included women of all colors and many nations, ...from street girls to university lecturers."(4)

Kyemba recalled being summoned to Idi's office from time to time to listen to his boss talk about his sexual conquests. As the former minister said, "He had an extraordinary sex life." The dictator also enjoyed telling his ministers that if anyone wanted his wife Medina they could take her as she was readily available. To other army officers Idi would remark on the sexual performance of his wives. He called Kay "an animal in bed" but complained that Nora was "cold." Idi was partial to using sexual hardware such as vibrators and tickler-condoms. Oral sex was also popular with him but only one way. He liked to be fellated but would not do cunnilingus. As well, he bragged about the number of children he fathered and how he was able to keep all his wives content.(5)

One rather naive biographer reported Idi was fair in dividing his attentions and gifts among his wives and believed the dictator when he said, "It is a man's duty to divide his love fairly among his wives and to make them feel wanted and happy." In truth they were neglected by their husband and quite unhappy. By March, 1974, the first three wives, Sarah, Kay and Nora, had banded together. For two years they had been virtually isolated and all had taken lovers. On March 25, united in their hatred of Idi, they threw a party for their lovers. Amin was informed of this by a phone call from one of his bodyguards. Furious, he phoned the wives and threatened to throw them out. By then they were all drunk and told the dictator that he could keep Medina and go to hell.

The next day Amin announced he had divorced all three of them. As a Muslim he could do this by simply stating "I divorce thee" three times. For public consumption Idi said he divorced Sara and Nora because they were involved in business - they were as Idi had given each a textile store in 1971. Kay had to be divorced, he said, because she was his cousin and he was responding to complaints that they were too closely related to stay married.(6)

A month after the divorce Sarah was arrested for alleged smuggling. She was fined and released. A year later the car she was driving was rammed by one containing Idi's bodyguards. Sarah was hospitalized with a broken leg and arm. Her former husband visited her in jail and gave her a tongue lashing for being such a poor driver. When she was released from the hospital she fled to London in late 1975, and never returned to Uganda. Sarah had to leave behind her six children to be raised by Idi's other women. Not that the one loyal wife, Medina, fared much better. Idi often beat her. During one severe beating in 1975 she suffered bruises, a black eye, and a broken jaw. Another severe beating took place in January, 1977 when she was two or three months pregnant. On that occasion he also kicked her.(7)

Ex-wife Kay was found murdered in August, 1974. Her dismembered body was stuffed into the trunk of a car. The most widely accepted story of the circumstances surrounding her death has it that she died accidentally at the hands of a doctor called Mhalu-Mukasa, while undergoing an abortion. The doctor was also the father of the child and panicked when she died, fearing he would he subject to Idi's wrath when the story came out. The doctor cut up the body and stashed it in his car planning to dispose of it later, with the help of a friend. However, the friend was arrested first and spilled out the story. Knowing he would soon be arrested the doctor killed himself with a drug overdose rather than face torture at the hands of the dictator. A minority opinion is that Amin learned of Kay's affair with the doctor, murdered her, or ordered it done, and then planted the body in the doctor's car to frame him. The doctor found the body and then committed suicide. Or even that Amin had Kay killed because he thought she was an informant.(8)

While he may not have murdered Kay several sources note that on different occasions Idi has killed men to take their women as his mistresses, and even in one case as his wife. Which is what happened to the woman destined to be Amin's fifth wife, Sarah Kyolaba. Idi first met her in 1974 when she was eighteen and he forced her to have sex with him. Sarah was living then with a boyfriend by whom she was pregnant. After she gave birth and returned home to her boyfriend from the hospital in early 1975, Amin announced he was the father of the child. Once or twice a week Sarah was ordered to Amin's residence for sex. The boyfriend finally objected and tried to stop the practice. The next day he was taken away by soldiers and never seen again. Sarah knew Idi had killed her boyfriend but she could do nothing about it. They married in 1975 although Sarah always hated him. He beat her regularly.(9)

His casual affairs and one night stands were "too numerous to count" and his sex life extended into every corner of his administration. No ministry or department was left untouched. A woman who had never personally met Idi might receive a summons, through an aide, to appear at the dictator's residence at a certain time on a certain day. The reason wasn't stated but it was obvious. Amin had seen the woman and taken a fancy to her. A woman summoned once might never be called again or she might be called regularly for a period of time before suddenly being dropped. A female who ignored one of these "requests" did so at her own peril. Something would happen to her or someone in her family. Sometimes a woman summoned in this manner would abandon her position and flee the country rather than submit. In bed Amin liked his women to move around a lot and to make lots of noise; or, as he put it, "It's no good taking a girl to bed if she is shy - do you get my point?" When they didn't he wasn't pleased and the woman in question might be subject to a beating.(10)

Strangely enough, while he did commit what amounted to rape, there was no shortage of females who submitted to him willingly. Idi claimed to have had sex with hundreds of white women. This is an exaggeration but reports are that he had plenty. The former US ambassador to Uganda, Thomas Melady, reported that some educated women were attracted to him. Godfrey Lule, the former Ugandan Justice Minister, said that Idi was a "sex fanatic and often talked of little else." The dictator argued, Lule said, "that a man's mental ability directly related to his sexual capacity and he boasted of being able to handle four women a night."(11)

Some sources say that there was no evidence at the time of his ouster that Idi then had VD. Others maintain that he was suffering from syphilis. One of his girlfriends, a nurse, claimed Amin had infected her with the disease and left her infertile. He lectured students and soldiers on the need to avoid spreading venereal disease. Said Amin to them: "You must make yourself very smart, very clean, very healthy. I find that the VD is very high. If you are a sick man, sick woman, you had better go to the hospital, make yourself clean or you will find that you will infect the whole population. I like you very much and I don't want you spoiled by gonorrhea."(12)

At the time of his ouster from power Idi had an estimated thirty or so mistresses and thirty-four children. As one writer noted, "His treatment of women has its counterpart in his treatment of the country."(13)

JOHN F. KENNEDY

Without doubt Jack Kennedy was the worst womanizer to ever occupy the White House. Lyndon Johnson runs him a respectable - but very distant - second. He treated women with contempt, objects to he conquered and discarded. Throughout his running around - which was pathological - he displayed towering arrogance. Today JFK is revered as a hero, almost a demigod. John Fitzgerald Kennedy was born on May 29, 1917 and assassinated on November 22, 1963. On September 12, 1953, he married Jacqueline Lee Bouvier, twelve years his junior. He was the president of the USA from 1961 to 1963.

JFK's womanizing didn't become general public knowledge until the mid 1970s when Judith Campbell, his mob connected mistress, went public. Since that time details from one source or another have literally poured out. The womanizing itself started much earlier. In 1933 Jack had his first reported sex experience when he and his friend Lem Billings went to a whorehouse in Harlem to get laid. They went wearing full evening dress and wanted to lose their virginity to the same woman. The prostitutes were white and the charge was $3. Later that night they returned to Choate, where they were both students, and went to see school mate Ralph Norton Jr., worried they would get VD. Norton accompanied the pair to a hospital where they picked up some creams and salves. Returning to the school they tried to sleep but couldn't. In the middle of the night Jack decided they should see a doctor. They woke one up and went over. Kennedy also made use of another $3 brothel, the Gypsy Tea Room, in West Palm Beach, an area the Kennedy family went to vacation.(1)

About one of his very early conquests Jack wrote to a friend "she got quite a scare when I gave it to her... However I couldn't feel any maidenhead and she is quite sexy." A few years later he wrote to

Billings and bragged, "I can now get tail as often and as free as I want which is a step in the right direction." While father Joseph Kennedy was ambassador to London the family lived there and Jack engaged in a competition with his brother, Joseph Jr., for feminine conquests. Publicist Tex McCrary, who knew them during the war said of them, "They were the best swordsmen in the ETO." While in London before the war Jack was described as a man who was "silent, sulky, and talked mostly about girls." In the navy his nickname was "Shafty."(2)

The first serious involvement JFK had with a woman began in 1941 when he met Inga Arvad, who worked for a Washington newspaper. By the fall of that year the couple were living together in a Washington apartment. Until he met Inga, Jack had rarely slept with the same woman twice. Nicknamed "Inga-Binga" by Jack, she was married but not living with her husband. The affair was serious enough that JFK briefly thought of marrying her. Joseph was furious at the idea and told his son, "Damn it, Jack, she's already married." Newspapers went so far as to speculate that Joe would contribute a large sum of money to the Catholic Church, thus paving the way for an annulment so Inga and Jack could wed. Inga had other black marks against her. In the 1930s she had briefly spent time in Germany where she moved in high Nazi circles. After attending the wedding of Field Marshal Goering - at which Adolf Hitler was the best man - Inga interviewed the Fuhrer himself later. She also had at least one man in her life who was suspected of espionage. With this background Inga was under FBI surveillance as a suspected German spy. JFK was doing intelligence work for the navy when they first got together. In Washington J. Edgar Hoover had both the apartment and hotel rooms they sometimes slept in tapped. Hoover found they had "engaged in sexual intercourse on a number of occasions." The FBI boss also felt JFK talked too freely and too loosely about his work to Inga. To break up this affair Joseph stepped in and saw to it that his son was transferred to Charleston, South Carolina. The affair continued, however, with Inga traveling down for visits. During one such visit, her hotel room was bugged on orders from Frances Biddle, the Attorney General. This tape eventually made its way right up to President Roosevelt, who heard "Jack talking unguardedly about his work in between the sounds of their lovemaking."

Joseph had another talk with his son telling him it was one thing to have a fling but something quite different to continue a relationship with a non-Catholic married woman who was under investigation as a Nazi spy. More strings were pulled by Joe and Jack was assigned to sea duty. Thus, if JFK hadn't been screwing a suspected Nazi spy he never would have gone to sea where he earned, erroneously, the label of war hero. It was a label that would help him in his future electioneering. Inga gave birth to a son nine months after her last encounter with Kennedy. Six months before the birth she married actor Tim McCoy. Many years later she told her son, Ronald McCoy, that his father was not Tim, but JFK. While he campaigned in Pennsylvania for the presidency in 1960 an aide who knew of Jack's passion for Inga during his navy days suggested they visit Inga, who then lived in Pennsylvania. Jack almost recoiled, "Inga? Why she must be forty years old."(3)

While he was at sea during the war he wrote to his many girlfriends. One of them, Charlotte McDonnell, got a letter from him and "When I opened it up, I saw it wasn't meant for me. He had written two letters and got the envelopes mixed up." Nick Nikoloric was one of the PT boat men associated with JFK and said, remembering those years, "Girls were almost an obsession with him. We liked them too, but we didn't make a career out of it the way he did."

Jim and Jewel Reed were a married couple friendly with Jack around 1944. He would ask Jim to accompany him to parties but not Jewel. She thought of it as a male prowling thing and said JFK couldn't understand why Jim wouldn't leave his wife behind to prowl around with him. Said Jewel, "I think Jack felt this was being manly. But it seemed to me, he had a contempt for women." Jim Reed added, "I think he looked on women in a different way than I do... They were sort of chattel. He treated them that way... I think he had the feeling it was a war between the sexes, in a sense. A man would always try to conquer a woman. And she was there to sort of be conquered."(4)

During the last half of the 1940s, Jack had affairs with some famous women such as British tennis star Kay Stammers and actress Gene Tierney but most were unknown people. He also had a penchant for Broadway show girls and singer Morton Downey bawled him out saying, "You know, you damn fool, if you ever want to get any place in politics, you'd better cut out this nonsense with these long-stemmed beauties from Billy Rose's nightclub." Amongst those women with ordinary jobs, airline stewardesses and secretaries were popular. They appeared almost every night at his Georgetown residence in such numbers that Jack often didn't bother to learn their names, referring to them as "kiddo" or "sweetie" the next morning. They arrived at his place late at night and early the next morning were driven, without ceremony, by aide Billy Sutton, to their offices or air terminal. A male friend stayed over one night at Jack's apartment and remembered him coming home late at night after a movie with a girl. Later a second one came to the apartment. The friend went to bed and in the morning a completely different girl came down the stairs for breakfast. "They were a dime a dozen," said the friend. One woman who aroused more than passing interest was Florence Pritchett, who a few claim was the love of his life. In 1948 she married Earl Smith, who became President Eisenhower's ambassador to Cuba. JFK made more than a dozen trips to Havana to see her. The Smiths also had a house in Palm Beach which conveniently adjoined the Kennedy compound."(5)

When Victor Lasky published *J.F.K. The Man and the Myth* in 1963, it created quite a stir. It was one of the pioneer books in what might he called the "negative" biography genre. Despite the bias of the author there was absolutely nothing about Jack's womanizing in his book, although there was no lack of raw material. This illustrates just how little mentioned such a topic was. Either Lasky found nothing, or the publisher removed anything Lasky had included, or Lasky found such material but decided not to use it. Perhaps, as well, no one interviewed would volunteer such information.

The one thing Lasky does bring out is JFK's "first" marriage. So bland is it today that most recent books on JFK don't even bother with it. Kennedy and a socialite by the name of Durie Malcolm Desloge were a hot item in 1947, in Florida. A decade later, in 1957, a professional genealogist, Louis Blauvelt, published a genealogy of his family - Durie was a member - after thirty years of research. Blauvelt died within a year of publication of the book. One entry in the book stated that Durie, twice married and divorced, had taken JFK as her third husband. A reporter checked with Durie and the White House and received denials from both. No records to confirm this rumor could ever be found.(6)

One more recent book does cover this story. According to this author when JFK learned that *Look* magazine was going to do a story on the marriage, Jack warned one of the editors "If you run that story I may wind up buying *Look* magazine." He also instructed his lawyer to warn the New York *Daily News* that they could publish that story "at their peril." *Newsweek* did do a story, with JFK's agreement, and the two reporters assigned were said to have been intrigued when they interviewed Kennedy and he "never flatly denied it." Joseph Kennedy had also heard the story and he dispatched his personal lawyer, James Landis, to Europe - where the wedding was rumored to have taken place - to investigate. Landis roamed around Europe and discovered that Durie and Jack had been together in southern France when they unexpectedly ran into one of his mother's friends. "From the way Jack introduced Durie, the woman understood Durie was Jack's wife." No other supporting facts were uncovered by Landis.(7)

The story about this marriage is likely not true. The genealogist just made a mistake, although the Kennedy family is certainly capable of engineering large and massive cover-ups, and have done so; Teddy and Chappaquiddick, Robert and Marilyn Monroe, for example. What is most interesting about this story is the behavior of Joseph Kennedy in calling in a man to spend time and energy to check it out. If Joseph asked Jack about the rumor he didn't believe a "no" answer or he would not have investigated. If he got a "yes" answer he would have got all the facts and not needed a man to wander Europe. Joseph either didn't ask his own son about the story or if he did, he didn't believe the answer he got. When confronted with a similar situation with regard to his brother, Robert Kennedy would handle it in the same way - go somewhere else.

George Smathers was a Senate colleague and fellow philanderer of Jack's. They used to "hunt" together and arrange to meet women at an apartment hideout in Washington that the pair used. Said Smathers, "Jack liked to go over there and meet a couple of young secretaries. He liked groups." Smathers recalled, "We had a nice little place on the river when we were both senators and we'd go there sometimes with a couple of girls... Once he had me called back to the Senate so that he could chase around ... it dawned on me that I couldn't be wanted back there because the Senate was in recess... So I turned around and drove back and entered the place... There was the old rascal chasing both of the girls around, having himself a fine old time." When JFK was President Smathers claims he found him and a "highly disarranged, pretty young woman" in the Cabinet room. Never one to let politics interfere with womanizing, JFK, while running for Congress, once left in the middle of a parade in Boston to catch a train because he had a date in New York City.(8)

Sometimes Kennedy's womanizing was even too much for Smathers. When Jack failed to win the Vice-presidential nomination at the 1956 Democratic convention he and Smathers went off for a yachting trip on the Mediterranean. The eight month pregnant Jackie stayed home. The trip turned into an orgy with several young women getting on and off at every port of call. One crew member said that, "Unique among them was a stunning but not particularly intelligent blonde who didn't seem to have a name but referred to herself in the third person as *Pooh*. She fascinated Jack." When JFK received word that Jackie had given birth to a stillborn child he was in no hurry to go home because he was having such a good time. Three days later he did, but only after an urging to do so from Smathers, who insisted he had to patch up his crumbling marriage if he wanted to advance in national politics. "Jack liked girls," said Smathers. "He liked girls very much. He came by it naturally. His daddy liked girls. He was a chaser." JFK once told Clare Booth Luce, "Dad told all the boys to get laid as often as possible."(9)

His appeal to women was said to be magnetic. Recalled a friend when he was a Congressman, "I could walk with Jack into a room full of a hundred women and at least eighty-five of them would be willing to sacrifice their honor and everything else if they could get into a pad with him. And he loved it."(10)

Jack's marriage to Jackie was a union of opposites. She had no interest in politics and was into the arts while JFK was more of a low brow jock type. When they were courting, she knew of his reputation as a womanizer but was reportedly not daunted. Frank Waldrup was the editor on the newspaper which employed Jackie and, aware of

Jack's reputation, told Jackie what he knew about him to try and keep her from getting hurt. While she may have been aware of his philandering, Jackie was probably unprepared for just how flagrant it would he. One observer said, "She found herself stranded at parties while he sneaked out with someone who'd caught his eye, she found herself the object of the barbed pity of other women in her circle." Kennedy assured friends that his wife didn't know about his running around but one friend reported, "After the first year they were together, Jackie was wandering around looking like the survivor of an airplane crash." The marriage had soured early even though many early books on Kennedy painted a picture of a growing love between the couple up to the time of his death. More accurate is the report that just after his presidential inauguration the marriage had become "little more than a matter of mutual convenience ... any romantic love that might have once existed between them had long since evaporated and ... all that was left was a need to put the best public face on things."(11)

In the early days of their marriage Jackie had considered divorce from Jack because of his womanizing. She discussed the matter with the Kennedy family and her own family. Reportedly Joseph Kennedy offered his daughter-in-law one million dollars in cash to stay married to his son and that Jackie accepted the offer. Igor Cassini was the source for the story and said Joseph Kennedy told him. While there is no proof for the story, it has never been denied.(12)

At a party Kennedy would openly flirt with any female who took his fancy, as he always did, even if his wife was with him. A friend of the couple, Betty Spalding, said, "He was obviously not very conscious of how much he hurt his wife." Male friends of the couple would often bring girls around for JFK and Jackie once said to one who didn't that he was "one of the few friends who didn't bring women to Jack." To another friend Jackie grimly commented, "I don't think there are many men who are faithful to their wives."(13)

Two young women, each about twenty, worked in the White House. One worked for Evelyn Lincoln and the other was employed by Pierre Salinger. The pair had no real discernible duties and one or the other or both often joined JFK on his travels. Reporters noted that "both women were available to the President at all hours, that one of them always accompanied the President on his trips." The Secret Service code named them *Fiddle* and *Faddle* and soon that's what everybody called them. The pair hosted many parties in Georgetown for Kennedy Administration people. At Palm Beach, a reporter was dining with Fiddle when she was called to the phone. When she returned she told the newsman, "It's the President. He wants me. Right now. I've got to go." Jackie knew about them and referred to them contemptuously as "the White House dogs." While giving a White House tour to a French photographer, she opened a door and came across either Fiddle or Faddle. She turned to the photographer and said, "This is the young lady who is supposed to be sleeping with my husband." On another occasion Jackie found a pair of panties in her pillow case and disdainfully handed them to Jack saying, "Here, would you find out who these belong to. They're not my size."(14)

JFK had an affair with Pamela Turnure, whom he met at a wedding when she was twenty and he was forty. She then worked for him for a couple of years as a receptionist when he was a Senator. Pam's landlady, Mrs. Leonard Kater, claims that JFK was a regular visitor to Pam's upstairs apartment. Once she heard him throwing pebbles at her window at 1 AM. Mrs. Kater and her husband set up tape recorders to pick up sounds from the bedroom. She concluded that "he was not a very loquacious lover." Finally she paraded up and down in front of the White House with a picket sign which said, "Do you want an adulterer in the White House?" A reporter at a White House party recalled, "I remembered the President suddenly disappeared from the party, and soon afterwards, I saw Pam discreetly heading for the elevator to go to the upstairs family rooms." Jackie was away that day but she knew about Pamela. As President JFK decided that Jackie needed a press secretary of her own - she hadn't asked for one - and he sent her Pamela to fill the post. It was something Jackie had to accept. Reportedly, Kennedy enjoyed the idea of having his mistress work for his wife.(15)

The strain between the couple was evident in other ways. A female once asked JFK if he discussed politics with his wife to which he retorted, "What are you, one of those feminists." James McGregor Burns was running for Congress and asked Jack for an endorsement.

JFK agreed and Burns returned later with a script that involved both Jack and Jackie. Kennedy looked it over and said, "Please cut out any references to my wife." Charles Bartlett had introduced the couple and years later said Jack, "Was pleased with the whole setup... But I don't know how much of an asset he really was to her. He was a lousy husband... So, if I was doing it over, I don't know how hard I would push her." Writer Truman Capote knew the couple and used to have dinner with them. Often he dined alone with Jackie because JFK was out of town. She didn't talk about it but Capote knew she was hurt because her husband "was having all those other broads."(16)

While he campaigned for the presidency in 1960, Kennedy continued his affairs. Morton Downey told Roy Cohn how the Kennedys had managed to assure the silence of a woman with whom Jack had an affair during the campaign. On the night he was nominated in 1960 by the Democrats in Los Angeles, reporters caught him climbing over a back yard fence near where he was staying. JFK shouted that he was off "to meet my father." In fact he was on his way to a liaison with the wife of a former diplomat. He made a series of notes when he had laryngitis at one stage during that campaign. Notes that were thought to have been destroyed and only surfaced on what would have been his seventieth birthday. In one note he worried that if he won the election "my poor [philandering] days are over." After winning the presidency, he told friend and newsman Charles Bartlett that he planned to curb his womanizing ways in the White House. Said Bartlett, "He told me he was going to keep the White House white." One must assume his tongue was firmly in his cheek. At the same time he was arranging to "have his pretty, obliging stewardess, Janet des Rosiers, put on the payroll of the White House secretarial staff." She had been the stewardess on his campaign plane. More accurate with regard to White House purity was the aide who joked to Jack that "The Kennedy administration will be known for its screwing, the way the Eisenhower administration will be known for its golf." To which JFK replied, "You mean nineteen holes in one day."(17)

It was business as usual for JFK in the White House. When Jackie was away from the White House - which was very frequently - the Secret Service provided cover for assignations that took place behind the closed doors of the family quarters. Said one observer, "Jack was well supplied with stars and starlets through Sinatra and the Hollywood connection." The Secret Service was sworn to silence about these liaisons but the servants weren't. JFK had his attorney prepare a statement for those employees to sign which pledged them to not speak or write about their experiences in the White House. When word of this reached the press it caused an uproar. The President then asked one of his aides - the chief usher - to take the blame for initiating the idea.(18)

One of the President's long term affairs was with Mary Meyer. She shared an apartment with Pamela Turnure - it has been said of Jack's women that they liked each other and befriended each other. According to Mary, JFK first asked her to sleep with him in December, 1961, but the affair didn't start until early in 1962. She visited the White House several times a week when Jackie was out of town. Mary was supposedly a good friend of Jackie. She and Kennedy were together at least thirty times from 1962 until Jack's death. She once brought six marijuana joints with her to the White House and the President smoked three. Finally he wouldn't smoke any more saying, "Suppose the Russians do something now." Meyer was mysteriously murdered a few months after the President's assassination. The crime was never solved. Throughout her affair, Mary kept a diary and left instructions for it to be destroyed after her death. For a while the diary couldn't be located. When it was finally found it was turned over to a CIA friend of Meyer's who did destroy it. The diary contained several dozen references to JFK.(19)

Kennedy had no trouble getting his own girls but close male friends were always happy to send some over. One reporter was once overheard telling a woman how to get into the White House with a note he wanted delivered to the President. JFK called the man afterwards to report, "I got your message - both of them." Airline stewardesses were frequent visitors to the mansion. Nor was Kennedy overly concerned with being discreet. One afternoon the President was in bed with a woman when they were interrupted by a knock on the door. Opening the door an angry JFK found two foreign affairs advisers with a batch of cables and a clear view of the woman in bed.

Kennedy didn't bother to close the door. He read the cables, made his decisions and went back to the woman.(20)

Traphes Bryant was the kennel keeper at the White House and he claimed to have seen several nude male (including JFK) and female swimmers in the pool. All were drinking. Then the alarm went off which indicated Jackie had returned home unexpectedly - a service performed by the Secret Service for JFK. There was a rush to get rid of the booze and the bodies. Bryant also said he saw a naked blonde once come out of the elevator. His liking for blondes was a source of complaint by the upstairs maids whom Bryant overheard say, "Why can't he make it easier for us? Why do we always have to be searching for blonde hairs and blonde hobby pins? Why can't he get himself a steady brunette?" Jackie was a brunette(21)

In the summer of 1963 it came to light that there was a private retreat on Capitol Hill that catered to government officials. One hostess was Ellen Rometsch who charged $200 a night for her services. Before publishing his story on this reporter Clark Mollenhoff went to Attorney General Robert Kennedy to see what he knew of the situation. Bobby checked it out and found that nobody in the White House had yet been "entertained" by her. Bobby knew, however, that Jack had asked to meet Rometsch. To protect his brother, Bobby acted swiftly and by August Ellen and her husband were deported from the US and the club shut. After both brothers were dead, another episode of Bobby stepping in to protect his brother came to light. In 1975 William Safire got some documents from the files of J. Edgar Hoover showing that early in 1961 Robert had paid a $500,000 settlement to a woman who claimed she had been engaged to Jack in 1951 and had sued for breach of promise. According to the documents, RFK had not denied paying the settlement for his brother and therefore Hoover believed the story was true.(22)

The idea that JFK used prostitutes-- or wanted to-- as with Rometsch, has other support. A whore was once sent to Roy Cohn on his boat. This woman claimed to have been one of JFK's girls at the White House. A staffer at the White House recalled being stopped on his rounds of that building by a Secret Service agent who said, "The President has got a hundred-dollar hooker with him right now." Another source in Los Angeles remembers getting requests from the Secret Service to "find a woman for the President." Sometimes the order was for two girls at a time. The evidence seems to indicate that Kennedy liked group sex.(23)

The President's Palm Beach retreat in Florida was another favorite spot for dalliances. A regular ritual was a leisurely stroll down North Avenue with an aide, pointing out women who took his fancy. The aide took note of all this, presumably, for many of these women later found their way to the President's bed, if not at his place then at the home of a friend or neighbor. Newsmen saw them sneaking in at night and/or coming out early in the morning. CBS's Robert Pierpoint remembered seeing a young woman and Kennedy emerging from a cottage one morning. They embraced before she stepped into a waiting limousine. JFK entered the limo for another quick embrace. Then one of the President's sisters drove up in a convertible and yelled, "Come on, Mildred!" Mildred gave Jack another lingering kiss and left the limo to join the sister.(24)

When he wasn't having sex he liked to think about it, and to talk about it, and joke about it. He loved to talk about sex and gossip about the sex lives of others. He was said to be able to remember the plot of a dirty movie seen years earlier. He liked to fantasize about sex with the help of movies. One time Bobby Baker came across Kennedy in the Congressional dining room seated with a stunning blonde and a friend named Bill Thompson. Put up to it by Kennedy, Thompson called Baker over to the table and said, about the woman, "She gives the best head in the United States." The woman seemed oblivious to it all while JFK broke up with laughter and then said to the embarrassed Baker, "Relax Bobby. She's German and she doesn't understand a word of English. But what Bill's saying is absolutely right." A Kennedy aide said that the President asked him to try and make it with Letitia Baldrige, Jackie's social secretary, and then report back to JFK as to how she was in bed. The aide declined and suggested Jack find out for himself.(25)

A reporter for *Look* magazine by the name of Laura Bergquist interviewed Jack and recalled, "I can't believe this guy! He's the president of the United States and when I go up there for an interview, he's in his shorts, that's all. And they're shorts that don't even fit! And he's sitting around scratching himself in various places and the first thing he says to me is 'Hi Laura, getting much?'" She had just returned from a Cuban trip where she'd interviewed Che Guevara. Kennedy wanted to know about the Cuban. Laura started to tell him then JFK announced, "I think you have the hots for Che." Kennedy then left the room. Thought Laura, "That burned me. Here I'd come back from Cuba with all kinds of information that might have some value for him and he dismissed it all with that macho remark."

After another trip to Havana, Laura met with the president again. He wanted Laura to tell him about Fidel Castro. His first question was, "Who's Fidel sleeping with?" Annoyed again Bergquist thought, "Well, I didn't know who Fidel was sleeping with. It didn't matter to me, but it did matter to him. It burned me because I had so much to tell him about Castro, and he didn't ask me!"(26)

In another one of those notes he scribbled out while he had laryngitis during the 1960 campaign he bragged, "I got into the blonde." A woman reported that Kennedy thought there was only one place for women and that was horizontal. Said a friend, "I think he was discreet to an extent and yet I think he wanted people to know he was better with women than his father was." Nor was he concerned with being caught for the friend added that JFK told him, "They can't touch me while I'm alive and after I'm dead who cares." When another friend told Kennedy he was thinking about getting a divorce, the President advised him, "Why don't you try it the way I'm doing it?" The friend noted that he had to go home five nights a week while Kennedy often didn't. A few days later JFK called the man and said, "You're right. If I had to go home three nights a week, I'd go up the wall."(27)

One woman that he pursued but never bedded remarked, "The whole thing with him was pursuit. I think he was secretly disappointed when a woman gave in. It meant that the low esteem in which he held women was once again validated." She once asked him about his excessive womanizing to which he said, "I don't know, really. I guess I just can't help it." Journalist John White had dated sister Kathleen Kennedy and thought of JFK's philandering that, "He was completely driven to dominate them. Once he got them, he lost interest and moved on to the next." Author Gary Wills reported that in 1960 a woman he talked to thought that if Jack's womanizing was known it would help him politically - that it had political appeal. Whether it was power over Khrushchev or power over women it was appealing. Kathleen wrote to her brother, "It's just that sort of treatment that women really like." Wills added that perhaps women could trust a man who "treats 'em rough" to be tough in other contexts as well. When JFK first took up with his mob mistress, Judith Campbell, Ted Kennedy had asked her for a date also, but was refused. According to Campbell, Jack never forgot that and on several occasions when they were in bed together he said to her, "Boy, if Teddy only knew, he'd be eating his heart out."(28)

Certainly JFK was a prodigious cocksman. Smathers, no slouch himself, said, "He had the most active libido of any man I have ever known." Said a fellow congressman, "Travelling with him was like travelling with a bull." Yet, like most super studs - Mussolini for another example - he was a lousy lay, judging from the few available reports. A conquest in England reported that, at a party, she found herself ushered into a bedroom alone with Kennedy. He talked briefly about England while he locked the door and undressed. Then they had a "hurried sexual encounter" followed by a discreet return to the party. Another one reported that, "He was as compulsive as Mussolini. Up against the wall *Signora*, if you have five minutes, that sort of thing. He was not a cozy, touching sort of man." A third conquest said, "Sex was something to have done, not to be doing." He wasn't in it for the cuddling." Judith Campbell used to assume the top position when the President's back acted up. Gradually it was the only position they used. "I was there to service him," said Campbell. His early love, Inga Arvad, reported, "If he wanted to make love, you'd make love - now." If they had fifteen minutes to get somewhere and Inga said no, that they didn't have time for sex, Jack would look at his watch and say, "we've got ten minutes, let's go."(29)

As for Jack's equipment - and all the Kennedy brothers - Truman Capote has provided an interesting account. "What I don't understand is why everybody said the Kennedys were so sexy," he reported. "I know a lot about cocks - I've seen an awful lot of them - and if you put all the Kennedys together, you wouldn't have one good one. I used to see Jack when I was staying with Loel and Gloria Guinness in

Palm Beach. I had a little guest cottage with its own private beach, and he would come down so he could swim in the nude. He had absolutely nothin'! Bobby was the same way; I don't know how he had all those children. As for Teddy - forget it."(30)

One of JFK's better known paramours was Judith Campbell, who went public in 1975 - then Judith Campbell Exner - and opened the floodgates to a tide of revelations about Kennedy. The couple met on February 17, 1960 in Las Vegas. JFK was electioneering at the time and had his campaign plane stop at the Nevada City. He took a couple of men with him to Frank Sinatra's suite at the Sands Hotel. It was there that JFK was introduced, by Sinatra, to Judith Campbell. Their first sexual encounter was March 9, 1960, at the Plaza Hotel in New York. It was disappointing for Judith, who got the impression she was just there to service the candidate and said, "He did not appear to want to give very much, just take." They continued to meet, some twenty times in the White House, lunch in the Oval Office and in various other locales such as New Hampshire, Los Angeles and New York. The White House log recorded seventy phone calls between the President and Campbell from the end of 1960 to mid 1962.

Within a month or so of meeting Kennedy, Campbell was introduced, by Sinatra again, to reputed Mafia boss Salvatore "Sam" Giancana, the man recruited by the CIA to kill Castro. Judith began a relationship with him and claimed she sometimes went from the bed of one to the other. A few of her phone calls to JFK came from Giancana's house. Apparently Sam pursued Campbell vigorously when he found out she was seeing the President. Hoping perhaps to have a connection to avoid future prosecutions. Judith was said to be well connected in the worlds of show business and organized crime "where she was regularly passed around among a certain set of not-too-reliable characters" In her memoirs Judith claimed JFK never knew she was seeing Sam but later she told her co-author, Ovid Demaris, that she had lied about that and had in fact told Kennedy that she was seeing him.(31)

Word of this indiscretion reached J. Edgar Hoover and he met with Bobby on February 27, 1962, when he detailed the relationship to the Attorney General. Hoover worried about the possibility of blackmail and that Campbell had been planted to incriminate the President. What Bobby said is unknown, but he met with his brother on March 22 for a private discussion. JFK's affair with Judith ended abruptly thereafter.(32)

So wide ranging was JFK's womanizing that stories have linked him with several women who were associated with Stephen Ward of the Profumo scandal fame in England. A connection with Ward is possible since Ward, an osteopath, had treated Joseph Kennedy and Averell Harriman. The latter was a member of the Kennedy administration. One of the women was Suzy Chang, who was born in China in 1955. Her family settled in the US during the 1950s but Suzy first lived in London. She was a friend of Ward and allegedly had an affair with JFK in 1960, in the US. Author Anthony Summers has official US documents on the woman and she attracted intense federal interest at the time of the Profumo scandal. In June, 1963, Kennedy was in London, on an official visit when the New York *Journal-American* printed an item which linked her with "one of the biggest names in American politics." It was hinted that an ever bigger scandal lay hidden in the Profumo affair. JFK's name wasn't specifically mentioned.

As soon as the item appeared, JFK received a phone call at Prime Minister Macmillan's home. The President immediately assigned Robert to damage control. The news story ran in just one edition of the *Journal-American* and was then pulled from all later editions. Within 48 hours the two authors of the story were in Bobby's Washington office. After ascertaining the man referred to was JFK Robert asked the reporters for their sources. The men refused and the meeting ended in a deadlock. Also present at the meeting was Courtney Evans, Hoover's liaison man. After the meeting RFK "admonished" Evans "not to write a memorandum" on what took place. Evans told Hoover and the next day Robert said he hoped Evans didn't misunderstand what he had said previously. The Attorney General threatened an anti-trust suit against the paper if the story was pursued. It was dropped. In the latter part of the 1980s Chang reportedly had a new name and lived on the US eastern seaboard.(33)

Another Ward woman who claimed an affair with JFK, after he was elected President but before his inauguration, was Mariella

Novotny, who was eighteen at the time. Mariella was a Czech and said she was related to Anton Novotny, then leader of that country. On the day she left England on the trip to the US where she claimed she dallied with Jack, she saw Stephen Ward. Later she would claim she thought she was a pawn in a plot to compromise the President-elect.

At one of Ward's parties Novotny met a US man named Harry Towers, connected somehow to show business. He asked her to accompany him to the US and she did. They arrived in the US on December 14, 1960, and lived together in New York hotels. Novotny said she turned to prostitution after Towers arranged dates for her. Towers denied such charges. Mariella was arrested in March, 1961, and charged with prostitution. Towers was also arrested. Both were released on low bail. Harry jumped bail that year and fled behind the Iron Curtain where he stayed for two decades. Mariella also jumped bail and left the US by boat on May 31, 1961. An FBI report stated that Mariella "Was obviously aided by persons unknown to leave the US."(34)

While in the US Novotny said Towers introduced her to Peter Lawford, then took her to a number of parties. At one party hosted by singer Vic Damone she met Kennedy and the pair had quick sex. This encounter was arranged by Lawford. Dean Martin's former wife Jeanne said of Lawford, "I saw Peter in the role of pimp for Jack Kennedy." Later Mariella said she participated in a group sex game with JFK. Two prostitutes were used who played doctor and nurse, with uniforms, to Kennedy's patient. Lawford recruited the hookers and after a teasing session they all had sex together.

Novotny also said, "she visited the President at a house in Washington and also had sex with the President's brother, Robert." When she arrived back in England, Mariella told her story to reporter Peter Earle of the *News of the World*. Most of her story was never published - for diplomatic reasons. Earle still believed her story years later although most don't. Mariella gave the FBI an address book listing names of her New York clients, many of whom were said to be well known. The FBI says the book has been destroyed. In 1983 Novotny died of a drug overdose.(35)

55--Sex and Politicians

Before she died in 1967, actress Jayne Mansfield said she'd had a sporadic three year affair with Jack. Lawford had introduced them and JFK was turned on, said Peter, the first time he met her because she was pregnant. Leslie Devereux was an expensive New York hooker who was given an address by Lawford and told to meet him there. It turned out to be the Carlyle and when the pair reached Kennedy's suite, Jack smiled and said, "All right, Peter, disappear." Leslie had four or five meetings with JFK with standard sex at first, drifting into kinky. Devereux said they did a little S&M with Leslie tying Jack's hands and feet to the bedposts, blindfolding him and teasing him with a feather and her fingernails.

On inauguration night, after many parties, Lawford imported six Hollywood starlets who all wanted to be with the President. Peter arranged a line-up of them and the President selected two to close out his first day in office.(36)

The major female figure in the Profumo case was Christine Keeler. In July, 1965, she claimed to have had sex with Kennedy. Little attention was paid to this as she was not considered credible and most thought she hoped to get money from such a statement. The president monitored developments in the Profumo case very closely and ordered all cables on the subject from the embassy in London sent to him personally. A friend, Charles Spaulding, noted, "He felt terribly sorry for Profumo and he sympathized with the way Profumo was caught. Jack also thought the girls involved were kind of cute." Keeler and Mandy Rice-Davies arrived in New York City in July, 1962, and stayed there for about a week. They began with more grandiose plans of making it in the US and going on to Hollywood. However, they ran out of money and returned home. The FBI and Hoover became aware of the trip when they were checking out the American end of the Profumo scandal. On July 2, 1963, RFK asked Hoover if he could tell him exactly what Keeler and Rice-Davies did when they visited New York. It seems a strange thing to do. Why would he have any interest in what two then unknown women did on a seven day visit to New York. Unless he was worried that his brother had been involved with one or the other or both and wanted to know for certain to prepare for damage control in the event of a scandal. The Profumo affair had broken less than one month earlier. Since the

Kennedys and Hoover disliked each other intensely it must have been a difficult request for Bobby to make to Hoover. Yet, like Joseph Kennedy before, Robert couldn't, for whatever reason, ask his own brother about it.(37)

Kennedy's most famous affair was the one with Marilyn Monroe. She wasn't the only star he was involved with, however. Other names linked with his include: Angie Dickinson, Kim Novak, Janet Leigh and Rhonda Fleming. None acknowledges any such connection. JFK had two main conduits to the stars. One was Frank Sinatra and the other was his brother-in-law Peter Lawford.

The first to expose the JFK/Monroe affair was columnist Earl Wilson in his 1974 book *Show Business Laid Bare*. Wilson said the affair started around 1961 and that it was pursued in New York's Carlyle Hotel, the Beverly Hills Hotel, Peter Lawford's Santa Monica home and other locales. She used to call him "The Prez" and thought her screwing him helped ease his chronic backache. One famous gathering was at the Carlyle Hotel in May, 1962, where Monroe, dressed in "skin and beads" sang Happy Birthday to Jack at a party in his honor. At that hotel Kennedy had a private penthouse suite. So private was it that when the Washington pouch was delivered to him there he came down to the lobby to get it. Said an aide, "Whatever happened in there, nobody ever knew." Reportedly he used it for a variety of assignations.(38)

Before the hideaway at the Carlyle, JFK had kept a suite on the 8th floor of Washington's Mayfair Hotel from 1955 to the end of 1959. An FBI informant referred to it as "Kennedy's personal playpen." This individual attended a party at the suite during which Jack and Senator Estes Kefauver and "their respective dates made love in plain view of the other partygoers. When they were done, the two senators simply exchanged mates and began anew."(39)

When JFK was with Monroe at parties at Lawford's place he would take her for a stroll around the pool "and tell her raunchy stories while his hands roamed around her body." He was sitting beside her at dinner one time and put one hand under the table. He put it on her leg and moved it up until he found she wore no underwear. He quickly took his hand away. Marilyn said with a smile, "He hadn't counted on going that far."(40)

Later research has shown their affair began much earlier, as early perhaps as 1951. There are memories from that time of a young JFK and Monroe attending parties given by Charles Feldman, a frequent host to the Kennedys and Marilyn's agent. Two of her friends said she was seeing JFK during the last few months of her marriage to Joe DiMaggio. By early 1960, Marilyn was often seen at the Lawford beach house for campaign meetings and parties. By the time of the 1960 Democratic convention in July, 1960 in Los Angeles, rumors of an affair between them were widespread. So much so that bandleader Freddy Karger, a former Monroe flame, refused to book his band for a convention ball at which JFK would attend. Humorist Art Buchwald wrote a humorous piece about the couple for his newspaper just after the November election.(41)

The affair may have started later with the introduction by Peter Lawford. The actor arranged many of the meetings for the couple and on at least one occasion he took photos of Marilyn performing a sex act on JFK while he lounged in a large marble bathtub.(42)

Deborah Gould, Lawford's third wife, said "Peter told me that Jack had always wanted to meet Marilyn Monroe. It was one of his fantasies. Could Peter arrange for that? He did - he would do anything he was asked to do." Marilyn told some of her friends about her affair with Jack. One was Paula Strasberg. Another was reporter Sidney Skolsky whom she told that when she and JFK were alone in Lawford's house they had to leave a light on. If the light went out the Secret Service would break down the door and burst in. Another favorite trysting place for them was the Carlyle. Marilyn, like other women, found JFK to be an inadequate lover who "had little time for the preliminaries of lovemaking." To reporter James Bacon, Monroe said Kennedy "wouldn't indulge in foreplay."(43)

George Smathers said he heard about the Monroe liaison from JFK himself and said, "I never did believe that Jack Kennedy had a big deal going with Marilyn Monroe until after Bobby. He took her away from Bobby, something like that - Jack would take a girl away from his brothers, or a friend, for a short relationship, at any time." Smathers was wrong about the specifics in this case but perhaps accurate in general.(44)

Just hours before she died in August, 1962, Monroe reportedly phoned Peter Lawford and whispered, "Say good-bye to the President."(45)

JFK and British PM Harold Macmillan met in the Bahamas in December, 1962. One evening the pair were sitting around talking in Nassau. Kennedy eyed a young woman nearby and said to Macmillan, "You know, it's funny, but if I go too long without a woman, I get a headache."(46)

ROBERT F. KENNEDY

Always considered to have been the "moral" brother of the Kennedy clan Robert Kennedy's only indiscretion was thought to have been with Marilyn Monroe. More recent evidence, while brief and sketchy, suggests that RFK was much more of a womanizer than previously thought. He was born on November 20, 1925 and served as Attorney General during his brother's presidency. In 1964 he was elected US Senator from the state of New York. Bobby was assassinated on June 6, 1968 while campaigning for the Democratic presidential nomination. Robert married Ethel Skakel in 1950 and by 1960 the couple had seven children and RFK had just been named "Father of the Year."

Much of his reputation for morality may date back to his reported attitude toward sex as a young man. At seventeen it was said that he would never exceed what he considered proper behavior with a girl. Schoolmate Sam Adams said, "To Bobby, women were supposed to be as much Catholic, and as much beyond reproach, as he was... He was very intolerant of smutty jokes. He wouldn't laugh at them, wouldn't even listen. It may have been part of his religious approach to purity and cleanliness." The Kennedy family considered him to be a prig and he and Jack clashed over JFK's liaison with Inga Arvad. RFK didn't like the open sexual relationship his brother had outside of marriage. Said one observer, "Robert was shocked at his brother's flagrant disregard of the moral code he himself prized... This argument over Jack's sexual practices would continue all their lives." Sam Adams added about RFK that at Harvard, "He never joined in the sexual escapades of the other boys. Once in a while, the other fellows would make a trip to the local red light district in the Boston area. Bobby never went along."(1)

Either such reports were erroneous or sometime along the way Robert changed his ways. Even some books about him less than a decade old report no other affair except with Monroe. One, by Kennedy family friend Arthur Schlesinger Jr., even, indirectly, discounts the Monroe liaison with the author writing, "I doubt whether they had seen each other more than half a dozen times." Yet Schlesinger knew more than he wrote. Years later he gave a telling comment, orally, about Bobby to writer Anthony Summers when he said, "Bobby was human. He liked to drink and he liked young women. He indulged that liking when he traveled - and he had to travel a great deal."(2)

As well there is a claim by Mariella Novotny, connected to the Stephen Ward/John Profumo scandal in the UK that she had sex with both Robert and Jack. Other evidence comes from Jeanne Martin, former wife of entertainer Dean, who moved in the Peter Lawford circle. While seeing Lawford as a pimp for JFK, she added, "It was a nasty business - they were just too gleeful about it, not discreet at all. Of course there was nothing discreet about either of the Kennedys, Bob or Jack. It was like high-school time, very sophomoric. The things that went on in that beach house were just mind-boggling. Ethel could be in one room and Bobby could be in another with this or that woman. Yes, Bobby was a grabber, but not in the terms that Jack was... Bobby didn't have eyes for me, but I do know this. I have a friend that was in the library with him, and before she knew it the door was locked and he threw her on the couch."(3)

RFK and Marilyn may have first met shortly after the 1960 presidential election. The introduction took place at a party hosted by Lawford at his Santa Monica beach house. According to the story they slipped away from the party and had sex in the back seat of a parked car. It was a relationship that would last until Marilyn's death although the first public appearance of the couple wasn't until the May, 1962 birthday party for Jack in New York City. RFK's affair with Marilyn overlapped with that of JFK's. Robert's interest in her was obvious at that party. Adlai Stevenson joked that to talk to her he had to break "through the strong defenses established by Robert Kennedy, who was dodging around her like a moth around a flame." Bobby hovered around her all night. A reporter spoke to Kennedy brother-in-law Steve Smith and brought up the question about an affair between Monroe and JFK. Smith replied, "Jack? But I thought it was Bobby."(4)

A neighbor of Marilyn in Los Angeles, Jeanne Carmen, recalled opening the door of Monroe's apartment in the summer or fall of 1961 and finding a surprised Bobby on the doorstep. She kept saying, "Come in" but he kept standing there. Finally Marilyn came out of the bathroom and kissed him. These two women dressed RFK up another time in a false beard that belonged to Jack Benny, a baseball cap and sunglasses and dared him to go to a nearby nudist beach telling him he would never be recognized. They did go and he wasn't spotted. Monroe's studio maid and another friend both remember hour long phone calls from RFK to Monroe. The actress started to keep a diary after Bobby got annoyed with her once saying she didn't remember things he told her. Jeanne Martin had sometimes seen Marilyn at the Lawford beach house and was "quite sure" that Marilyn had an affair with both brothers.(5)

After the actress died a handwritten note on Kennedy stationery was found among her things. Written by Kennedy sister Jean Smith, and undated, it thanked Monroe for sending her father a note and added, "Understand that you and Bobby are the new item! We all think you should come with him when he comes back East!" Through her husband Steve Smith, Jean claimed no recollection of the note but didn't actually deny writing it. Joseph Kennedy had a stroke in December, 1961 which may have been the reason Marilyn wrote to the father. The note indicates the Kennedys knew of the affair.(6)

During the summer of 1962 RFK made several trips to the West Coast. Ostensibly the reason was for discussions about a film version of his book. While there he and Monroe met several times - usually at parties at Lawford's house. Neighbors of the actress claim to have seen him visit Monroe's Brentwood home a number of times during June and July. She also placed many phone calls to Bobby's Washington office.

Marilyn's affair with Bobby was much more serious than her fling with his brother. As one writer said, "She was not drawn to Bobby physically, as he was to her. But he took a personal interest in her, while the President did not. This was far more dangerous to Marilyn than a strictly sexual attraction would have been." By early in 1962 she hinted to friends that she might marry again and it might be to a very important man in government. Those who assumed she meant Robert were surprised at her lack of discretion and realism. One of her oldest friends, Robert Slatzer, stated that Marilyn showed him her diary which outlined meetings with RFK and told him "Robert Kennedy promised to marry me. What do you think of that?" Near the end of her life the actress had many conversations with journalist W.J. Weatherby. A little after the May, 1962 birthday party she told him she might remarry someday. When Weatherby asked who it might be, Marilyn replied, "Only problem is, he's married right now. And he's famous so we have to meet in secret... He's in politics... In Washington." Weatherby added, "Her pride wouldn't allow her to seem of only passing interest." With the Kennedys she would be. One observer had RFK describe Monroe as "a dumb broad." Another, likely more accurate, had him call her a "very remarkable girl."(7)

The affair between RFK and Monroe had deteriorated badly by July, 1962. Slatzer termed it "a troubled love affair that had apparently gone too far." Near the end Slatzer described her as paranoid about the relationship, convinced her phone was tapped and "terrified of something or someone." Her friend claimed Marilyn recorded Bobby's pillow talk in her diary, including the details of a CIA plot to kill Fidel Castro. Slatzer warned her that the diary was dangerous. Marilyn said she had a press conference scheduled to blow the whole affair wide open unless RFK contacted her. Slatzer advised her to drop the idea and forget what she herself called a "bad experience." The actress died two days before this supposed press conference was due to be held. There was also a reported quarrel between the couple during which Monroe told Bobby that she was tired of being "passed around like a piece of meat," that she had had it and "didn't want Jack or Bobby to use her anymore."(8)

Marilyn Monroe died of a drug overdose on the night of August 4, 1962. A full investigation of her death by a grand jury was never done. A thorough autopsy was never done. People changed their stories over time. No drug traces were found in her stomach. Other ways of overdosing include by injection - no needle marks on the body were ever mentioned - or by enema. If the latter was used traces of drugs would have appeared in the intestines. They weren't checked at the autopsy. When they arrived on the scene of the death the police were surprised at the tidiness of the room - usually a convulsive overdose victim leaves disorder behind. RFK is said to have made a deposition to the police - a deposition which later, said the police, went missing. Monroe's telephone records were spirited away by the police, in two separate groups. One group of records was taken by the FBI while a different set was taken by an LA police captain named James Hamilton, a friend of RFK. These records remained "lost" for two decades until the ones Hamilton had taken surfaced. One year after Monroe's death Hamilton retired from the police force and became the chief security officer for the National Football League. One of those who recommended him for the job was Bobby. The telephone records were important because they showed a large number of calls between Bobby and Marilyn, some to his private number in Washington. A special ABC news program on the subject of Monroe's death was canned from the air, in the mid 1980s, at the last possible minute by station chief Roone Arledge, a friend of Ethel Kennedy.(9)

Until about six weeks before she died, Marilyn used to call Robert in Washington on his private number at the Justice Department. However, after June 25 she began to call the general switchboard number instead. RFK had disconnected the private line, evidence he was trying to break off the affair. Her indiscrete behavior and her own mob links - through former lover Frank Sinatra - perhaps made her too great a risk for the Kennedys to bother with her anymore. On June 26 Bobby was in LA and he and the actress had dinner at the Lawfords. The next day RFK went to Monroe's house and spent an hour there, according to the house keeper. Apparently she was told never to call or contact the Kennedy brothers again. During the next month Marilyn was still trying to reach Robert and complained to Slatzer that RFK "had got what he wanted" and that men "used her only as a plaything."(10)

On the weekend that Marilyn died, August 3 to 5, RFK said he was staying at the ranch of his friend John Bates in Gilroy, California, 350 miles from Los Angeles. With him were his wife Ethel and some of their children. Bates claims there was no way Robert could have slipped off to Los Angeles during that weekend. Yet several people swear that he was in LA. Monroe's house-keeper, Eunice Murray, claims RFK was there on August 4 arguing with the actress at her home. Earlier, though, Murray had said he wasn't. Peter Lawford publicly said that RFK wasn't in town that weekend but privately told a friend that Bobby was in town, saw Monroe and left, and then Monroe phoned Lawford. Two senior police officers say that Bobby was in town the night Monroe died."(11)

There is no shortage of theories to explain the actress's death, that RFK killed her or that the Mafia killed her to try and set up Bobby. RFK, the reasoning goes, might have wanted to kill her because she threatened to expose him. The story about the press conference is likely false as she had never done anything like that in her life. The Kennedy brothers, all of them, treated women with total contempt and arrogance and it would never occur to them to kill something as inconsequential or harmless as a woman. Monroe had mental problems enough of her own at the time of her death, exacerbated no doubt by dealing with the Kennedys, and probably did commit suicide. However, there has been a massive coverup of the details.

What might have happened, at a minimum, that night is that RFK saw the actress on August 4 to break off for good. A distraught Monroe phoned Lawford later. Recognizing trouble in her voice Lawford and perhaps RFK as well, went to Monroe's house where she was dead or dying. They delayed reporting the situation to the police for several hours - there was indeed a delay of many hours - while Robert got out of town via a helicopter to the airport while Lawford stayed behind to remove any and all evidence connecting her with either of the Kennedys. The police aided whatever coverup went on by conducting an abysmally poor investigation and by losing many of the important pieces of evidence. Truman Capote said, "The Kennedys didn't kill her... She committed suicide. But they did pay one of her best friends to keep quiet about their relationship with her. The friend knew where all the skeletons were, and after Marilyn died, they sent her on a year-long cruise around the world. For a whole year no one knew where she was."(12)

When RFK ran for the Senate in New York in 1964 right-wingers circulated a booklet called *The Strange Death of Marilyn Monroe*. In it they charged RFK had Monroe killed by Communist agents under his control after she threatened to expose him. No such rumors were used against him in 1968 when he started his presidential run.(13)

One man who had strong feelings was Joe DiMaggio. The baseball star had wed Monroe in 1954 but the union had lasted only nine months. After Marilyn's death Joe instructed the funeral directors, "Be sure that none of those damned Kennedys come to the funeral." At an Old Timer's Day baseball event at New York's Yankee Stadium the two men met. Robert extended his hand to DiMaggio but Joe refused to shake it.(14)

EDWARD M. KENNEDY

As the last of the Kennedy boys, Edward M. Kennedy was as aggressive and thoughtless a womanizer as his brother Jack. Where Ted differed from his brothers was in turning to booze. Not only was he a womanizer but usually a staggering drunk to boot. His womanizing led to the infamous Chappaquiddick incident and, with his gross behavior during and after that event, combined to kill his chances for a run at the presidency. Edward Moore Kennedy was born on February 22, 1932, and elected to the Senate from Massachusetts in 1962. He married Virginia Joan Bennett in 1958. They were divorced in 1985.

While he was a student at Harvard in the spring of 1951, Edward paid his roommate's brother to take a Spanish exam for him. Within hours the cheating was discovered and both men were expelled. Ted was readmitted to the university in the fall of 1953. For ten years the Kennedy family kept the incident covered up. At law school he was arrested at least four times for reckless driving. Before marrying Joan, Edward showed up at every party where he drank heavily and then drove recklessly, earning the nickname "Cadillac Eddie." Along with a classmate Ted kept "a list of girls who were rated from A (top quality) to E (only in an emergency)." Other classmates agreed that he dated mainly As and Bs. When he did, he made his intentions clear from the start. "If the dates indicated they would not go to bed with him, he would be too polite to ditch them, but they never got another call."(1)

After Jack Kennedy was elected President in November, 1960, his Massachusetts Senate seat came vacant. Patriarch Joseph Kennedy wasn't about to let it go and said, of that seat, "Look, I paid for it. It belongs in the family." Since a senator had to be at least thirty years old Edward was then too young to fill it. The problem was solved when JFK had the Massachusetts governor appoint Benjamin Smith, JFK's former college roommate, to fill the vacancy with the understanding that Smith would vacate the seat in 1962 when Ted turned thirty. Smith did.(2)

Ted met Judith Campbell the same time JFK did, in February, 1960, in Las Vegas at Frank Sinatra's hotel suite. JFK had made a lunch date with Campbell for the next day. The evening they met, Edward tried to persuade her to fly to Denver with him the following day in a manner Campbell considered as "childishly temperamental." When Judith told JFK of the attempted pick-up he was amused and agreed with Campbell's assessment of his brother adding that he was unlikely to fulfill the Kennedy destiny.(3)

One of Edward's biographers, James MacGregor Burns, a Kennedy friend, admitted that reporters, Senators, their staff people, friendly or hostile, have no doubt "that Kennedy is involved, and has been for some time, in a series of brief flirtations and longer, more intense involvements." A congressional friend of Ted's remarked, "He is the least discreet guy on the Hill. I have told him ten times 'Ted, you're acting like a fool. Everybody knows you wherever you go. Jack could smuggle girls up the back way of the Carlyle Hotel. But you're not nearly so discreet as you should be.'" Ted replied to his friend, "Yeah, I guess you're right." But he never listened. A Washington reporter added, "The important thing here is that it shows how reckless Kennedy is with his career. He just doesn't care. He wants to have his fun. He knows he can get caught any time, yet he makes no effort to be discreet."(4)

In the two years before Chappaquiddick Kennedy had been having an affair with a woman named Countess Llana Campbell whom he took to rented cottages several times for long weekend parties on Martha's Vineyard. At the time of Chappaquiddick, Ted was involved with Helga Wagner, who lived in Key Biscayne, Florida. After his car went into the water, but before he notified the police, Kennedy made many phone calls. One of them was to Wagner.(5)

By early 1969, Ted had reportedly reverted to his "Cadillac Eddie" image for he was drinking heavily and driving recklessly. Many reporters witnessed an incoherent and drunken Kennedy on a plane and while some filed memos with their publications nothing was published. John Lindsay of *Newsweek* wrote that he thought Ted was "an accident waiting to happen." Nothing was printed because "of what was virtually a journalistic safe passage still granted by the media to the Kennedys on questions involving their personal life." Kennedy's marriage was badly strained at the time.(6)

On July 18, 1969, Kennedy left a party on Chappaquiddick Island accompanied by 28 year old Mary Jo Kopechne. He drove his car off a bridge into a pond. Ted escaped but Mary Jo didn't and died in the submerged vehicle. The party that day on the island - which is just east of Martha's Vineyard - was to honor the "boiler room girls," the secretaries who had helped Robert Kennedy the most on his presidential campaign the previous year. Attending the party were six women all of whom were unmarried and in their twenties and six men all in their thirties and all but one married. None of the wives were in attendance. It would have been easier to hold the party across the narrow channel in a restaurant or hotel in Edgartown but instead an isolated cottage on a relatively isolated island was chosen. The women were all checked into an Edgartown hotel. The man who rented the cottage told its owner that it would be used only by himself, his wife and his children. It's easy to see what the real purpose of the affair was, at least in the minds of the men who organized it.(7)

Kennedy said the pair left the party at 11:15 PM and were heading to the ferry to return to Edgartown. He got lost and went off the paved road leading to the ferry onto a dirt road and then off of it into a small pond. Ted made several dives to try and rescue Mary Jo, after he got out of the car, but failed. Then he walked the one and a half miles back to the party and got two of the men there, Joseph Gargan and Paul Markham, and the three returned to the scene. They all made more dives but once again failed to rescue Mary Jo. Edward told the men to return to the party and that he would go to Edgartown and report the accident to the police. The channel across to Edgartown was 500 feet. The scheduled ferry service stopped at midnight. However, the ferryman was required by his contract to operate at any hour if called. Outside normal hours he could charge a fee. Ted didn't call him though, he swam across the channel, he said, and went to his hotel - the Shiretown Inn. No one saw him arrive in wet clothes but at 2:25 AM one of the owners saw Ted standing, in dry clothes in the lobby. The owner asked if Ted wanted something. Kennedy said no that he had been awakened by a noise, looked for his watch to see the time but couldn't find it. Then he asked the owner for the time and was told it. This rather strange behavior seems to have been Kennedy establishing an alibi for a plan that was never used. That plan called for Joe Gargan, Ted's cousin, to shoulder full responsibility for the incident.(8)

By 7:30 AM Kennedy was in yachting clothes and chatting amiably with other hotel guests. Gargan and Markham showed up at the hotel and the three retired to Ted's room where he told them he hadn't phoned the police. Around 8:50 AM, the trio left and caught the ferry to Chappaquiddick. When they landed they hung around the dock. The ferry went back to Edgartown and returned. This time it contained a wrecker and when they engaged him in casual conversation, he told them he was on his way to the accident scene. Kennedy then knew he had no choice but to report the accident. He took the ferry back to Edgartown and phoned the police. The Senator made a brief statement to the police which didn't mention Gargan or Markham. Nor was the party situation explained. It was ten hours after the accident before he finally reported it. Ted claimed he was dazed, confused, injured and didn't know what he was doing. After making his statement, Ted left immediately for the Kennedy family compound at Hyannis Port where he would stay secluded for a week as legal experts and advisers from all over the US were flown to the compound. The party site was cleaned up by Kennedy aides - the booze removed and the attenders returned to from whence they came - all without the knowledge of the police. One Kennedy aide, Dun Gifford, was charged with the sole task of getting rid of the body. By that afternoon the body was embalmed and a death certificate issued listing the cause of death as drowning with no evidence of foul play. Delayed by bad weather it was noon the next day, July 20, before he flew the body out to the Kopechne family in Pennsylvania - and thus away from the jurisdiction of the state of Massachusetts. The doctor who issued the death certificate didn't recommend an autopsy and none was performed although he hadn't conferred with the District Attorney. As it turned out the DA had badly wanted an autopsy.(9)

Mary Jo's funeral was held on July 22. Ted Kennedy attended, wearing a very conspicuous white neck brace, for the injuries he supposedly suffered in the accident. Never again, before or after the funeral, was he seen wearing the brace. The local investigation was cursory at best. The state DA opened his own investigation but Kennedy lawyers used legal tactics to delay it. A deal was cut with the local prosecutor in Edgartown, an acquaintance of Ted's, and Kennedy pled guilty to a charge of leaving the scene of an accident. He received a suspended sentence of two months in jail.(10)

About a week after the accident, Kennedy took his case to the public, the voters of Massachusetts, on TV and radio. He mentioned Gargan and Markham for the first time and said, "I regard as indefensible the fact that I did not report the accident to the police immediately." The consensus on his statement described it as "rambling, banal, self-pitying" and that it "turned the stomachs of alert people all over the country." This was even true of Kennedy friends such as Theodore Sorenson, who was then working on a book about the family. Sorenson called Ted's actions indefensible and also took out several passages from his book - then in the proof stage - alluding to Edward's "bright political future."(11)

No inquest would have been held except that a public uproar became so loud one was finally scheduled but not until January, 1970. The results of that inquest weren't released for a further nine months. Kennedy claimed he'd never been on Chappaquiddick before July 18, that he was unfamiliar with it and that's why he got lost and went onto the wrong road. Several residents of Martha's Vineyard testified that he had been there several times prior to that. On July 18, he had twice driven the paved road to the ferry and twice driven the dirt road to the beach. He was familiar with the area. Ted knew where he was going.

Kennedy said he left the party at 11:15 PM, yet Sheriff Look had seen a car parked with two passengers in it at 12:45 AM. Kennedy probably gave the earlier time because the ferry stopped at midnight. At the inquest Kennedy said he was taking Mary Jo back to the hotel because she wasn't feeling well. However, the couple didn't say goodbye to anyone at the party and Mary Jo left her purse at the party cottage. When Gargan and Markham returned to the party, after joining Ted in rescue dives, they and their clothes were not wet. No attempt was made to rescue Mary Jo.(12)

A man in the area claimed to have seen three men in a small boat crossing the Edgartown channel at around 2 AM. Gargan and Markham had told the girls they were looking for a boat. The next morning a young boy discovered his rowboat was used during the night and tied up at a different spot. Kennedy had not swam across the channel. When he first walked to the party cottage from where his car went into the pond Ted passed two lit buildings. One was a cottage where he could have gotten help. The second was a fire station that was unoccupied but where he could have pulled the alarm and gotten help within a few minutes. Ted did neither. During those hours between the time of the accident and his reporting of it - when he was "dazed and confused" - he managed to make sixteen or seventeen phone calls, including one to his Florida girlfriend. That list of calls, seen by several people, wasn't introduced at the inquest because by then it was "lost." An attempt to exhume the body for an autopsy failed. The application was denied by the Pennsylvania courts largely because the parents, who were strong Catholics, objected. Cardinal Cushing had urged them to help to deny an autopsy because it "desecrates" the body. While it's unlikely the Kopechnes knew Cardinal Cushing personally, the Kennedys certainly did. Did they ask him to pressure the Kopechnes?(13)

In his inquest report, the presiding judge stated: "I... believe that Edward Kennedy operated his motor vehicle negligently... and such operation appears to have contributed to the death of Mary Jo Kopechne." Nothing came of this. He also determined that Ted and Mary Jo didn't intend to return to Edgartown at that time and that Kennedy's turn onto the dirt road was deliberate. As one writer has noted of this affair, "One need not be an admirer of Edward Kennedy to acknowledge that he and his attorneys manipulated everything and everyone - federal, state and local officials, the press, the public, his friends, and events themselves - in a most remarkable way."(14)

Saddest of all is that Mary Jo probably didn't have to die. When the car was pulled out of the water about ten hours after it went in, there were still a few air pockets in the vehicle. Mary Jo's face was pushed into one such pocket. Likely she suffocated rather than drowned, after using up the oxygen from that pocket. Perhaps she survived for several hours before suffocating. Had Ted stopped for help at one of those buildings, she may have been saved. At the inquest, "Experts testified that if Ted had pulled the fire alarm Mary Jo could likely have been saved." Mary Jo's parents paid a visit to Chappaquiddick in 1975 and said "they were not satisfied with the Senator's account."(15)

One of the rumors after Mary Jo's death was that she was pregnant by Ted. An autopsy could have quickly put an end to such a rumor. Yet it was the Kennedys who worked to see that one was not held.

At the time of the incident, Kennedy was considered a shoo-in for the Democratic presidential nomination in 1972 but, despite the massive Kennedy cover-up, his chances ended that night. In the fall of 1974 Ted was believed getting ready to take a run at the nomination. Reporters began to dig into the Kopechne affair again. Ted announced in September, 1974, that he was withdrawing, partly because the *Boston Globe* had done a massive investigation of the affair pointing out over one hundred discrepancies between Ted's testimony and that of others. They were ready to run the story before Ted withdrew.(16)

Ted announced his candidacy for the presidency in 1979 but it never got very far off the ground. His marriage was then a shambles, at least partly due to his womanizing. Rumors had Ted involved in liaisons with women such as Margaret Trudeau, socialite Amanda Burden, skier Suzy Chaffee, and others. So widespread was Kennedy's reported womanizing that the *New Republic* commissioned feminist Suzannah Lessard to do an article on Ted's woman problem. The owner of that publication then refused to print what he had commissioned when he read the article. Ultimately it was published in *Washington Monthly* and concluded Ted had a "severe case of arrested development, a kind of narcissistic intemperance, a large babyish ego that must be constantly fed." Chappaquiddick was raised again and again as Ted tried to campaign and he was unable to handle those questions as he was reduced to mumbling, fumbling and stumbling. Once again his presidential chances collapsed as the press openly mocked him and nicknamed him FRK (for Fat, Rich Kid - a name first coined by a Carter aide).(17)

Ted's womanizing is not a response to his "terrible tragedies" - he was like that long before any happened, and his womanizing caused some of them. In trying to analyze why voters would choose Ted, one writer suggested, speaking of Kennedys in general, "the Kennedy reaffirms the qualities they sense in themselves: compulsiveness, a cult of toughness, sexism, greed and hyperacquisitiveness, a lack of moral vision and courage." It all applies to Ted - except that he's not tough.(18)

Truman Capote commented: "Teddy is crazy. He's a menace. He's a wild Irish drunk who goes into terrible rages. I'd want anybody to be President before him."(19)

GOATS

The Goats are a step down from the *Lady Killers*. None of the women involved with these men found herself prematurely dead under mysterious circumstances. On the surface they are a disparate and unconnected group. There's an Italian Fascist, a Middle East ruler, a Caribbean strongman, an Asian dictator, a crude and vulgar Texan, and an African despot.

What connects them solidly is a compulsive womanizing. Under other situations and circumstances these men could have been great friends. They were soul mates. "All pecker" might be the best way to describe them. They tended to want to fuck anything that moved. Young females were always preferred but any age would do in a pinch. So voracious were these men that some reverted to procurers - part time or full time, official or unofficial - to keep up a steady supply of females. What little is known of their sexual technique indicates it was quick and tough, and brief as a minute or two. Women were treated roughly by these men but it apparently dissuaded few from returning. When they weren't actually having sex they liked to talk about it. Toilet humor was favored as was the habit of regaling their buddies with stories of their sexual feats - often in lurid and intimate detail.

Discreet was not the style of any of these men. The masses may have been unaware but the inner circle knew. Wives were aware of their husband's doings but it put no brake on their macho behavior. Or they were allowed virtually unlimited wives. In their wake they left children scattered everywhere. Most fathered illegitimate ones. Another thing they had in common was a dislike of women in general and a low opinion of them as people. All saw females only as creatures to be conquered sexually. And they were also useful for cooking, cleaning, raising children and so on. In their quest for higher and higher numbers, an expanding body count, some of these men, as they aged, resorted more and more to the use of aphrodisiacs. That's more than a little ironic considering the prodigious cocksmanship of the group without such aids. All of them presided over regimes that were violent at home and/or outside their own borders - both in some cases. They screwed a lot and they fought a lot. A motley and sleazy crew the Goats do not represent the best and the brightest.

BENITO MUSSOLINI

Italian dictator Benito Mussolini was, by all accounts, callous and brutal to women. He was a fan of the quick in-and-out given to shouting curses when he climaxed. American cowboys are supposed to want to die with their boots on. That's how Mussolini went. It's also how he preferred to fuck. Benito was born on July 29, 1883 and ruled Italy from 1922 until his death.

Initiated into sex at about age sixteen, Benito divided himself between a long series of casual encounters and regular Sunday visits to brothels. The first contact was with a prostitute whom Mussolini recalled "exuded grease at every pore."(1) He was left, he said, feeling "dirty - staggering like a drunken man."

However, he found himself hooked on women and took them on river banks, on staircases and up against trees. "I've been undressing every girl I see with my eyes," he said.(2) Very early on he caught some form of VD which may or may not have been the syphilis which would later plague him.

A girl of twenty, whose soldier husband was away on military duty, became the first woman to become more than a one night stand. She became his mistress in 1902. "Our love was wild and jealous," he recalled. "I did what I liked with her." They fornicated and fought with the same furious abandon that was always part of his youthful affairs. One time he stabbed her in the thigh with his pocket knife right to the hilt. He "always abused her and bullied her and made love to her violently and selfishly."(3)

Another early conquest was a girl named Virginia who had a nice complexion and was reasonably good-looking. Taking a fancy to her he recalled that "I caught her on the stairs, threw her into a corner behind a door, and made her mine. When she got up weeping and humiliated, she insulted me by saying I had robbed her of her honour and it is not impossible she spoke the truth. But I ask you, what kind of honour can she have meant?"(4)

Virginia remained his lover for three months. Mussolini moved around a lot in his youth and he left behind him a chain of disconsolate mistresses. A favorite technique to win sexual favors was to use the old line of promising to marry the girl.

Around 1906 Benito turned to school teaching and continued his womanizing unabated. One of the dictator's biographers wrote of the Friuli region where Mussolini taught that "The man who does not drink, eat and make love in whole-hearted fashion is not held to be a man worthy of the name."(5)

He contracted syphilis in 1907 and was treated for the disease for some fifteen years. During a bout of ill-health in the early 1920s samples of his blood were sent to England for lab tests. The test for syphilis finally showed him free of the disease. Since rumors abounded that the dictator had VD Benito decided he should proclaim his favorable results to the public in a communique and put an end to the gossip. Aides were able to dissuade him from that idea.(6)

The woman destined to be the dictator's only wife was Rachele Guidi. The couple met in 1908 or 1909 and began to live together a year later. He was 26 and she was 16. They would have five children. Rachele was the daughter of his father's mistress. Jokes were made that she was Mussolini's half-sister.

The year he met Rachele he was away in the city of Trent for seven months. Benito didn't write to her even once during that period and fathered a child by a woman in Trent. Rachele and Mussolini had a civil wedding on December 15, 1915. They had a church wedding on December 29, 1925 when the dictator decided that as the leader of a nation he should conform to the religion professed by his subjects. A second reason was that Pope Pius XI had asked him to marry. Hooking up with Rachele did nothing to diminish his "promiscuous ardour."(7)

Just one month before his civil wedding, Benito had a son by a beauty parlour operator named Ida Dalser. This was the only illegitimate child the dictator would ever acknowledge. It was also one of the stormiest relationships he had. When he wrote to her, he signed himself "your savage lover."(8)

Dalser had been involved with Mussolini for several years and he had lived with her off and on before finally abandoning her in 1915. She could not, however, be brushed aside so easily. Ida once marched to her lover's office in Milan, with their son on her hip, and dared him to come down to the street. From his office window, Mussolini threatened her with a pistol. Once she was in a hotel room where she set fire to the furniture and generally trashed the place as she screamed she was the dictator's wife. A steady stream of harassing letters were sent Benito's way by Ida in which she demanded he keep his promise to marry her.(9)

A maintenance allowance wasn't enough to buy her off and she always insisted that Mussolini had promised to marry her or that she was, in fact, his wife. Desperate to avoid a public scandal - the average Italian wasn't aware of his sexual exploits - Mussolini had Ida forcibly confined to a mental hospital around 1925. She died there ten years later.(10) Reports on the son are contradictory. One has him as mentally and physically deformed, dying in another institution in 1941. A second account claims the son may have been normal and died in action during World War II.

Countless other liaisons took place during those years. One was with Margherita Sarfatti, who lived in Milan. Mussolini moved to Rome permanently at the end of 1922 to run Italy. Rachele didn't join him there for five more years. She lived in Milan. Benito made the journey to Milan a few times a year. Sometimes those visits were to see Sarfatti. On one such visit in 1924 when he was in Milan for a funeral, he stayed for ten days living with Sarfatti. He told Rachele he was sleeping in his office. Knowing of some of his liaisons Rachele had gotten wind of this one and left Milan in a huff. Sarfatti was a regular visitor to Rome during the dictator's time there and he visited her at a hotel. He didn't break with her completely until the mid 1930s. She was a Jewess.(11)

Leda Rafanelli was unsuccessfully pursued by Benito in 1913-1914. He told her he had no family ties or any other encumbrances. When she found this was completely false he blithely explained that his wife was used to his infidelities. He told her he "needed a talented woman to support him as his official mistress." One writer has noted that none of his women, except perhaps Clara Petacci, were pretty: "the others were sometimes called ugly and positively unattractive. His taste in such matters was something of a puzzle to his associates."(12)

Claretta, or Clara, Petacci was the other major involvement of his life. Born in 1912 and almost thirty years younger than the Italian strongman, Clara first met him in 1932. She had always worshipped him. Rachele claimed Clara first met Benito's two sons in a Rome confectionery store where she tried to get one of them interested in her. When that failed, she moved on to the father. Clara is also painted here as ambitious and involved in political decisions. A minority position to say the least.(13)

Clara's first few meetings with Mussolini were said to be platonic. During this period Clara married but the union was short lived. The relationship with the *Duce* resumed in 1936. Mussolini phoned her daily and soon installed her in his private apartment. "There she arrived at about three o'clock every afternoon and waited patiently for the appearance of her lord." She had to be there but he didn't always show up. The husband from whom she was separated was exiled to Japan by Mussolini, to avoid a scandal, who admitted of this liaison that "Italian public opinion would not approve and that he was running a political risk."(14) In fact this affair didn't become public knowledge until the end of 1942 when it became the subject of widespread gossip. "His sexual prowess subsequently became legend-ary."(15)

While in Rome he continued to womanize at a voracious rate. One foreign artist to whom he gave a few sittings came away with a work of art and a child. A French actress or journalist known as Mademoiselle Fontages - real name Magda Coraboeuf - came to Rome in 1937. When she returned to Paris she revealed she had been Benito's mistress. His first act of courtship, she said, was to remove her silk scarf and pretend to strangle her. "I stayed in Rome two months and the Duce had me twenty times," she related. This caused quite a scandal and Mussolini gave the word to the police and the French embassy that she was not to be allowed into Italy again. Fontages reacted by first trying to poison herself and then shooting and wounding the French ambassador whom she felt had made her "lose the love of the world's most wonderful man."(16)

The Duce's own sexual activities colored his law making. As dictator he imposed a tax on "unjustified celibacy." This measure was to help raise the birth rate. Severe punishments were prescribed for adultery, more severe for females than males. And "infection with syphilis was, by Mussolini's personal wish, made a crime."(17)

Mussolini's sexual exploits were, he knew, a source of grief to Rachele but it made no difference. His promiscuity continued. In fact, when it came to a choice between affairs of state and affairs of the genitals the outcome was a toss-up. As head of state he frequently yielded to his loins and disappeared to some assignation leaving staff and police in a state of anxiety.

Women came to his office or he went to them. His chauffeur, Ercole Boratto, drove him to addresses all over Rome. They came to his office "to be hurled bodily on to the floor or the window-seat by the inflamed Duce... he rarely took time to remove either his trousers or shoes." He told Boratto that "a man should have a little engine to wind up in his back. That's the only way he could manage to satisfy them all."(18)

Another writer noted that he liked all women indiscriminately as long as they weren't thin. His only requirement was "that they should smell strongly, either of scent if their bodies had little natural smell or preferably of sweat." He didn't mind if they weren't clean. No thought was given to their pleasure or comfort. He used the uncarpeted floor in his office or the concrete window-seat, cushioned, as his favorite fucking spots in his office. Pants and shoes remained on and sex was over in a minute or two.(19)

Of his lightning fast technique Clara once lamented that "he did not even take off his boots." It may have been quick but it was also noisy for "he could not make love in silence, and while he held the woman in his arms he would keep up a running commentary of exclamations, curses and shouts." This may have been the reason that he kept a deaf attendant attached to the rooms where he met Clara.(20)

These women fucked by Benito ran the gamut - married, single, journalists, actresses, maids, countesses, foreign visitors, wives of fascists - and they "spoke of their experiences afterwards without regret and frequently with pride." One returned because she couldn't "refuse a man of such importance." Others were "enraptured by the unfettered sensuality of his love-making, particularly when his brutality and savage curses in the moment of climax were followed by words of tenderness." They found his unselfconscious clumsiness appealing.(21) Mussolini would have agreed for he felt women "prefer brutality in a man to courtesy."

In addition to his callous sexual treatment of women Benito felt the intervention of females into politics was disastrous. He summoned his women when they were required and abruptly dismissed them. Clara knew about her lover's many other liaisons and was jealous and worried about being supplanted by one of these females. Mussolini "recognized Claretta's right to be jealous and his own right to pursue any opportunity that came his way." Complaining to a friend, Clara said, "He has these women seven at a time."(22)

The *Duce* often bragged about his sexual conquests to Clara. It was his way of keeping her "in her place." His favorite women of the time would get his private phone number but the dictator would swiftly change it as soon as he tired of them.(23)

Rachele was one of the last to learn of her husband's involvement with Clara. She learned of the affair from her servant in the middle of 1943. She stewed and fumed for months before confronting her rival. When she arrived at Clara's home the guard wouldn't admit her and stalled for time while he phoned Benito for instructions. The *Duce* gave the okay for the meeting and the guard returned to find Rachele trying to scale a nine foot high fence around the property. Rachele acidly commented on Petacci's clothes saying, "What elegance! The kept woman is really elegant! This is how a woman dresses when she's kept by the head of a nation - and look at me, I'm married to him." More insults followed, from both sides, and gave way to screaming. A Mussolini aide, present throughout, had to step between them. Clara fainted. Said Rachele, "I know these faints - I know them! Nobody dies from such a trifle."

Petacci was revived and called Benito on the phone saying Rachele called her a whore. A nervous *Duce* spoke to his aide and told him to keep things reasonable. Rachele moved to the attack again and demanded that Clara step aside. Clara said that Mussolini needed her and his letters proved it. "Show me," demanded Rachele. Petacci called Benito and got his permission to read some of the letters. He said, "Well, all right - but don't let the situation become worse."

When Clara got the letters and started to read them, Rachele ripped them out of her hands and the aide had to step in again, suffering a deep finger-nail wound from the wife in the process. After two hours, a bitter Rachele acknowledged defeat and stormed out of the house.(24)

That night Rachele tried to commit suicide by taking poison. For a couple of nights following the argument, Mussolini actually did sleep in his office.

By 1943 the dictator had grown tired of Petacci and tried to end the affair. He confided to a friend that he found his mistress "revolting." Once he had a guard bar her entrance to his residence. However, she pushed her way through. Mussolini told her, "I consider the cycle closed." Clara pleaded though, and he took her back. Several more times he tried to get rid of her but always relented after she pleaded with him. Once he said to her, "Please leave me alone. The war is going badly. The people might criticize me for my weakness. There's already been one woman who made me do stupid things and I don't intend to put up with it again."(25)

On the night of April 28, 1945 Mussolini and Petacci were in a car trying to flee the country as the Allied forces advanced. They were caught by Italian partisans and shot to death. The next day their bodies were hung upside down from a girder in a public square in Milan where they were left on display for several hours. Clara did not have to have been in the car that day. She could have gotten safely away earlier and Mussolini had tried to get her to go. She refused and insisted on staying with her lover.

In her memoirs, published several decades later, Rachele had rationalized away much of her husband's womanizing. She claimed that his "tally was no greater than that of any attractive Italian male... My husband always slept at home - save when he was travelling." She insisted that "at no time did he pursue women." Rachele did admit that three women had hurt her: Dalser, Sarfatti, and Petacci."(26)

IBN SAUD

In terms of the number of females bedded, Ibn Saud may be the world champ, at least for the modern period. He did have a leg up in the competition; a religion more sexist than most, and he had a country of his own - named after his family. Ibn Saud was born sometime between 1876 and 1880. He created the Kingdom of Saudi Arabia in 1932 and ruled it until his death on November 9, 1953.

Marriage number one took place in Kuwait when Ibn was only fifteen or sixteen. His bride was younger but she died soon after. By the turn of the century, he had at least two marriages under his belt and perhaps more. When he was in his thirties Ibn Saud claimed to have 75 marriages behind him.(1)

Politics was often a factor and the desert ruler made a point of marrying into certain clans and tribes to form and/or cement alliances. As a Moslem, Ibn was faithful to the Koranic law on marriage. This law was strict and specific but easy to obey. A man was allowed four wives at once. The marriage ceremony took only minutes with whatever witnesses were around. Divorce was quicker. The man just had to declare, three times, to his wife that she was divorced and it was over. Ibn Saud never had more than four wives at a time.

Around 1915 Ibn was wounded in the thigh during a desert battle. As he lay in his tent recuperating, rumors spread that he had been shot in the genitals and was finished as a father and as a husband. In that macho land it was a dangerous rumor and pretenders to the throne prepared to step forward. Ibn Saud was warned of the gossip and frantically dispatched aides to the nearest village to bring him back a bride - quickly. He had less than four at the time. A girl was brought back. Ibn wed her on the spot and immediately put an end to the rumor.(2)

Sex and women were always an obsession with Ibn Saud. He once told an English visitor he had only three real pleasures in his life: "prayer, women, and perfume, in that order."(3) He told another visitor that he thought sex was a great pleasure and said the thing most worth living for was "to put his lips on the woman's lips, his body on her body and his feet on her feet."(4) One observer noted that "a passionate need for women was fundamental in his character, a part of the zest which gave him dominance over men and made him a ruler. As a ruler he had limitless chances to indulge it."(5)

While he never had more than four wives at once, Ibn Saud accumulated something like 300 wives in his lifetime. He died with a full complement of four. Every time he went on a trip Ibn made it a practice to divorce his least favorite wife of the time. This kept a spot on the roster open in case he became smitten while traveling or the possibility of a political alliance presented itself.

Women were veiled from head to foot. When Ibn, or his aides, chose his wives, they did so by their eyes, their voices, their demeanor and background, and any gossip which could be heard about their beauty.

In some cases he never did see their faces as unveiling the face wasn't always the first thing he did. If he was disappointed by a new woman he would divorce her in the morning after the wedding night. These women were returned to their fathers with Ibn's thanks and a present. Those who had children were pensioned off and given houses until the child was six or seven years old - old enough to join his family at the Palace.(5) Those divorced and tossed out after one night were free to marry again. It was said that divorce from the desert ruler carried no stigma.

The Koran required a man to treat his wives equally and Ibn's four wives each had their own house equipped with slaves and attendants. Ibn Saud visited each strictly in turn. His current wives were never seen by other men. Nor did he speak of them. Not that this meant he was all alone in the Palace. This was fully stocked with concubines - who had a status similar to wives - and slaves, women he had bought. These were all right in the eyes of the Koran. There was no restriction on numbers and Ibn Saud had an unknown number of each over his lifetime - probably in the hundreds.

Disciplinarian that he was Ibn Saud imposed limits on himself, using the number four as a base. He drew up the "A" team which was comprised of four wives, four concubines, and four slaves. These were the women he fucked. Specific individuals on the team could change daily, or hourly for that matter, but it always remained at twelve. Besides the "A" team, "he was in the habit of accepting as his natural due the night-time favors of any young girl who was presented to him by his hosts when travelling away from home." This was called an accepted Arab custom.(7)

Obviously his relations with women were fleeting. So removed from them was he that he once remarked he never saw a woman eat or drink. His conversation with them was limited to small talk. Nor did he have a high opinion of them. He said women could be allowed to listen to the reading of holy books, "but that other reading, and especially writing, were unsuitable accomplishments for them."(8) Another time he boasted, "I have no use for women older than thirty. I divorce them automatically when they reach that age."(9) He did keep some past that age. His second wife remained with him all of his life. She was divorced but a companion for some fifty years.

He fathered a large number of children with about 45 sons living to maturity - from at least 22 mothers. And at least that many daughters from a wider range of women. This was when infant mortality was about 75 to 80 percent.

According to one writer, his "sexual prowess was phenomenal through the greater part of his life."(10) He serviced at least one of the "A" team members each day and felt this was the minimum he could do to keep his reputation up. Seldom did he fuck more than once a day and never in the morning, which he thought was unhealthy.

Siesta time was a favorite time for fucking his slave girls. When he was finished with one, he might pass her along to a friend. He "discussed the bodies of his slave girls freely... Bawdy jokes, lingering sexual reminiscence and erotic discussion which was so earnest and technical it bordered on the academic, these were the staples of conversation among Ibn Saud's male intimates - and, as in the way with stag talk, it tended to be bragging."(11)

As he aged, Ibn produced fewer children and it began to prey on his mind. He became more ill-tempered than when he was in his prime. Four sons had been born in 1942-43, then none until 1947 and then a final birth in 1952.

In 1945 during this period of worry over declining potency the royal medicine chest was accidentally left on board a US ship. American officers discovered it to be filled with an extraordinary variety of aphrodisiacs. One of those responsible for procuring royal concubines kept recruiting younger and younger females on the theory that by contacting the flesh of nubile young girls a transfer of vitality might occur.

Even in death Ibn Saud wanted more than his share. The Koran spoke about promising a number of *houris* (heavenly companions) in Paradise. Ibn hoped to be granted an extra ration. He also hoped to be allowed more wives in Paradise and told friends "that he hoped in view of his special service to Islam to be so allowed a dispensation and to have four or more of them in Paradise."(12)

When Ibn Saud died, his son Saud succeeded to the throne and ruled until he was peacefully deposed in 1964. He was succeeded by another son, Faisal, who ruled from 1964 until he was assassinated in 1975.

Saud was born in 1902. He fathered about 55 sons and 54 daughters, maintained a vast harem and in 1962 had over one hundred wives. The total tally of wives and concubines is unknown.

Faisal, born between 1904 and 1906, had a wild youth and ran around a great deal in the 1920s and 1930s. Diplomats of the time thought he would never amount to anything because "he was so tied up by his women." However, after two early and brief marriages, he entered into a long, happy, and apparently faithful union. He never took advantage of polygamy. He fathered eight sons and nine daughters. Faisal died an austere and pious old king renowned throughout the Arab world for his aestheticism.

RAFAEL TRUJILLO

As strongman of the Dominican Republic from 1930 until his death in 1961 Rafael Trujillo ruled with an iron fist. His treatment of women was particularly callous and his weekly "cattle calls" were notorious. He and Idi Amin are the only men profiled in this book who practiced what amounted to rape.

Rafael was born on October 24, 1891 in San Cristobal, Dominican Republic. He entered the military in 1919 and in 1930 was president of his country. Little is known about his early life as Trujillo systematically destroyed all records from this period. What little remains paints an unflattering portrait of the young Trujillo. Sometime between 1910 and 1916, he was convicted of a crime and received a fine and a jail sentence. For some reason, he was able to avoid the jail sentence. Speculation is that he committed other illegal acts during this period and for a time may have been a pimp.

In 1913 he married Aminta Ledesma. Her parents were firmly opposed to the union as Rafael's reputation for fighting and fucking was even then well known. Aminta was pregnant though, and the wedding went ahead. Apparently Trujillo spent very little time with her and they were divorced in 1925. Described as "humble and colorless" Aminta was virtually banished after the divorce although she continued to live in the Dominican capital. Few people were aware of her existence.(1)

Toward the end of the 1920s, Trujillo was Army chief of staff but still rejected for membership in exclusive clubs and, in general, snubbed by Dominican society. To remedy this, Rafael focused his attention on wooing Bienvenida Ricart. She came from a family that was poor but had social standing. He inundated her with costly presents and sought to marry her. Ricart's family opposed the union as much as Ledesma's had, and for the same reasons. Once again Trujillo prevailed and he married Ricart in 1927. This didn't curtail his womanizing at all and Bienvenida immediately found Rafael engaging in "endless liaisons."(2)

Just a year after the marriage Trujillo became enamored by Maria Martinez. Her family was so outraged by the liaison that they shut their daughter out of the family home. Rafael set her up in her own apartment in an open arrangement which caused a social scandal. To counter this Trujillo invented a marriage for Maria - to a Cuban who never appeared in the Dominican Republic. Records were manufactured to try and document this lie. In June, 1929, Maria bore him a son, Ramfis.

Generally, Maria's name was kept out of the media and Ramfis and Bienvenida were mentioned together - to foster the idea they were mother and son. Things changed in 1934 when it was announced, in December of that year, that Bienvenida was going abroad for a few months on a pleasure trip. Her name was not mentioned again. Early in 1935 a new law of divorce was passed which allowed divorce on the following unusual ground, "the will of either spouse, if they have not procreated any children during the first five years of marriage or later." Benvenida hadn't and Trujillo was the first Dominican to take advantage of the new law. Rafael obtained a divorce in April and married Maria on September 28. The first media mention of any of this was on September 30 when it was announced that the dictator had wed. The leader's ferocious womanizing continued unabated and one writer noted that "his sensuality and sexual drive were extraordinary. He was not merely amoral but profoundly immoral... Trujillo's extreme interest in women was remarkable for its ferocity."(4)

During the month of December, 1936, Lina Lovaton was proclaimed Queen of a forthcoming carnival in Santo Domingo the following year. She stated her great admiration for the First Family. It was a sentiment that was reciprocated by Trujillo, who was taken with her. Lina's reign soon extended to a villa in Miami - where she lived at least through the 1970s - and a job in that city as vice consul for her brother Jose in 1943.

Maria and Lina engaged in a protracted struggle for the position of First Lady. It was only after a desperate battle that Maria reaffirmed her position and Lina left the Dominican Republic permanently. The specific spur to leave was an abortive assassination attempt by persons unknown. Maria had a long memory. Twenty years after Lina had been crowned, the Dominican Republic was picking its representative for the Miss Universe contest of 1956, to be held in Long Beach, California. Mrs. Trujillo informed the selection panel they could pick anyone entered except two. One was the prettiest girl and the other was a niece of Lina.(5)

The marriage remained stormy. During the 1940s, Maria once followed Rafael to an army base because she thought he was involved in some amorous meeting. Trujillo found out and was so incensed that he ordered some army officers to shoot her if she entered the base proper. In the early 1950s there were rumors of a final rift between them and an imminent divorce. Legend has it that Maria pulled a gun on her husband in their bedroom and told him that she would kill him if he tried to get a divorce. Fearing that his wife wasn't bluffing Trujillo cancelled any divorce plans he may have had.(6)

Maria kept her husband until death but she had to put up with his sexual conquests which ran into the untold thousands. As one writer noted he, "lives in a Latin country, where manhood still is measured by the number of females a man has been able to subdue. Trujillo's prowess with women commands a great deal of public attention." His hangers-on took the liberty of joking "boastfully about his exploits with women." Rafael was not a discreet womanizer.(7)

Vanity played no small part in the dictator's life. He squeezed himself into a corset to minimize his stout frame and tottered around on elevator shoes to maximize his 5' 8" height. With a pathological fear of illness he was always ready to test new medicine - in particular "products whose avowed purpose is to either rejuvenate or strengthen virility." A main topic of after-dinner conversation at the palace between Rafael and his aides was on the properties of the newest competitor to the aphrodisiac "Spanish Fly."(8)

Abelardo Nanita was the dictator's official biographer and he wrote of his subject that "handsome and striking in bearing, it hardly need be added that his enormous popularity with the fair sex stems from something other than politics. When he makes his way through enthusiastic crowds, many a look of admiration from feminine eyes and many sighs are sent his way for the man he is, independently of his being a national hero."(9) Obviously this was what Trujillo wanted to believe.

As a busy dictator Rafael didn't have enough time to court women and that chore was handled by aides. There were always friends and those who sought his favor who proposed women for his bed. Many a Dominican father or brother made their "fortune over the virtue of a beautiful and willing female relative or friend."

Rafael didn't go after the wives of other men. He liked to hold exclusive rights over his women. His favorites were all marked women whom no man could get close to without risk. Plump mulatto females were his favorite women. Among his thousands of conquests a thin woman was a rarity. Said to be gallant and full of finesse with a well-turned phrase, Rafael also liked to recite poetry to his choice for the night in the bedroom. He didn't patronize prostitutes and his choices came from diverse social backgrounds. Most were virgins.(10)

The selection process became more and more organized as time passed. Responsibility became formalized in the person of a palace staff official. Once or twice a week in his office this person assembled a group of eligible women - about thirty. Trujillo inspected the groups and indicated his choices for the week. Those selected were given instructions as to a time and place to report. The dictator fucked each woman once or twice. A few favorites were kept on a little longer. As a favorite they could have no other social life but once Rafael dismissed them permanently they were free to carry on with their lives. He provided financial support for any children he fathered but only very rarely did he legitimize them by acknowledging paternity.

Most of the women assembled for the cattle calls were there willingly but some were unaware, at first, of the real reason for their audience. Picked up perhaps by a palace procurer who wasn't truthful. Trujillo didn't force any of these women to have sex with him if they were chosen. However, they might suddenly find themselves out of a job or a male relative might be threatened with unemployment. In some cases a man close to the woman might come to physical harm. In most cases the woman came around.(11)

91--Sex and Politicians

In the last five years of his life the dictator's sexual cravings intensified and his taste went strongly to very young girls - sixteen, for example. The cattle calls were stepped up and often staged three times a week with as many as forty women assembled each time. Many men high in the regime were involved in rounding up and presenting women. The palace official who had overall charge of the operation was reimbursed by receiving a fee of ten percent on all public works projects.(12)

On the night of May 30, 1961, Trujillo was alone except for his chauffeur, being driven to an assignation with a current flame. On the way a carload of conspirators ambushed the dictator and wounded him slightly with one shot. The chauffeur wanted to try and drive away but Trujillo, the macho fighter/fucker to the end, declined. He stepped out of the car with his guns drawn. He was promptly cut down dead.(13)

SUKARNO

Indonesian strongman Sukarno's legendary sexual exploits began at an early age. Even though he was allowed four wives at a time it wasn't enough as he managed to be married to five women at one time.

He was born on June 6, 1901 in the Dutch East Indies, as Indonesia was then called. Involved in politics as a young man he found himself president of his country when it declared itself independent in 1945. Dictator was a better description of his position and he held power until 1966 when he was deposed in a military coup. Death came on June 21, 1970.

Around 1915 Sukarno was a teenager in high school. His fellow students were mainly Dutch and white. The adolescent felt the sting of racism, real or imagined, and vowed revenge. His way of getting even was to try and have sex with white girls. Of this period Sukarno later recalled, "it was the only way I knew to exert some form of superiority over the white race and make them bend to my will. That is always the aim, isn't it? For a brown skinned man to overpower the white man? It's some sort of goal to attain. Overpowering a white girl and making her want me became a matter of pride... I admit I deliberately went after the white girls." Evidently he was quite successful.

One of his early political mentors was a man named Tjokroaminoto and in 1921 he married his mentor's daughter, sixteen year old Siti Utari. The marriage was seen to be less of a love match than a symbolic coupling with her father. Sukarno would later claim that this marriage was never consummated and that he regarded Utari as only a sister and not a bedmate. Those familiar with him always greeted such claims with hoots of derision as his "tremendous sexual appetite" was well known.(2)

The couple divorced in 1923 at a time when Tjokroaminoto ran into political trouble. The procedure under Moslem law was simple and straightforward. The man only had to utter "talak, talak, talak" and return the woman to her father. Sukarno did this and he was free.

However, sex and not politics was the cause. The same year that he wed Utari, Sukarno moved away to another city for a time. He boarded at the home of a friend of his father-in-law. Inggit Garnish was the wife of the friend. She was about fourteen years older than Sukarno but he was immediately taken by her. Almost at once they began an affair. Once he was divorced he and Inggit were married. She had obtained her divorce during the interval. About his second wife the strongman wryly said, "Inggit and I shared a great deal. We both had the same interests... we both even shared love of Sukarno."-(3)

He remained faithful to Inggit for about a year, which may have been a record for him, but then he started coming home late at night on a more and more regular basis. Despite his womanizing the marriage endured until a serious affair in 1938 caused complications.

Sukarno was then living in exile on the west coast of Sumatra when he began an affair with a fifteen year old girl named Fatmawati, daughter of the local head man. Inggit was childless and fifty-one years old. Sukarno wanted to take Fatmawati as a second wife. As a Moslem he was entitled to four but problems developed. A storm of protest came from militant women's organizations when the news broke. There was also Inggit to deal with. When Sukarno told her of his plans to take a second wife so he could have children, Inggit refused to accept the idea and demanded a divorce. Sukarno told her, "I have no wish to cast you aside. It is my desire to consider you in the topmost position and for you to remain the first wife." Then he offered a deal. "Although I love Fatmawati, I will forget her if you find another whom you deem better suited for me."(4)

No deal was arranged and the matter was dropped, temporarily. Inggit could not initiate a divorce herself as it was the man's prerogative under Moslem law. Sukarno related his feelings for Fatmawati by saying, "to me she was just a pretty child... What I felt for her was fatherly affection." Cronies greeted this remark with more derision and countered by saying "what he really felt was an ache in his loins."(5)

His marriage continued for a few more years but it was under increasing strain. Sukarno continued to form liaisons with various secretaries and was a regular patron of geisha houses - Indonesia was then occupied by the Japanese. Returning home late one night following one such liaison Inggit could take so more and threw a cup at him beaning her husband on the head. In 1943 the couple divorced and Sukarno married Fatmawati.

Abu Hanifah, an associate of Sukarno, described the new wife as young and pretty. He also found her "completely unsophisticated. She had no dress sense and her manners were faulty. The young bride had really only her youth, her prettiness and her smile... Her social education and upbringing afterwards was Sukarno's work, she was really the product of Sukarno's imagination of how a first lady should be. That he afterwards became bored with his own creation is another question."(6)

Hanifah got some insight into Sukarno's wandering eye one day when he was out driving with the dictator and Fatmawati. Every time they passed a female Sukarno would stare and comment, "Look how pretty that one is, I bet she is not yet 20," or "What a mouth, what a bosom." Hanifah joked that all Sukarno had to do if he wanted to see a pretty woman was to look beside him - at his wife. Fatmawati replied, "You know Bung Karno. He never knows what he really wants. He wants to have everything. Yesterday he married an older, experienced woman, today he marries me, an ignorant virgin, God knows what he wants tomorrow."(7)

It was not until 1953 that the next major sexual crisis disrupted the leader's life. He began an affair that year with Mrs. Hartini Suwondo, an oil company official's wife. Since she lived in another, city she had to be flown in to Djakarta to liase with Sukarno. An army officer handled all the logistics of arranging the assignations.(8)

This affair quickly became widely known and was the subject of gossip and comment in the Indonesian press. Hartini was described as a sophisticated woman, more worldly than Fatmawati. The affair was so serious that it became a concern of the government. Ali Saetroamidjojo, the Indonesian prime minister, wanted to avoid a scandal. Sukarno was determined to marry the woman. Ali pointed out the mass of problems a marriage might create and urged his leader to simply keep the woman as his mistress. Sukarno replied that he loved her and that "it would be immoral, in the circumstances, to keep her as a mistress. The honest thing to do - the only thing for him to do - was to marry her openly."(9)

At the time of this involvement a small group of Indonesians was working to pass into law a bill on monogamous marriages. Sukarno's actions created another storm of protest with women staging marches against him. While Sukarno was distressed by all the commotion he took no action against the protesters. This showed, he believed, that he was not a tyrant. He married Hartini in 1953.

Nor did this action go down any easier at home. Fatmawati was just as angry as Inggit had been a decade and a half earlier. She wouldn't share a house with wife number two and moved out of the palace into a place of her own. Hartini was never advanced to the position of First Lady in any formal sense. It was a promise Sukarno had made to his son by Fatmawati. This meant that, due to protocol, Hartini could not join the dictator on the podium at public functions or sit with the ministers and their wives. Sukarno acknowledged that Fatmawati was bitterly angry about the marriage. He felt she had no grounds for her anger and said that "my first and second wives are devout Moslems well aware of our holy laws. And they understand. Or should, anyway."(10)

While Hartini was attending a women's congress in 1963, she allowed the group to consider a resolution that she be accepted as the country's First Lady. Sukarno heard that was happening. He abruptly broke off his own morning's business and hurried over to the meeting place. He took Hartini out of the hall and ordered her to go back home.

As a well known leader on the world's political stage Sukarno gave free reign to his womanizing tendencies. As he traveled the globe, he engaged in a lifelong series of liaisons with Dutch, Russian, American, Chinese, Japanese, Filipino, and Mexican women, to name only a few.

One of his most notorious junkets was a 1956 world tour which included visits to West Germany, the USA, China, and Russia. An orgy of sexual exploits ensued and some Indonesian observers contended "that the Communist governments were able to gather sufficient compromising evidence on film and tape to blackmail

Sukarno and to force him closer to the Marxist block."(11) This claim is likely fanciful as Sukarno made little effort to hide his activities and didn't seem overly worried about who knew what.

French newspapers referred to him as *"le grand seducteur"* while the American media called him a "lecher" and a "skirtchaser." In Britain reports claimed he had sired up to 150 children.(12) His wives bore him a total of eight children five by Fatmawati, two by Hartini, and one by a later wife.

During his infamous 1956 tour the dictator visited California where Marilyn Monroe was invited to a diplomatic dinner at Sukarno's request. He was clearly taken with the actress and rumors spread that they saw each other afterward. The Indonesian loved to brag about his sexual conquests but never bragged about Monroe and the rumors appear groundless. In 1958, however, according to a CIA officer in Asia, a plan was devised to bring Sukarno and Monroe together in an attempt to make him more favorably disposed to the United States. It was a plan that was never put into effect.(13)

Like most compulsive womanizers Sukarno had a low opinion of the gender. Around 1940 he announced that he was in favor of the separation of the sexes, saying, "I reject their association in the Western manner."(14) Much later Fatmawati asked him what type of woman he preferred. The dictator replied, "I like the unsophisticated type... I prefer old-fashioned women who tend their husband and fetch his slippers. I do not like the new generation of American women who, I have heard, make their husbands do the dishes."(15) In the mid 1960s his third wife asked him a political question to which he replied, "You don't understand these matters. They are more complicated than a woman can understand."(16) He had fixed ideas about age as well and liked to joke that, "a woman is like a rubber tree. She's not good after thirty years."(17)

During the 1960s Sukarno greatly enlarged his string of wives. Wife number three was Ratna Sari Dewi, a Japanese bar girl he had met in Tokyo in 1959. Next came a woman named Hariati and then Yurike Sanger who was wife number five. This was over the limit of four and Yurike was not recognized, in Moslem eyes, as formally married to him.

The dictator's choice of wives didn't pass unnoticed when students demonstrated in 1965 against the Sukarno regime. Word filtered through to the protesters that Dewi had made an expensive shopping trip to Europe and New York buying, among other items, mink coats and emeralds. Angry students wrote slogans on the walls of Sukarno's palace "We don't need Japanese dolls in Indonesia" and "Stop importing wives from Japan." At the home of Hartini the students wrote slogans which said: "Here lives the Supreme prostitute; this is the house of VD."(18)

One of Sukarno's biographers, J.D. Legge, claimed his subject had been faithful to Inggit for 19 years and that he didn't become obsessed with sex until the 1950s and 1960s. Legge then argued it was the result of the dictator's declining powers and fear of death reviving his insecurity.(19)

Legge was mistaken. Sukarno was obsessed with sex from early on. He didn't become a proverbial dirty old man. He had started out as one and never changed. Sex was a subject he loved to talk about. He used to say things like, "Women must never eat pineapple. It dries them up sexually." He owned many pictures and statues of nude women. Rarely could he pass one of these objects without touching the parts. One of his favorite pastimes was to regale his listeners with accounts of his sexual adventures.(20)

Faced with the choice of death or sex there was never much doubt as to which he would pick. In 1964 he went to his doctor after a bout of ill health. The physician advised him to ease up on his sexual acrobatics in the future. The patient asked how long he would live if he stayed away from women. When the doctor replied "two years" Sukarno laughed and said, "Why should I bother then to prolong my life if I must stay away from women."(21)

He did go to a lot of bother in the hope of enhancing his sexual powers. To that end he took large doses of Arab honey, Japanese syrup and American vitamins. Well-wishers often brought him other "guaranteed aphrodisiacs" such as Dutch serums, Korean chocolates, or dried snake udders. Sukarno admitted, "I'm a very a physical man. I must have sex every day."(22)

After his ouster from power, Sukarno lost not only his power but most of his wives as Hariati, Dewi, and Fatmawati all divorced him over the following few years. The day before he died, Dewi flew in, at his request, to see him. She brought his daughter, then about three, whom he had never seen before. His funeral was attended by his wives and children. Inggit was 83 years old.

LYNDON JOHNSON

Following in the footsteps of Jack Kennedy was no easy matter - at least in termS of womanizing. However, Lyndon Baines Johnson gave an extraordinarily good account of himself. While unable to duplicate JFK's volume, Johnson matched his predecessor in vulgarity and low opinion of the gender as a whole. Lyndon was born in Texas on August 27, 1908. Politically he worked his way up to Vice President, from 1961 to 1963, and then President of the United States from 1963 to 1969. He died on January 22, 1973.

As a young boy Lyndon had a knack for flattering women. He hugged and kissed all the mothers and grandmothers and it was said that all the women in town loved him. It was a talent that would never leave him. As a teenager he was also known as a brawler and often got into fights.

Another widespread belief was that Johnson was determined to marry for money. He had three major involvements before marrying the third woman and in each case the girls' fathers were the richest men in their respective small Texas towns. In 1924 he courted Kitty Clyde Ross, who was a year older than him and daughter of the richest man in Johnson City. Kitty's father disliked the Johnson family and two decades earlier his own wife had been forbidden to marry Lyndon's father. Kitty was ordered not to see Lyndon and the family kept her constantly busy to help kill the romance.

While in college Johnson started dating Carol Davis, who was two years older than he was. Lyndon personally spread the news that he was dating the daughter of San Marcos's richest man. This was 1928. Carol had a big white convertible, courtesy of her father. Lyndon would drive it and honk the horn conspicuously whenever he passed fellow students or others he knew.

One fellow student recalled that Lyndon did plenty of boasting about his sexual progress with Carol and that he "made a production" of the romance. He bragged that Carol paid and told students, "We've been to the movies in Austin, and Carol paid." Johnson constantly reminded people how rich the Davis family was. Said one student, "She was a rich man's daughter, and Lyndon was always looking for a way to help himself." Added another, "He was hinting: he wanted to find a girl who had a lot of money. So preoccupied was he with marrying for money that it became the topic of a college newspaper joke.(1)

Carol's father also disliked the Johnson clan and told his daughter not to get mixed up with them. She remembered that her father loved to sit on his porch and talk to people - except Lyndon to whom he wouldn't speak. The couple had very little in common - Lyndon was interested only in politics - and the romance soon ended. One source has it that LBJ formally proposed to Carol but was rejected.(2)

On campus he talked a lot about girls. His brother, Sam Houston Johnson, recalled that on more than one occasion he had visited his brother on campus and Lyndon came back to his room naked after a shower. The future president would take his penis in his hand and say, "Well, I've gotta take ol' Jumbo here and give him some exercise. I wonder who I'll fuck tonight."(3)

All his boasting about sexual conquests gave him a reputation as a ladies' man - "except among those students who were ladies' men." The truth was that Lyndon had trouble getting dates even though women outnumbered men three to one on campus. A student recalled, "I mean, we all boasted and bragged about girls. But Lyndon's boasting and bragging were to an extent that was ridiculous. Nobody believed him."(4)

The other reputation he took away from college when he graduated in 1930 was that of a man determined to marry money. The school yearbook for 1930 contained a fake ad to enrol students in a lonely hearts club. One of the lines read, "Lyndon, some of our girls are rich." Lyndon also acquired the nickname *Bull* - for bullshit - and was renowned for sucking up to people. Another line in the yearbook ran "Believe It Or Not - Bull Johnson has never taken a course in suction."(5) His wish came true on November 17, 1934

when LBJ married Claudia Alta Taylor - Lady Bird. Her father was
the richest man in Karnack, Texas.

A few years later, in 1937 when Johnson was a freshman Congress-
man in Washington, he met Charles E. Marsh, who owned the *Austin
American-Statesman* - that city's most influential newspaper. He and
Lady Bird spent a weekend at Marsh's Virginia estate which was called
Longlea. It was also home to Alice Glass a stunning woman said to
combine brains and beauty. She was Marsh's mistress. Marsh had left
his wife and children for her and constantly asked her to marry him.
She always refused.

LBJ and Alice became drawn to each other after a few more visits
to Longlea. Alice told her sister she thought Lyndon was "a young
man who was going to save the world." Also admired were what she
saw as his idealism and lack of desire for his own political advance-
ment.

Sometime in 1938 Glass informed her sister that she and Johnson
were lovers and had been for a few months. Sometimes LBJ visited
Longlea with Lady Bird, but more frequently he came alone. Recalled
Alice's sister, "he would leave her on weekends, weekend after
weekend." The couple also met at a Washington apartment maintained by Marsh - if he wasn't in town.

Part of the attraction was sexual. At the time Marsh was 50, Alice
26, and LBJ 29. Alice "liked men" and was "absolutely mad" for LBJ.
Alice told friends that Lyndon discussed marriage and said he would
get a divorce. It was an era when a divorce could kill a man's
political career and if he said it he likely didn't really mean it.(6)

His character was said to be changed when he was with Alice. He
sat quietly while she read poetry to him. He tried to eat more
normally instead of ramming huge loads of food into his mouth.
Marsh never learned of the affair and Johnson continued to suck up
to the man. It paid off since Marsh helped him financially. The
consensus was that Lady Bird knew of the affair.(7)

Passion faded from the liaison and Alice married Marsh. She
divorced him quickly and married several times after that. They
continued to meet from time to time. A breach occurred in 1941
when LBJ sought higher office - showing he was ambitious. When
LBJ was a Senator, he sometimes dismissed his chauffeur for the day

and drove the ninety miles to rendezvous with her. A final split didn't take place until the Vietnam War. A bitter and disillusioned Alice told friends she had burned all his love letters because she didn't want her granddaughter to know she had been associated with the man responsible for Vietnam.(8)

By the time LBJ got to the Senate at the end of the 1940s, he was known to his friends as an "incurable womanizer" and a man who had a "prodigious extramarital life." It was all, apparently, known to his wife.(9)

Many were appalled by - both his humor and his manners. He would scratch his crotch or pick his nose in mixed company. If he had an injury such as a hernia, he would drop his pants to show it even if women were around. In conference with a fastidious male, Johnson delighted in going to the toilet, insisting the man accompany him, and then continuing the conference there while he, Johnson, took a shit. One observer described him as a "crude bastard." Another termed him a "real, vulgar, low-class American." He loved sexual jokes. When asked his opinion of Jerry Ford, he said, "Ford's economics is the worst thing that's happened to this country since pantyhose ruined finger-fucking."(10) He enjoyed watching bovine copulation.

During his Senate years when Lady Bird was out of town - and sometimes when she wasn't - he would take a woman, perhaps one of his secretaries, to a social affair and introduce her to people saying "Wantcha to meet mah girl."

A staff member of the White House once had an experience on the LBJ ranch in Texas during a stay there. She was surprised to find there were no locks on the bedroom doors. However, she felt safe with so many Secret Service agents around. In the middle of the night she felt the presence of someone in her room. She was just about to scream when she heard a familiar voice say, "Move over, honey; this is yore president."(11)

During the Democratic Convention in Los Angeles in 1960, LBJ was standing in a reception line. He was then a candidate for the presidential nomination. As the line moved by, he reached out to shake the hand of a young woman only to find a hotel room key in his hand. Lyndon pocketed the key and turned to the next person in line without missing a beat. Later he went to the room and-exclaimed, "Here ah am honey." They fucked, slept for half an hour and then he left. As he departed he said, "Ah want to thank you for yore help to mah campaign."(12)

Most of his affairs were short term but a few were longer. One that only came to public light in 1987 was a liaison with Madeleine Brown. Most of those involved were long dead and while she had little documentation to support her claims, the story of Brown and LBJ appears to be taken seriously.

Madeleine first met Johnson in Austin, Texas in 1948 when she was 23. The occasion was a radio reception at Station KTBC - owned by the Johnson family. Brown worked for an advertising agency. Three weeks later they met accidentally at another party. Madeleine said, "He looked at me like I was an ice cream cone on a hot day." After a short time, he told her, "Well, I'll see you up in my apartment." Brown went on, "He had a certain amount of roughness about him, and maybe that's what I liked, you know. He commanded. I've been told that every woman needs to act like a whore in bed, and I guess that's what I did."(13)

From the beginning LBJ told her to keep everything secret. "You see nothing, you hear nothing, you say nothing." KTBC station manager, and Johnson family confidant Jesse Kellam, had introduced them and acted as a go-between. Whenever LBJ returned from Washington and wanted to see Brown, it was Kellam, who contacted her.

Madeleine lived in Dallas and once she got the word she would be on a plane within the hour for Austin. Met by a KTBC mobile van, she would be driven to the Driskill Hotel for the rendezvous.

Usually they spent about half an hour together. Their longest liaison was three hours - the shortest was fifteen minutes. On the latter occasion LBJ greeted her by saying "Honey, I can give you 15 minutes of my valuable time." Asked about Johnson's sexual habits, Brown said, "He was a little kinky and I loved every second of it. So did he." Their relationship was purely physical. They never talked about politics or world affairs. "We spent our time doing, not talking," said Brown.(14)

A bomb was dropped in April, 1950 when Madeleine told LBJ she was pregnant. He became irate an yelled, "How could you be such a dumb Dora." Later, when his anger had passed, LBJ promised he would take care of her financially. One of his lawyers, Jerome Ragsdale, handled the arrangements. A son, Steven, was born in December, 1950.

Madeleine later claimed that LBJ set her up in a two bedroom house, gave her a new car every two years, a live-in maid, and all the charge cards she wanted. The affair continued through the 1950s and 1960s. Brown was on her way to meet LBJ in Austin when the news of JFK's assassination came. She returned home that day but a few weeks later Kellam phoned to set up a meeting with the new president in the usual place.

The relationship ended around 1965 but they had one last meeting in 1969. Brown told LBJ he owed it to Steven to acknowledge him but LBJ said, "Oh, I can't do that. I've got the girls to consider, and Lady Bird." Madeleine thought, "what a fool I had been to take seconds. But that's what I did." In 1973 Kellam called to tell Brown that LBJ had died.(15)

Steven had never been told the truth about his father - his birth certificate listed Brown's first husband James as the father - until 1987. Brown told her son then because she'd had a heart attack and thought she was dying. In June, 1987, Steven initiated a $10.5 million suit against Lady Bird Johnson alleging he had been "deprived of his birthright." Steven is said to have a profile, hairline and frame very similar to those of LBJ. As proof, Brown offered a letter from Ragsdale, written shortly after LBJ's death, which states, "You have my personal assurance that I will continue with the financial arrangements that Lyndon provided for you and Steve throughout the past." The payments stopped two years after Johnson's death.(16)

One of LBJ's close associates was George Reedy, who noted in his memoirs that Lyndon was not a man to sublimate his macho instincts. "They were well developed." Of his womanizing another aide joked that LBJ had "extra glands." Reedy joked back that he didn't believe that - only that the glands he had were in good working order and "frequently exercised."(17)

Speaking about the kinds of females LBJ selected, Gene Latimer, referring to the 1930s, said Johnson "had an eye for girls with pretty faces and figures and did not regard too much what was behind those faces."(18) Reedy, a friend of Lyndon - and speaking of a later period - remarked that those he picked could sometimes be described "as second-rate only through the utmost exercise of charity." Lady Bird was excepted.(19) His women had to be young, cheerful and malleable.

When he was taken with a woman, LBJ would pour out his dreams and aspirations and that he needed the woman for a top spot in his organization. When she agreed she found the highest she could go was a position as his private secretary. This queen of the day did get some perks out of it. She got to travel under luxurious conditions, received expensive clothes, and attended some glamorous social functions with the Johnsons. Lyndon always arranged a safe male escort for this favorite.

Her time at the top was usually brief and soon she was moved downward from private secretary to ordinary member of the secretarial pool, which was known to the males on staff as "the harem." Sometimes LBJ referred to what Reedy described as a "dumb Dora" type as his "top-assistant." The real work of the office was performed by more intelligent women who had a "much lower display quotient... He liked his females spectacular - not just pretty."

Because his favorite constantly changed and because she ran the secretarial pool, and because she often wasn't very bright there was a constant state of turmoil in his office and morale was dismally low. Many of the more intelligent women, who didn't fuck LBJ, couldn't rise above the rank of secretary.

One of the things Johnson enjoyed was to travel with a large number of women over whom he could fuss - admonishing them, buying their clothes, supervising their diets, and telling them to "put on fresh lipstick." Reedy summed him up by saying he was "just a country boy from the central hills of Texas but he had many of the instincts of a Turkish sultan in Istanbul."(20)

A couple of old ideas about womanizing were trotted out by Johnson associates. Wilbur J. Cohen said, "I think he loved Mrs. Johnson... but he also was a man," the genetic theory. Erv Duggan opined that "Lyndon was a notorious wolf... but I think he also loved women and had a high regard for them"(21) the more you fuck them the more you love them theory.

However, like most goats, LBJ didn't like or respect women. Reedy has noted that Johnson saw females only as bed mates, housekeepers, cooks secretaries, and mothers. The greatest destiny LBJ could envision for a woman was that of being a dominant male's helpmate. Lyndon had, said Reedy, no respect for the political intelligence of any woman.(22) He enjoyed telling stories to cronies about the most intimate details of his conquests.

From the time he married Lady Bird he totally dominated her. In public he would shout orders at her which had to be instantly obeyed. Recalled an observer, "He'd embarrass her in public. Just yell at her across the room, tell her to do something. All the people in Texas felt sorry for Lady Bird. For decades those who knew the Johnsons used an oft repeated phrase, "I don't know how she stands it." Lady Bird had to bring Johnson coffee in bed, and the newspapers. She had to lay out his clothes and put all his belongings into the proper pockets of his clothes. She had to shine his shoes. Johnson insisted she do all these things and Lady Bird did them."(23)

Mrs. Johnson knew about most of LBJ's womanizing. When she was questioned about it, however, on Barbara Walters TV show after her husband's death, she said, "Lyndon was a people lover and that did not exclude half the people in the world - women. Oh, I think perhaps there was a time or two... if all those ladies had some good points that I didn't have, I hope I had the good sense to learn a little bit from it."(24)

When he was President, Lyndon took a couple of reporters on a tour of the private quarters in the White House. The reporters were friends of JFK and Johnson liked to needle them about the late President's womanizing. As they passed in front of the master bedroom, LBJ said to them, "I don't have to tomcat around Georgetown. I got all I want right in there. Rolled over on the Bird last night and again this morning. Not bad for a man of fifty-seven, is it?"(25)

JEAN-BEDEL BOKASSA

The ruler of the tiny Central African Republic, Jean-Bedel Bokassa, was cast in the same mould as Idi Amin. For years he systematically looted the treasury, killed opponents and children, practiced cannibalism, and committed other atrocities before he was finally deposed. He was born around 1921. At the age of six his father was beaten to death by the French colonial masters and a week later his mother committed suicide. Jean-Bedel was one of twelve orphans left to be raised by 32 uncles. As a young man he joined the army and served France well, fighting for them in Europe during the Second World War and later in Indochina. By 1965, Bokassa was the army chief of staff in his country and on New Year's Eve of that year, he led a coup which toppled his cousin, David Dacko, from power and installed Jean-Bedel as president. Years later, he declared himself to be President-for-life and after that he named himself Emperor. The 1977 coronation ceremony cost $25 million, about one third of the impoverished country's entire budget.(1)

The number of wives Bokassa had is uncertain but nine wives at the time of his coronation is a popular number. The number of officially recognized children ranged from 29 to 55. The other women, mistresses and one night stands, have been too numerous to enumerate. Bokassa's favorite wife has always been Catherine, a Central African and former stewardess for Air Zaire. One of her colleagues remembered a flight he piloted during which Bokassa, his entourage and the stewardesses all became involved in an orgy. Catherine wasn't on that flight. It was Catherine who was crowned Empress during the coronation ceremony. Wife number two, in terms of Jean-Bedel's favor, was a strapping blond Rumanian cabaret singer known only as

La Roumaine. The wives and mistresses all had their own villas. They were kept under guard in virtual imprisonment.(2)

Often Bokassa wouldn't show up for weeks on end and La Roumaine would get bored. She would get somebody to drive her to Bokassa's palace where she would throw an hysterical tantrum in front of everybody and call her husband an "ugly monkey." Once she persuaded the cook at her villa to lend her his motor scooter which she took for a spin outside the compound. This was a no-no and when another servant told Bokassa, the infuriated dictator had the cook murdered with pepper which was stuffed in his ears, nose, eyes and elsewhere. A maid at La Roumaine's villa told Jean-Bedel that her mistress and another maid were both screwing the security guards. One night Bokassa crept up to the villa on foot and caught his wife in the act with a guard. He also found explicit photographs of the two women and four guards. Three of the men were quickly murdered but one survived. At his trial Bokassa said, "I couldn't tolerate such conduct between my wife, my maid, and the security guards, which is why I had them arrested and ordered to be killed." La Roumaine was spared and allowed to leave the country.(3)

Periodically Bokassa had beggars with shriveled limbs, and others with birth defects, rounded up off the streets of the capital, flown up in planes and dropped into the river. Thieves had ears cut off. Newsmen were invited to watch his soldiers club petty thieves who were then left in the sun where many died. In 1971 the dictator celebrated Mother's Day by having everyone who was in prison for a crime against a woman taken out and hung at dawn.

In 1970 Bokassa launched a major effort to find the daughter he had fathered in Vietnam. All he knew about her was that she was seventeen and her name was Martine. Stacks of photos were forwarded from the French Embassy in Saigon and the dictator finally made his choice. Martine was located selling cigarettes in a Saigon slum. Flown to the Central African Republic she received an official state reception and was welcomed by a tearful Bokassa into his large family of fifty or so recognized children. A month later the real Martine was located and the whole process was repeated. Both Martines were allowed to stay. The real Martine married a doctor while the false one married Eidel Obrou, who became the commander of the presidential guard. In 1976 Obrou tried unsuccessfully to assassinate Bokassa and was summarily executed. The next day the false Martine, who was pregnant, entered a hospital and was delivered of a son by the real Martine's husband. A few days later the baby died mysteriously - poisoned on orders from Bokassa.(4)

At his palace, to accommodate his one night stands, Bokassa had eight love nests on the first floor. To choose from he had a bevy of black and white secretaries, a shop full of seamstresses, and a female army regiment. The main job for his chief of protocol was to keep the boss supplied with women. If the dictator was out in the streets in an official procession and a woman caught his eye it was not uncommon for him to stop the procession and say, "Bring her to me tonight." He would even cruise the city streets himself with a suitcase full of money, looking for women. Bokassa had a special fondness for blondes and for twelve-year-olds. To appease the parents of these children he would give them money, or a motor scooter, or even a house if they would let him have sex with their daughters.(5)

In 1979 the dictator decided school kids should buy new $24 uniforms for school. They could only be purchased from a shop owned by his wife Catherine. Civil servants hadn't been paid for months and so, as the parents of these children couldn't afford to buy the uniforms, the kids staged some mild protests. They were rounded up and jailed. Bokassa killed one eight year old personally with a pistol shot to the head from close range. He split open the skulls of several more with a large and heavy cane he habitually carried. As well, he gouged out the eyes of one of these boys. Soldiers beat and killed many more of them. So outraged was world opinion that the French sent in paratroopers who overthrew Bokassa, reinstalling David Dacko as President.

Reluctantly, after pressure from the French, the Ivory Coast took in the exiled Bokassa, who stayed four years. He married a woman from that country during his exile but mostly he stayed drunk. When they couldn't stand him anymore the Ivory Coast threw him out and he went to France where he lived on the outskirts of Paris for three more years of exile. With him went his Ivory Coast wife, fifteen children, and twenty other women. Tried in absentia by the Central

African Republic in 1980 he was sentenced to death for various crimes.(6)

Bokassa created a scandal in France when he published his memoirs, *My Truth*. In it he claimed French President Giscard d'Estaing, on his trips to Bokassa's country, "bought girls." That he had sex with many local women. Bokassa also alleged that Giscard had gotten Catherine pregnant and arranged an abortion. Giscard brought a suit to block the book's publication and in May, 1985, the court held that passages in the book were defamatory and ordered all copies of it seized. Thousands of copies were burned later that summer.(7)

For unknown reasons, Bokassa voluntarily returned to the Central African Republic in 1986. Some speculate he thought he would he welcomed with open arms and somehow return to power. Instead, Bokassa was arrested and put on trial for numerous crimes. In 1987 he was sentenced to death after being convicted of murdering a number of political opponents. The following year the sentence was commuted to life.

MACHO MEN

These men come a notch below the Goats. Unlike the latter, the *Macho Men* do not seem to be under the almost total influence of their genitals, although at times they might be: Chiang Kai-shek, for example, during a period of his life, the Shah of Iran for some of the time, and Bob Hawke whenever he had too much to drink - which at one time was frequently.

What ties the *Macho Men* to the *Goats*, and to the *Lady Killers*, is the blatantly cavalier, callous and chauvinistic treatment of women. All of the men in these groups have openly flaunted their womanizing - or at least made no attempt to conceal it - in front of their own inner circle, journalists, and their wives, and so on. The ordinary citizens living under these men may not have been aware of any or all of what was happening but those that really counted did. That of course is part of being a Macho Man, or a Goat, or a Lady Killer. Others must know of your prowess, your ability to conquer and take scalps. All of these Macho Men have openly conducted and/or flaunted their affairs in front of their wives except Peron. Being a Macho Man is as much concerned with displaying scalps as it is with taking scalps.

As always these men have gone after young women, carried to ludicrous extremes by Peron. They have callously cast aside an old woman for a new one as soon as it suited them. Chiang unloaded old wives and concubines for a politically advantageous wife. Marcos unloaded his common law wife, with their three kids, again for a politically beneficial union. Bob Hawke remained married to the same woman as he drunkenly lurched from one affair to another.

The Shah cast off a wife because she didn't bear a son. Mao tossed off a wife who became worn out after not only accompanying her husband on the Long March but also giving birth on the way. The Anastasio Somozas, father and son, also kept the same wives but left illegitimate children as well as being more extreme in the flaunting of mistresses. Having sex with children was Peron's specialty.

Of all the men profiled in this book the only hint of strong women are to be found in some who were married to Macho Men. Others such as the wives of Anthony Eden, Pierre Trudeau, and Idi Amin took a measure of revenge by cuckolding their husbands but by far the average wife of a man in this book took all of her husband's abuse with little or no public demonstration. An extreme example is Lady Bird Johnson - a model of obsequiousness. Virtually all were not political. Imelda Marcos took revenge on her husband's womanizing by extracting a deal which allowed her to basically loot her country's treasury as she saw fit. Mao's last wife was forced to be nonpolitical for decades - part of another deal - and then exploded in a fury with awful results. Only Peron and his wife Eva functioned in any sense as a team. While Peron was clearly the boss Eva was strengthening her position when her untimely death left her potential unknown and unrealized.

CHIANG KAI-SHEK

Chiang Kai-shek got an early start with women - he was just a young teenager when he first married. Born on October 31, 1887, Chiang led the Chinese Nationalist government from 1928 until his death on April 7, 1975. From 1949 onward that government was based in Taiwan.

Schooling began for the young boy at the age of five and he seemed to have a different tutor each year. At thirteen he was tutored by a woman named Mao Feng-mei. During the winter of 1901-02 the fourteen year old Chiang was married to Mao, who was a few years older than her groom. It was a parentally arranged match.(1)

Apparently Chiang ran around a good deal during this marriage. Mao also confided to friends that she lived in fear "of her husband's brutal nature and his beatings." He seems to have hit his stride during the period from about 1911 to 1921 when he spent a good deal of his time in the city of Shanghai. He was termed "a notable womanizer, on familiar terms with the brothels of Shanghai."(2)

It was while he was a banquet guest at a Shanghai brothel in 1912 that he was smitten by Yao Yi-ching, who worked as a parlour maid to a prostitute of that establishment. The pair exchanged amorous glances and soon Chiang claimed her as his concubine. He brought her to his home to live.

Chiang became a father twice during the period 1908 to 1913. The older son was by Mao while the parentage of the younger son was in doubt. The story circulated in the 1930s that the boy was the child of one of Chiang's close friends and a Japanese teahouse girl. The man had died and Chiang adopted the child. Years later, it was rumored that Kai-shek was the actual father. He had been in Japan at the appropriate time.(3)

In his Shanghai period, Chiang was involved in a period of "riotous living" and a contemporary condemned him for his "unredeemed moral degeneration." His myriad liaisons of this period must have been well known for early in the 1920s he wrote to a friend trying to explain his behavior. "Everybody says that I am given to lust, but they do not know that this is a thing of last resort, in a state of utter desperation."(4)

A crossroads of sorts was reached by the leader in 1921. His mother died in June of that year. Politics demanded more and more of his time. After a period of reflection Kai-shek made the decision to commit himself fully to politics. To clear the decks he made arrangements, in November, 1921 to separate from his wife Mao and concubine Yao as well as for the division of the family estate between his two sons.

Some speculated that Chiang took the death of his mother as a sign from heaven which partially released him from family obligations and pointed the way to politics. Chiang finished the disencumbering and by the end of 1921 he was a free man ready "to dedicate my energy to the revolution with all my heart."(5)

If this decision meant he planned to give up women his resolve didn't last very long. In 1922 he was taken with a harlot who enraptured him. Her name was Ch'en Chieh-ju. They lived together when his duties allowed. Either she was his concubine or they had lawfully married. She was generally known as Madame Chiang and most thought of her as his wife. Between 1922 and 1927 he took another woman - this one as a concubine.(6)

Chiang first met Soong Mayling in 1922 but didn't pursue her in earnest for a couple years. Being the sister of the country's Finance Minister and the sister of Madame Sun Yat-sen, she was very well connected politically. Sun Yat-sen was the most powerful politician in China.

The courtship didn't proceed smoothly. When he first broached the idea of marriage. Sun was agreeable but Madame Sun was opposed. The major stumbling block the hopeful suitor had to remove was the gossip about his past marriages and his many liaisons.(7) Madame Sun was livid at the idea and angrily told her husband that Chiang was not moral. "Mayling must never marry such a rogue!

Why, even at that moment some woman was living with him!" she said. Sun reported this back to Chiang and told his protege to wait a bit until his wife had time to cool off. Madame Sun's attitude puzzled Kai-shek since, in his universe, "women didn't make a fuss over things like that."(8)

Cleaning up his act Chiang disencumbered himself once more. Ch'en went off to live in the United States. To those who met her it was clear she wasn't strapped for cash. In time she settled in California and eventually wrote her biography. Planning to offer the manuscript to New York publishers in 1967 horrified officials in Taiwan got wind of her intentions. A large amount of cash was produced by them. It was enough to buy the manuscript.(9)

When Ch'en was packed off and out of China, Chiang told watching newsmen that he had divorced her in accord with Chinese custom. He also showed Mayling's family proof that he was divorced from his first wife. All these efforts paid off and in 1927 Chiang and Soong were married. The union was viewed as a political match which Chiang undertook "to resume his position as the Commander-in-Chief of the army."(10)

On his wedding day, Chiang made a public declaration that the couple would dedicate their united strength to the work of the Revolution. However, he still found some strength for females. In 1942-43, gossip about his womanizing was so rampant that his wife felt compelled to confront him. She told him gossip was coming from everywhere, that Chiang had several concubines and "that he was openly visiting some women regularly every day." A divorce was said to be imminent.

To deal with the problem, Chiang gave a large tea party to which were invited both Chinese and foreigners. When all were assembled, he gave a speech in which he detailed the rumors of his sexual endeavors and denied them all. He noted that in leading his countrymen he relied on his integrity and character. Chiang told the crowd that if he were guilty of such conduct he was unworthy of being the leader of China. However, since he was the leader of China he couldn't be guilty of such conduct. After that speech, Madame Chiang gave one of her own. She said she never had a single doubt about her husband.(11)

As one writer noted, "Being a married man had never weighed very much on Chiang's conscience... it had not interfered with... any sort of dalliance that came his way."(12)

FERDINAND MARCOS

Even though he was the undisputed ruler of his country it wasn't enough to prevent him from being humiliated by his sexual activities. The whole country got to listen to the sounds of his screwing, over the radio. Ferdinand Marcos was born on September 11, 1917. He was president, and dictator of the Philippines from 1965 to 1986.

Nothing appears to have been written on the sexual doings of his early years other than the note that "Marcos was a notorious philanderer, but most of his affairs went unnoticed." He remained that way all of his life. Partly, it was said, because in the Philippines emphasis was placed on machismo and an affair wasn't just tolerated but was expected. It often enhanced a man's image.

In 1950 Marcos met Carmen Ortega, who was a poor girl from the country. Ferdinand offered to sponsor her in a beauty contest - Miss Press Photography. Soon she was his full time mistress and moved into the house Marcos shared with his mother, Josefa. Carmen was known around town as Mrs. Marcos. Ferdinand once took her on a shopping spree holiday to the USA. At his bank when he was withdrawing $50,000 for the trip he introduced her to bank officials as his wife. Josefa always hoped her son would marry Ortega. By 1954 they had three children.(2)

Then Marcos met Imelda and everything changed. Carmen was not politically valuable. She had little or no political clout. Imelda had plenty. Ferdinand and Imelda married on May 1, 1954. At the time Imelda knew of her new husband's reputation as a ladies' man but may not have been prepared for the extent of it. While the newlyweds honeymooned, Carmen and her kids were bundled out of mom's house and relocated to a house in the suburbs. This cleared the way for Imelda to be moved in and installed as Mrs. Marcos.

When Imelda learned the entire Carmen story she was dismayed and wanted them all to move because the Marcos house was located on Ortega Street. Josefa and Ferdinand gave that idea thumbs down.

Adding to her anguish the new wife heard that Ferdinand was still seeing Carmen on the sly. Imelda paid her a visit and asked her to stop "entertaining" Marcos. Carmen was then pregnant with child number four - a conception which took place after Imelda's wedding - and declined the suggestion.

Imelda found she could do nothing. Divorce wasn't possible then - the Philippines was a Catholic country - no annulment was possible and she couldn't stop her husband from seeing Carmen. So despondent did she become that Marcos took her to New York City for three months of psychiatric care. When she recovered she flew on to Portugal on a pilgrimage to the shrine of Our Lady of Fatima. She prayed for children, which she hoped would secure her position, and then returned to Manila. She gave birth in late 1955 to the first of her three children.(3)

By the end of the 1950s the marriage had deteriorated significantly. As one writer noted "through the years, Imelda Marcos had endured the usual seedy little affairs of a philandering husband."(4) Marcos confided to some of his sexual conquests that Imelda was frigid and that he couldn't perform, that he was impotent with her. He told someone else that his wife had "virginitis."(5)

During the 1965 election campaign in the Philippines Imelda saw little of him. Some of his disappearances had nothing to do with the election and what Imelda "learned in those days was to accept that there would be other women in Marcos' life, especially as he grew in political stature and wealth."(6) Marcos enjoyed his reputation as a playboy and frequently joked about it.

When the 1969 election approached Ferdinand decided that, as one of his public relations projects, he would make a film about his own war exploits. It would be a full length jungle epic. A group of his businessmen cronies, including Potenciano Ilusorio, were given charge of the project. An American woman, to play his film sweetheart, had to be cast.

Ilusorio got in touch with Paul Mason in Hollywood, a minor producer associated with Universal Studios. Mason came up with two women he thought appropriate - Joyce Reese and Dovie Beams. These two arrived in Manila in December, 1968. Initially Beams had been wary. She'd heard that American girls were brought to the Philippines to "audition" for film roles and were then drugged and used sexually. Nonetheless, Dovie decided to take a chance.

In a day or so the women were taken to a party where they met a man introduced to them only as "Fred." Reese told Dovie she recognized Marcos right away. They talked a while and then "Fred" zeroed in on Beams. The pair talked for a few more hours and Joyce was forgotten. Fred finally admitted he was the president. As he left that night he kissed her lightly and said "I'm in love with you." The next day he returned and they became lovers. She got the part. Dovie was born on August 5, 1932. She was 36 when she met Ferdinand but passed herself off as 23. She supported herself in Hollywood as a minor actress.(7)

Beams was immediately installed in a fancy house, undergoing renovations, in the exclusive Manila suburb of Greenhills. Also provided for her use was a staff of servants, a bodyguard and her own secretary. When the affair commenced, Ferdinand told Dovie he was impotent with Imelda and that they had not had sex for years. Dovie also learned about Carmen. Once, after they had had a fight, Ferdinand went off in a huff to be consoled by Carmen.

Soon Marcos treated his new flame to a vacation trip to Hong Kong. One purchase she brought back was a cassette recorder so Marcos could teach her words and phrases in Spanish and Tagalog for the film. Ferdinand was writing some of the dialogue. From time to time these language lessons would be interrupted for a session of fucking - with the machine still running. Marcos would sometimes serenade his mistress with a love song. No fool was Dovie. Soon she had a collection of incriminating tapes.

When Imelda was out of the country, Marcos spent all of his time at Greenhills or brought Dovie to the palace. If he fell asleep Dovie would use the time to root around looking for any interesting documents to stash away for a rainy day. Her collection grew. If Imelda was in town the couple often met in a cottage located on the palace golf course.

Aware of her husband's philandering, Imelda and/or her agents were always on the watch. Imelda would order the palace security guard staff "to drive her around Manila searching for her husband or his car... We always knew where the president was, so we always drove her somewhere else."(8) Main point man for Marcos was Colonel Ver, who was always around his boss watching who was watching him. When Marcos took a break at the presidential retreat, Ver would smuggle Dovie in and out on the floor of his car.

The affair started to run out of steam. Dovie came home one day to find her belongings being packed up. Spies were watching the house said Marcos and she would be safer somewhere else. Dovie agreed. However, later she found it was all a lie. Carmen and her kids were moved into the newly renovated home - that was Marcos' intention all along. Tensions grew. They fought frequently. Dovie made two more tapes of them making it in bed in January, 1970. This time it wasn't accidental. She hid the recorder under the bed. Ferdinand was unaware. These tapes were sent out of Manila to the US, for safekeeping, to join her other items, such as documents and articles of his clothing.

One night he took some Polaroid shots of her in the nude and some porno shots of her on the bed. Ferdinand asked her to give him a lock of her pubic hair. She agreed, but only if he gave one of his to her. By then, Dovie's film was finished and was in rough cut. Marcos wasn't satisfied with it. He claimed it was poor quality and miscast. He wouldn't allow it to be shown. This was the final straw for an angry Dovie, who left Manila in a fury swearing revenge.

A few months later, in August, 1970, she was back in Manila for a showdown. Big bucks were demanded - $150,000 or perhaps more. Ilusorio refused to pay and lodged a complaint against her with the National Bureau of Investigation. That night secret police picked up Dovie and drove her to a confrontation with Marcos. They had a vicious row. It ended with Ferdinand wanting to kiss and make up. Dovie declined and claimed she was then taken away to a hotel room and tortured.

The story hit the newspapers and the city was in an uproar. Despite her spies, it was through the papers that Imelda learned of her husband's most recent, and most humiliating, escapade. Dovie contacted the US embassy in Manila whose officials tried to help Imelda buy Beams off with $100,000. When Dovie told them of the material she had collected, the embassy staff kept a close watch on her.

Dovie then called a press conference. Since the press was constrained against libeling the republic's president, she referred to Marcos only as Fred which allowed newsmen to quote her freely. She played one of her tapes complete with moans, groans, murmurs, and a creaking bed. Fred sang a love song which everyone knew as Marcos' favorite.(9) He told Dovie he liked her more than Imelda. Copies of tapes were made and a group of student protestors played some over a campus station. A bemused nation listened as Ferdinand begged Dovie to perform oral sex on him.

The US embassy officials put Beams on a plane to Hong Kong. Imelda managed to put a professional killer, Delfin Cueto, on the same plane but he failed to do his job. A few days later when Dovie tried to board a plane from Hong Kong to Los Angeles, Imelda's agents made another attempt - foiled this time by British plainclothes police who took the actress into protective custody for a few days.

After she was safely in California, Dovie produced all her evidence including Ferdinand's pubic hair. Periodically, over the following years, agents from Imelda would approach Dovie to try and retrieve her material. Imelda was worried the continuing scandal would ruin her own chances of someday becoming president of her country. Dovie, for safety, had stashed multiple copies of her collection here and there.

Eventually she told her story in a book *Marcos' Lovie Dovie*, authored by journalist Hermie Rotea. Once published, it began to disappear. Imelda's agents scooped it out of libraries across the US, including the Library of Congress.(10)

The tapes became collector items in the Philippines with copies being bought for as much as $500. Marcos' main political foe, Benigno Aquino, was said to have purchased one. The tapes became a favorite source of amusement in anti-Marcos households.

If Ferdinand was humiliated by the whole affair, Imelda was outraged. All of her repressed fury over her husband's many affairs came out and focused on the Dovie business. Five years after the fact,

Imelda said to a group of very surprised American bankers, as she pointed at her husband: "See that man? He prefers a slut to me."(11) Over the years, Imelda would haul out the nude photos of Dovie and, in a rage, show them to friends. In her bedroom she kept a detailed file on the affair. A file that claimed Beams relations with Ferdinand were "mere hallucinations." When she and Marcos fled to Honolulu in exile in 1986, she had that file with her.(12)

There have been persistent rumors over time that Dovie was a plant either by the CIA or some of Marcos' political foes to humiliate and undermine him. Or, even more fanciful, that she was some sort of payoff to Marcos from the Mafia. There appears to be no substance to these rumors. It was just a dumb thing Marcos did to himself.

Ferdinand's passion for American women extended beyond Dovie for, over the years, he was said to have had affairs with several wives of US service personnel. This resulted in the husbands being hastily transferred to other countries.(13)

Filipino singer Carmen Soriano was another who yielded to Ferdinand's charms. Imelda, accompanied by adviser Ernesto Villatuya, visited her in her San Francisco apartment in 1970. The First Lady demanded that Soriano sign a prepared statement that she had never gone to bed with Marcos. Carmen told Imelda to go to hell. Imelda took a wild swing at her rival, missed, and decked Ernesto.

Another possibly violent episode occurred when Imelda was suddenly and secretly hospitalized after a trip to Rome. The rumor was that Ferdinand had beaten her up thinking she had been running around. While the First Lady liked the company of men, to flirt with them, and be seen in public with them, the prevailing opinion was that she wasn't having affairs. Imelda seemed to have little interest in the sex act and, as one wit put it, "she wouldn't break her hair."(14)

The couple were cruising on a yacht in Manila Bay in 1972 when the subject of Imelda's ambitions came up. This resulted in a heated argument during which Imelda scratched Marcos on the face. Ferdinand responded by hitting her hard enough to drop her to the deck.

123--Sex and Politicians

The Dovie affair had long term political ramifications. Imelda's clan delivered a large block of votes and political support to Marcos. It was support he needed. They cut a deal after Dovie left. She would continue to deliver that support, stay married to him, and work for him - but at a price. In return she got a hands-off deal in which she could indulge herself limitlessly and Marcos would not attempt to stop her or interfere in any way. And so Imelda engaged in large scale and widespread corruption as she looted the treasury - clothes, jewels, international real estate and, of course, an awesome collection of shoes. Said one observer: "In the Philippines a philandering husband has to pay for the rest of his life. Marcos just used our taxes."(15)

BOB
HAWKE

Australia's Bob Hawke is one of the few world leaders to have ever publicly declared, on a television show, that he had been unfaithful to his wife. Hawke was born on December 9, 1929, was active in the trade union movement and became Prime Minister of his country in 1983.

While he was at university in the late 1940s and early 1950s, Bob firmly established two reputations for himself. One was that of a womanizer; the other was that of a drinker. So prodigious were his drinking accomplishments that he made it into the *Guinness Book of Records* around that time for speed drinking. He downed two and one half pints of beer in twelve seconds.(1) Hawke remained a heavy drinker for decades but after a couple of false starts he gave up alcohol permanently at the end of the 1970s.

The story is that he lost his virginity while at university, in 1949. A friend of those days recalled, "He could always line up girls, for himself and his friends. It was a case of 'you provide the beer and I'll bring the girls.'"(2) Another student commented that, "Hawke always had an extraordinary attraction for women. There are many men who are good in women's company but useless in the change room. Bob got on well in both."(3)

At university he screwed around a great deal and "was and continued to be a womanizer." He went out to conquer women to show that he could do it. His emotional involvement in all these entanglements was thought to be minimal. It is said that he fascinates women. That even those who don't like him admit that "he's got something, not necessarily attractive, but something." On March 3, 1956, he married Hazel Masterson, whom he had known since he was 17 years old.

During the 1950s when Hawke worked in the labor movement he joined a staff that worked in crowded quarters. Bob was given space on the top floor by himself but the secretary assigned to him wasn't allowed to work up there since they would have been alone and "Hawke's reputation for wenching was already known." The secretary worked on a floor below him. Modesty boards were installed on the fronts of all the secretaries' desks, as one recalled, so he "wouldn't look at our legs."(4)

Bob was on one side of an acrimonious debate that took place in 1971 - whether or not a South African rugby team should tour Australia - which sparked riots and generated hate mail towards both sides, including the future PM. He had always tried to keep his sexual affairs separate from his family life. However, the hate letters directed to his home gave people the opportunity to tell Hazel everything they knew about Hawke's peccadillos - with flourish.

Throughout the 1970s Hawke was known as a die-hard chauvinist. When asked by a dress designer what he thought of pant suits on females he replied, "Depends on the lady - but I prefer pants suits off a lady."(5) Appearing on a TV program with a feminist, he offended her by feeling her shoulder to see if she was wearing a bra. In the early 1970s, an Australian feminist magazine named Hawke Male Chauvinist of the Month.(6)

During the 1977 Labour party conference, feminist Ann Giles said, "Hawke approached women as sex objects and victims." Newspaper columnist Mamie Smith believed "that women thought Hawke was a bastard but they approached him believing that they would be the exception." The media down played both his womanizing and his heavy drinking.(7)

One of his biographers summed him up during this time by saying, "There was much that was known about Hawke - his drunken bad temper; his womanizing, including outrageous public propositioning of women when he was drunk - that was never reported and that journalists, the world's most avid gossips, were unwilling to discuss."(8)

It was said that his very demeanor showed open hostility to women - the way he stood, his excessively virile swagger - and every public gesture revealed dominance and that included sexual dominance.

Feminists had only to look at Hawke to see "The Enemy." Smugness was predominant in his approach to women.

By the end of the 1970s, his womanizing was beginning to receive a certain amount of public attention. This sparked a strange reaction. Females he had never met would write to him, or phone, and suggest a liaison. Hawke thought himself to he irresistible to women. When he was drunk he would solicit any female who caught his eye. Wrote a biographer: "He always thought of himself as a man who liked women - as womanizers invariably do; it took him years to acknowledge that his 'liking' was possibly not what it seemed on the surface."(9)

In March, 1989, Hawke appeared on a TV interview show in Australia. He surprised most people by admitting on that show that he had been unfaithful to his wife. There was nothing to tell the extent of his womanizing and Hawke could have been admitting to just one indiscretion instead of the countless numbers he had actually had. The interviewer, male, didn't probe the issue at all and quickly dropped the matter. Hawke made the admission with tears in his eyes and a claim that he was now faithful. Cynics felt that an election call might be coming - it didn't. Most political observers felt thc PM's admission would have no effect on his political future. On the TV show, Hawke added, "I guess there are not many women who would have put up with me."(10)

SHAH
OF IRAN

The Iranian ruler was another prodigious cocksman who started early and continued until he died. Mohammed Reza Pahlavi was born on October 26, 1919. He became Shah of Iran in 1941 and ruled until he was ousted into exile in 1979 - he had been briefly exiled from his country once before, in the 1950s. He died on July 27, 1980.

As a seventeen year old at a private school In Switzerland, he became involved with a chambermaid who was fired immediately. This may have been his first sexual encounter. Back in Iran a couple years later he was a compulsive teenage playboy. Every girl in town was at his beck and call and he had "no qualms about taking advantage of his position... passing from one pretty girl to another, according to the whim of the moment."(1)

The family decided it was time for him to marry and one was arranged by parents on both sides. The wedding took place in 1939. The bride was Fawzia, the seventeen year old sister of King Farouk of Egypt. This union was not a happy or successful one. By 1941, the couple occupied separate apartments - at least for a time. Fawzia resented her husband's infidelities, of which there were many. Those women who yielded to his advances the Shah referred to as his "shepherdesses."

In 1944, Fawzia was said to have surprised her husband in bed with a woman. A bad marriage became worse and in 1945, or maybe 1947, Fawzia left Iran on the excuse she was visiting her family in Egypt. She never returned and some time later a communique from the court was issued to say the couple was divorced. That was in 1948.(2)

The ruler of Iran went back to his old pursuit of bar hopping and he had innumerable liaisons. He was in Paris in 1948 and the man who was an attache at the Iranian embassy there recalled, "He had one or two evenings free, and spent them in nightclubs in the company of call-girls procured by his friends. He loaded these girls with sumptuous gifts." A few months later this man was at a reception where he met a young woman who had been bedded by his leader. She proudly flashed a diamond he had bestowed on her.(3)

On a trip to the USA in 1949 the Shah fell in love with a 23 year old American painter. The pair became inseparable until his sister urgently cabled him to come home - to break up the affair. Through the 1940s and 1950s he had affairs with women from Tehran's top society and movie stars. The type of women he preferred were "tall blond Europeans, especially the Scandinavian type, and they arrived in droves... though he tended sometimes to treat them cavalierly."(4)

His second wife, Soraya, agreed that the woman that "appealed to him most was the European... so far as I know he never considered marrying any of these other women. He had far too much common sense for that."(5)

Eighteen year old Soraya Esfandiary married the Shah in 1950, or 1951. She also resented her husband's infidelities but found she could do nothing about them as they continued unabated. Soraya was also rumored to have caught the Shah in bed with a woman.

This marriage ended in 1958 in divorce. The chief reason seems to be that Soraya failed to produce any children. The Shah's mother was driving him to come up with a male heir. Soraya saw a gynecologist about the problem and told him "Four times a night and twice every afternoon. Still I don't have a baby." The doctor told her it was sometimes difficult for the egg and sperm to coincide and to keep the Shah interested. Said Soraya, "All I'm asking you to do is find something to break up my eggs. I'll see the Shah goes on making omelettes."(6) After the divorce it was alleged that, for years, the Shah rendezvoused for a brief fling with his ex-wife once a year in the posh Swiss ski resort of Gstaad. Around this time the Shah had a couple of aides who procured females for him - or, as it was euphemistically termed, "arranged entertainment" for their master. In 1959 the Shah wed a 21 year old Iranian student of architecture - Farah Diba. The following year she produced the coveted male heir.

The ruler's womanizing continued as before. Minou Reeves was on the Shah's staff and recalled some incidents that he witnessed. Once at the airport in Zurich the Shah left his wife and disappeared to spend the afternoon with a film actress. A few days after that, in Berne, Brigitte Bardot was sitting in a hotel bar. She had come to meet the Shah. When Reeves saw what went on, and how often, he understood why his boss was adamant about having separate bedrooms.

An affair with actress Ann Margret made big headlines. Back in Tehran the Shah's affairs were common knowledge. Since he was the ruler of an Islamic country he was entitled to up to four wives and as many concubines as he wanted. And since he seemed to prefer the Western mode of monogamy, combined with furtive affairs, he was considered relatively restrained.(7)

In other respects the Shah downgraded his wife. While Farah is considered to have opened the doors of the palace to art and culture, the Shah wasn't very interested and "seldom took her seriously." One day in 1973, she made a well received speech broadcast on the air. The talk was in favor of free speech. The Shah instructed an aide to "Tell my wife that she can't talk like that."(8)

During the 1970s, a rift developed between the couple. The Shah's womanizing had become intolerable. For many years a lot of his women came from Madame Claude in Paris, who ran a high-class call-girl operation. Hundreds of females from this establishment, and other services, passed through Tehran for the Shah, and other members of his court.

One of Madame Claude's girls spent several months in the Iranian capital in 1969. She was flown in first-class and booked into a hotel by a man from the Ministry of the Court who had a room beside hers. She had to wait three days before the Shah finally showed up to screw her. Meanwhile the Ministry man continually propositioned her. She had been warned that if she yielded she would be on the next plane out because "the Shah wanted his girls untouched by Iranian hands." For the next few months, the Shah came twice a week to fuck her. The rest of the time, this woman had little to do. She couldn't even go to the hotel pool without a guard. She was not allowed to see anybody besides the Shah and the man next door - who never stopped propositioning her. The boredom got to her and she left Tehran of her own accord after several months.(9)

Apparently all these prostitutes coming and going didn't bother Farah too much for "All this was taken for granted; it was part of the Pahlavi style but then something serious happened"- that being that the Shah fell in love with a 19 year old Iranian named Gilda. Rumors were that he had actually married her and installed her in a cottage on the palace grounds.

Farah was angry and left the country at the end of 1972. Speculating on the cause of this rift a CIA report said, "it seems more likely that the Shah's dalliance with another woman was the real cause." Farah returned but insisted the Shah get rid of Gilda. General Khatami, his brother-in-law saved him by taking Gilda on as his own mistress. The Shah was grateful.(10)

Author William Shawcross has listed some of the stories he uncovered. The Shah insisted on having sex with a minister's daughter in a helicopter while it was flying; that he had a love child in France; that one of his mistresses sent a bill for clothes to the embassy in Paris; that when the couple went to St. Moritz she would go to their villa while he went to a hotel room for a liaison; that of European women the Shah most liked blondes with big mouths; and that Lufthansa hostesses were once favored. Shawcross found that the Shah's court "reeked of sex" and that pimping was rampant. Business and sex were intertwined. As a courtier said, "you had to pimp to progress." Many of the closest advisers to the Shah procured women for him. Former Italian prime minister Giulio Andreotti remembered that the Shah once arrived at the Venice Film Festival and shocked the local prefect by asking for a woman for the night.(11)

When the Shah was ousted from Iran in 1979, he made stops in several countries. One was Panama. The US ambassador to that country once lost contact with the deposed ruler while he was there. Frantically he checked around. Finally he reached President Royo, who, after some prodding, told him to relax - that the Shah was having a little fun. He was with a woman. General Manuel Noriega was responsible. He had been talking to the Shah, who had related he was bored. Noriega explained the macho ethic of Latin America. Every man in Panama had a wife and a mistress. The Shah liked the idea and said he wanted to see more of Panamanian life. What he saw was the inside of a plush hotel room at the Panama Hotel. Noriega booked a room and arranged for a woman to come in. Not a whore he insisted. A woman who was from a good family.(12)

At the time of the Gilda affair, the Shah was interviewed by Oriana Fallaci, who asked the Shah if he had taken another wife. "A stupid, vile, disgusting libel" was the reply. The Shah agreed with her suggestion that he could if he wanted to, as a Moslem. But he would only do so in special circumstances such as if the wife was ill or refused to perform her wifely duties. The Shah elaborated: "Let's face it! One has to be a hypocrite or an innocent to believe that a husband will tolerate that kind of thing. In your society, when something like that occurs, doesn't a man take a mistress, or even more than one? Well, in our society, instead, a man can take another wife."(13)

WILLY BRANDT

When Germany's Willy Brandt resigned as Chancellor in 1974, several factors played a part in his decision - one of which was his sexual exploits. He was born Herbert Ernst Karl Frahm on December 18, 1913. Later he took the name of Willy Brandt, because it was so common, as a *nom de guerre*. He was Chancellor of Germany from 1969 to 1974.

Gertrud Meyer was an office worker and socialist and she became "the first of a number of women in his life."(1) Willy was sixteen at the time. In 1933 Brandt went into self-imposed exile in Norway from the Nazis. Meyer went with him and the couple set up housekeeping together in Oslo. Willy introduced her to some of his friends as his wife.

A few years later, in 1936, Gertrud had "married" a Norwegian man in order to obtain the safety of Norwegian citizenship. She was still living with Brandt and later used this sham husband to help Willy get a passport so he could travel. By 1939 the pair had become estranged. Willy was away a great deal and Meyer decided there was no real future with him. She left and went to the United States. Said Willy, "The war came between us - but not the war alone."(2)

Willy had some brief affairs - one in Paris with a German emigre - and a Norwegian friend said of Brandt, "He was always a woman charmer of great quality, with the greatest technique of all - patience." A major involvement started in 1939 when he began an affair with Carlota Thorkildsen. She was nine years older than he was and said to be more intellectual. They had a child in 1940.

When the Nazis took Norway, Brandt was forced to move to Sweden where he and Carlota married in 1941. The couple lived well enough in their new country to be able to hire a maid. Rut Hansen was her name. She was a 23 year old Norwegian who needed work. After spending a year in the Brandt's employ, she moved on to secretarial work. Although Rut was also married, she and Willy began an affair in 1944.

Later that same year, Carlota and Brandt separated, divorcing in 1948. A mutual friend said, "Willy exchanged the intellectual Carlota for the proletarian Rut. He didn't get warmth from Carlota, but challenge. He got warmth from Rut. There was disappointment on Carlota's side, for sure. But not hatred."(3)

Willy was back in Germany in 1947. Rut joined him later in that year. Her husband had died the year before. Soon she was pregnant and Brandt decided it was time they got married. Stationed in Berlin at the time was a Norwegian army brigade which had a chaplain. Willy approached this man but the chaplain refused to perform the ceremony for a divorced man who was living in sin. After some more shopping around someone was finally found who would perform the ceremony. The year was 1948 and Rut was eight months pregnant.

In the early 1950s, Willy spent many weeks away from home on business and "sought diversion in lively company after the often dreary hours of parliamentary work." In other words, he had a lot of affairs. One of the most memorable was with a 31 year old divorcee by the name of Suzanne Sievers which started in 1951.

Another politician, Herbert Wehner, remembered her showing up looking for work saying, "People say I have the prettiest thighs in Bonn." Wehner said, "I could only laugh - this whore." However, Willy was interested and began seeing her. This affair lasted over a year with the couple also swapping letters. Hers were signed "Puma" and his were signed "Bear." As it turned out Sievers had screwed other high ranking German politicos and was arrested in East Germany as a spy. She received a five year jail sentence. Suzanne had been trying to work both sides of the street.(4)

Commenting on Brandt's affairs of the time a female journalist said, "He was bored after a day's work and wanted to have some drinks and fun, and women were fun. I know dozens of men like that." Sievers showed up in Willy's office in 1955. Brandt had used his influence to have her sentence reduced to three years. A grateful Sievers wanted to resume the affair. Brandt declined. A few more years later, in 1960, a less than grateful Sievers was aligned with some politicians who were opposed to Willy. When some journalists learned of the feud, they got Sievers to agree to publish her account of the affair with Brandt. Sievers set to work with a writer and produced a manuscript. However, a last minute court order was obtained which restrained the book from being published.

In the early 1970s, it was said that "a number of extraneous women passed through his life." Virtually none held his fancy for any length of time. These sexual exploits were widely gossiped about and Brandt joked, "Some people seem to overestimate my strength at my age."

During the 1972 election, Willy's campaign train traveled the length and breadth of his country. It was equipped with private sleeping quarters for the Chancellor. If an attractive journalist was on board there was a good chance she would be invited forward to those sleeping quarters to spend some time with Willy. One woman who returned to the main car at two AM - after several hours with Willy - was "hailed with cheers by her male colleagues." A press spokesman for Brandt told the group to go ahead and write up that story. The press man boasted, "Our Chancellor is fifty-nine and can make five speeches a day and give eight interviews and still get it up." Nobody wrote it.(5)

Not everyone who received such an invitation accepted. One woman refused one such offer on the grounds that Willy was "too fat." While campaigning for the 1974 election, Brandt resumed the practice of inviting females to his private quarters on the train.

Brandt's world came crashing down in 1974 when he resigned as Chancellor. The primary reason was over a spy scandal that had broken. However, the "women stories" were also a factor. Rut had also confronted him about other women and she had been pushed to her own breaking point by her husband's endless affairs. Back in 1966, it was said of the couple that she "led her own life but was available when he needed her."

In his resignation speech, Willy said, in part, "I am no plaster saint and never claimed to be free of human weaknesses." One of the reasons he gave in the speech for resigning was "signs that my private life was going to be dragged into speculation concerning the spy affair."(6)

MAO ZEDONG

By most accounts Mao got a late start and showed little interest in women until he reached his mid twenties. He was never a great womanizer in the sense of rolling up big numbers, relative to others in this book, but he was cold and aloof and treated women selfishly and callously. Mao Zedong (Mao Tse-Tung) was born on December 26, 1893. He ruled China from 1949 until his death on September 9, 1976.

As a young boy, Mao underwent a marriage when he was just thirteen or fourteen. The match was arranged by his parents - as was the custom - and the bride was nineteen or twenty. While he acquiesced to this union, the marriage was never consummated and he never lived with the woman, or had much to do with her. He later repudiated the union. This woman was left living with his parents and working around the farmhouse for free. From time to time he received hand made gifts from her such as cloth slippers and clothes.-(1)

As a student and young man, Mao was serious and surrounded himself with like minded people. He recalled, "I was not interested in women... Quite aside from the discussion of feminine charm, which usually plays an important role in the lives of young men of this age, my companions even rejected talk of ordinary matters of daily life."(2)

Through until he was about 26 there is no reference to any sex life for Mao. He was as good as his word. Sometime in 1920 he opened the Cultural Bookstore along with a partner named Tao Ssu-yung. The couple seemed to be in love but Tao abruptly left the bookstore after a couple of months when she and Mao developed political differences.

That same year he began seeing Yang Kaihui, who was the daughter of one of his former professors and eight years younger than he. At first they lived together in a trial marriage but then formally wed - perhaps influenced by the impending birth of a child. By 1923, Zedong was on the run as a political agitator and the couple never again spent much time together. Yang would be executed in 1930 by Mao's political foes, the Kuomintang.

After this first "real" marriage, Mao became more interested in women and in sexual activities. A former officer recalled that Mao showed great interest in the females in his command, made suggestive remarks about them and asked what the relations were between them and their officers. The man explained that everyone was very busy and there was no time for any fooling around. Zedong told the officer, who was younger, that he, Mao, was old enough so that female beauty always produced "voluptuous feelings" in him.(3)

One of these voluptuous feelings was directed, in mid 1928, towards Ho Tzu-chen (He Zizhen). She was an eighteen year old high school student. Within a few days of meeting they were living together. Mao announced to his comrades, "Comrade He and I have fallen in love." The couple married around 1930 - before Kaihui's execution, according to one source, and after in others. Most of Mao's marriages, and divorces, were informal affairs having little or no paperwork or legal status as we know it.

On the Chinese leader's infamous "Long March" Zizhen was one of only 35 women to accompany the almost 100,000 men. She gave birth to their fourth child on the march and the fifth shortly thereafter. Zizhen was also wounded by shrapnel on the march and took 18 to 20 pieces of metal in her body. "Scarecrow thin" was how she was described at the end of that march.

After those 6,000 miles, as one observer recalled, "Ho was a physical wreck, appearing decrepit beyond her years. Mao lost interest in her."(4) Mao began to show interest in other women. Zizhen once confided to a friend: "Zedong treats me badly. We bickered and had a fight. He grabbed a bench and I grabbed a chair. Oh, it's clear we're finished."(5) Mao had seen his wife turn from a political comrade to a quiet housewife - a woman who had nervous disorders - perhaps as a result of the march. She behaved erratically by then and it was said she had developed the habit of beating her children. Zizhen was dispatched to Moscow for treatment and ended up in a Soviet asylum. Years later she was returned from Russia, uncured, and installed in a Shanghai mental institution.

One writer has noted that Mao "treated both Yang and Ho as sex objects, as long as it suited him." During this period in Yenan, he showed further chauvinism when he declared it was legal for Communist cadres to remain married to two wives at once on the grounds that the Sino-Japanese War had made it "impossible for a man to stay faithful to one wife when they could not be physically together due to the circumstances."(6) Mao and Zizhen would be divorced but only after repeated requests by Mao and not until around 1947 or 1948.

Thus Mao was on his own around 1937, with his wife in Moscow. Noted an observer of the time, "At the age of forty-four, he was as highly sexed as ever. He often boasted of his virility with some of his close comrades at lighter moments, attributing it to his fondness for chili peppers."(7) One affair was with a woman journalist named Ting Ling. They spent many hours together in his cave. A comrade said, a few years later, "Although he is now about fifty, his enthusiasm for women has not diminished in thirty years."(8)

Lily Wu was an actress with whom Zedong had a brief fling. While most sources state Zizhen was in Moscow during this time a couple claim she was with Mao during the Wu affair. She and Mao had a fierce argument over the actress with Zizhen formally charging Lily with alienating her husband's affections. Mao denied these allegations. Lily, at Zizhen's insistence, was asked to leave Yenan.(8) Throughout this period and into the 1940s, it was reported that women were drawn to him by his growing power.

Jiang Qing (Chiang Ch'ing) came on the scene in the period 1938 to 1940. She was an actress twenty years younger than Mao and going under the name Lan P'ing. Mao attended one of her performances and was enraptured. Said a comrade, "He applauded her performances so loudly that Ho Tzu-chen became jealous. The two of them often fought about this, with terrible results."(10) If Zizhen was present when Jiang first arrived in Yenan she was soon packed off to Russia.

Smitten by the actress, Mao and Jiang often spent nights together in his cave. Rumors spread quickly about the leader's new woman.

Soon she was pregnant and determined to become Chairman Mao's wife. One day she burst into a meeting of high ranking officials and announced, "I have good news to report to you. The Chairman and I have started living together."(11)

Zedong was also pushed by Jiang to do something to formalize the union. As a party member, Mao had to first receive the approval of the Central Committee. Mao stated his case before this group, claiming that Zizhen's "mental derangement" had forced him to abandon her for Chiang. Perhaps expecting rubber stamp approval, Mao was surprised to find most of the committee members opposed to the union.

The opposition revolved around that she was a pushy actress, that she had no solid political background, and that she was trying to force out a mother and veteran of the Long March. Most of the members of the committee had shared the march with Zizhen. Said one of those opposed, "Ho Tzu-chen has always been a good comrade to you, she is a reliable and faithful companion and has shown her true worth in battle and in work. Why are you no longer able to live together with a woman like this?"(12) However, Zedong was adamant and told the committee that if Jiang wasn't accepted as his wife he'd "go back to my native village and become a farmer." The party finally, and reluctantly, agreed to his demands.

Some conditions were imposed though. Jiang was to "remain a housewife and play no role in public affairs." These conditions laid down to restrict Jiang didn't bother Mao for he probably believed she just wanted to be his wife. As one biographer commented, "Like most older men, he chose to think that the much younger Chiang Ching loved him unconditionally."(13)

Pressure was still brought to bear and Jiang wasn't really regarded as Mao's wife until the time of the Communist victory in 1949. Under this pressure, Mao made her wash off her make-up and stay home to look after the kids. Many of the ordinary Chinese looked at the union, for Zedong, as a way of having "a concubine in red sleeves who tended the incense while one reads books." They felt that for Jiang the union was a way to achieve power and glory.

True to the agreement, Jiang didn't appear in public with her husband nor was she present when the wives of other leaders gathered

- for almost thirty years. She resented all of this bitterly and it was all vented in a fury during the Cultural Revolution and after when she was a member of China's notorious Gang of Four. Said Jiang about her early years with Mao, "sex is engaging in the first rounds but what sustains interest in the long run is power."(14)

By 1973, the couple lived apart and from then onward if she wanted to talk to her husband she had to submit reasons in writing to a liaison officer and receive Mao's permission beforehand. At least once, in 1974, Mao refused permission. He wrote back to her saying, "Nothing will be gained by seeing me. The books by Marx and Lenin, and my books too, are all there. You do not read books by Marx and Lenin, and you do not read my books. There is no point in seeing me."(15)

Back in the 1930s, the type of women who appealed to Zedong were described as feminine women who could make a home for him. He appreciated beauty, intelligence and wit. Above all he prized loyalty to himself and his ideas. He was always cold and aloof from his women. Around 1936, Mao was recounting some of his early life to a biographer. One of the most rapt listeners was Zizhen. They had been together for eight years but she had never heard most of the details before. One writer said of Mao's relations with women that the total record indicated his "capacity to ignore them, to use them, and to abandon them."(16)

ANASTASIO SOMOZA

Anastasio Somoza - both father and son - had a number of things in common besides genes. Both exercised dictatorial control over Nicaragua. And both were notorious womanizers. Anastasio the father, nicknamed Tacho, was born in 1896. By 1937, he was President and strongman of his country. He ruled until he died in 1956.

When he was nineteen years old, the maid in his house became pregnant and Tacho confessed. She gave birth to a son whom he acknowledged much later in his life. When his mother learned of the situation, she shipped Tacho off to the United States - to Philadelphia. It is said that the English and US vernacular he picked up while in Philadelphia later charmed the Americans, during the 1930s back in Nicaragua, when they helped him attain power.

In 1919 Tacho married Salvadora Debayle. Later he had an affair with the wife of an American minister by the name of Matthew Hanna. During the late 1940s, Tacho was visiting Austin, Texas as the guest of some businessmen who were interested in obtaining oil leases in the dictator's country. A secretary who had spent a lot of time organizing the trip wanted to meet Tacho. This was arranged one night over dinner at his hotel. Late the next day, his Texas hosts went looking for him. A tired security guard outside his door told them, "He's still in his room. That damned blonde went in there last night and they haven't left since."(1)

A liason with a Spanish woman resulted in her becoming pregnant and suddenly leaving Nicaragua. In the 1950s Tacho took a young mistress. The end came violently when he was assassinated in September, 1956. A son named Luis was head of the country for a few years. He was replaced by a puppet head until Anastasio the son, born on December 5, 1925, was named President in 1967. Anastasio ruled until he fled into exile in July 1979 - pressured out by the Sandinistas.

As a young man, Anastasio fell in love with a woman who worked on a newspaper. Tacho wasn't keen on his son's friend feeling that she wasn't good enough for his boy. Tacho suggested the liaison should be broken. Somoza tried to defend his choice. The father became irate and smashed his son in the face, loosening a tooth. That ended the romance. Accompanying officers of the National Guard Somoza was a regular visitor to the brothels in the 1940s. On December 20, 1950, he married his first cousin, Hope Somoza, who was an American.

The couple had little in common. Somoza had a reputation of being a boozer and a brawler - activities he preferred over being with his sedate and refined wife. Brothels remained among the spots he regularly visited in the 1950s. He also fathered a girl in this period whom he later acknowledged as his illegitimate child.

Somoza continued a long series of one night stands both with girls at home and on his regular trips abroad before he embarked on a long term liaison in 1965. That year he took as his mistress a seventeen year old telephone operator named Dinorah Sampson. Trysts took place in locations such as Somoza's old farmhouse and a warehouse. Dinorah never minded.

It was generally agreed that Anastasio was both unattractive and overweight around the time he met Dinorah. However, like other men in his position, he had an exaggerated idea of his physical appeal claiming that during an election campaign "all the women screamed for him."

The Dinorah affair quickly became common knowledge in Nicaragua and the triangle was always prime gossip at society gatherings. As time passed, the dictator spent more time with Dinorah and less with Hope. Sampson had "won the right to his pillow."(2) Tiring of clandestine meetings, Somoza built his mistress her own mansion at the end of the 1960s. Often both wife and mistress found themselves attending the same party. The group around Hope thinned while the one around Dinorah grew. It was a function of which woman was felt to have the most influence with the dictator.

Hope once summoned up her courage to confront her rival and have it out. By the time she reached Dinorah's house, she was in such an emotional state that she promptly fainted. After that she gradually separated from the dictator. In 1977, Anastasio said of his wife that she could be "a royal pain in the ass. Just too damned bossy, picks at me about everything." When someone asked him why he didn't get a divorce, he said it was because of "my religion and because of my position." Asked which was the most important, he quickly replied "religion."(3)

So jealous of his mistress was Somoza that he often changed her bodyguards fearing she was becoming too fond of the current group. He sometimes had her followed when she made trips to Miami. Anastasio had a heart attack in 1977 at Dinorah's villa. It may or may not have been in the middle of sex.

In the late 1970s, Anastasio found Dinorah weeping at a party because she thought a singer had insulted her. Somoza, drunk at the time, became irate and chased the man. He aimed a kick at the singer but missed and hit a rock. The swelling of his foot became so great that, a week or so later, he was x-rayed and discovered to have a broken big toe. A cast was placed on his foot and society made a big joke of the whole episode.(4)

After he fled Nicaragua, Somoza sought exile in Paraguay. In that country, in September, 1980, he met the same fate as his father - death by assassination.

JUAN
PERON

While Juan Peron could womanize with the best of them, there was a curious pattern involved. When he was married, he seems to have been faithful to his wife of the time. The periods between wives were the ones when he went wild. Most of the men in this book have gone after young females - no matter how old the men were. Peron took that to an extreme and hustled even children. Juan Peron was born on October 8, 1895. He was president of Argentina from 1946 until 1955 when he was ousted by the military. Following a long exile he returned, in failing health, to briefly lead his country again, from 1973 until his death on July 1, 1974.

Stories on Peron's early sex life, from his graduation from military school in 1913 until his first marriage in 1929, are contradictory. One biographer, Page, claims that Juan devoted himself entirely to military life and showed little interest in women until he married in 1929. Page draws on the memory of a military man to say that during the 1930s when fellow officers used to sit around in the barracks telling about their sex lives and conquests, Peron confessed he had nothing to contribute because he'd had sex with no one except his wife. This writer states further that it was unlikely he was involved with other women at all until after his first wife died in 1938.(1)

Other biographers tell a different story. One says that when Juan graduated from military college he had a reputation as a brawler and had a "certain predilection for very young girls." Another writes that Juan first had sex when he was at the academy and it was with prostitutes for, as Peron is quoted as saying, "In the epoch in which we were boys, we weren't accustomed to go to social parties, and it would not have occurred to us to go to a home and make love to a family girl."(2)

145--Sex and Politicians

On January 5, 1929, Juan married seventeen year old Aurelia Tizon. The union seemed to be an ordinary one but was childless. Peron never fathered a child during his life and the charge of being "sterile" was often thrown at him by political opponents. Aurelia died of uterine cancer on September 10, 1938.

Juan spent time in Europe in 1939-1940 and the rumors were that he had a German mistress during his stay in Italy. The dictator himself later asserted that while in Spain, he lived with a Catalan school teacher and possibly impregnated her. Some two decades later, while the deposed dictator was in exile in Spain, he sent emissaries out searching for this woman and the child. No trace of a child was ever uncovered. Neither was the woman found, or alternatively, she had died in a hospital in Florence. Likely the child story was a fabrication by pro Peronists to show their leader was as "virile" as other men. Being childless was a slap at one's manhood.

By 1943, Peron was a major public figure in Argentina. As such he was the subject of magazine articles in his country. Several pictured him living in his Buenos Aires apartment with his daughter. One article called her Maria Inez while another referred to her as Isabelita. No daughter at all she was just a teenage girl that Peron was living with. Juan had nicknamed her Piranha - because of her overbite - and that's all she was known by. She was described as plain in appearance, silent and bored with her role as "daughter." Peron took her to boxing matches and introduced her around as "my daughter."(3)

When Evita arrived on the scene, the young girl made a quick exit and articles never again made mention of Juan's "daughter." There are two stories on the exit of sixteen year old Piranha. One is that Evita showed up at Peron's apartment with her belongings in hand and ordered Piranha out. Thus presenting Juan with a fait accompli. The second, and more likely, version is that the dictator handled this change in women himself. About the time that Evita made her appearance, Juan was rumored to have been involved with another woman, a sister of Aurelia. In fact, according to the Tizon family, he was close to marrying the sister but was dissuaded by Evita.

Peron met Eva Duarte (Evita) in January, 1944 when Juan called out actors and actresses to help raise money for earthquake relief.

Soon the 24 year old actress and the 49 year old colonel were living together. They would be almost inseparable until her death in 1952. Peron remembered the first meeting with Eva and said, "I looked at her and felt that her words were overpowering me; I was almost overcome by the power of her voice and her look... Instinctively I perceived that the collaboration of a woman of this kind would be invaluable for the social task I had in mind... I had to prepare a woman who would be the feminine leader of my political movement."(4)

Having a mistress was no scandal but to openly live together and to be seen in public was. Peron was beset by criticism and problems. When she appeared in public with him Eva conducted herself in a "crude and uninhibited" way. Fellow army officers were shocked and many felt Peron was setting a bad example for the military. There were persistent rumors that Eva had been a prostitute but they were not true. Critics dismissed her as "one of those tiresome girls who screw all over the place in the hope that someone will give them a part."(5) To army critics, Juan retorted "They reproach me for going with an actress. What do they want me to do? Go with an actor?"

By September, 1944, the US embassy reported a decline in Peron's personal prestige "partly because of the Eva Duarte situation." The United States intensely disliked the Nazi leaning strongman. During the 1946 election campaign in Argentina the US media vigorously smeared Peron. *Life* magazine called his private life scandalous and compared Eva's position to that of Goering's actress wife in Nazi Germany.(6)

The New York Times Magazine called him a rabble rouser. Peron's success, the article said, came about because South Americans followed men and not ideas. Certain well defined characteristics were necessary to be a typical leader. "He must in the first place be a real he-man and prove it either by having many mistresses or by shooting many policeman... even though there is no suggestion that Peron ever shot a policeman, he is well up to specification on most of these points."(7) *Look* magazine stated Peron had taken nude photos of Indians and stashed them in his desk. This article also said that during his time at military college, Juan kept pinup photos of nude females and effeminate officers in his locker, which showed his real interests.(8)

Peron and Evita married on October 22, 1945. The public record subtracted three years from Eva's age so she could appear to have been born legitimately. She was born Eva Ibarguren in 1919 but became Eva Duarte, born in 1922. The birth record of a child who was born and died that year was used. Bribery was probably involved. The public record also listed Peron as single instead of as a widower and that a prenuptial medical exam had taken place - it hadn't.

About marriage, Peron said, "I'm firmly convinced you shouldn't marry a woman who pleases you physically, but one who has other qualities... Because physical beauty is only for a time, later comes spiritual beauty which lasts longer, and the intellectual, that lasts longest of all. The man who doesn't think of this... has a woman for a short time."(9)

Observers have concluded that the relationship between Peron and Evita had very little to do with sex. One writer said that Peron's urgent need was to have a woman hovering around, for a listener, for company, and for domesticity. He concluded that the sex drive was not highly developed in Peron. The same was said about Evita. That she had a low level of passion and was little interested in sex. The marriage was a union of two passions for power, not a marriage of love. Yet another writer states that "Each was highly useful to the other, but conjugal love and affection probably had little if any part in their relationship."(10)

Evidence for this lack of love came from the cynical way the dictator handled Eva's death. An undertaker had been installed in a nearby hotel - on standby - as his wife neared the end. Embalming began within minutes of death, conditions for exhibiting the body were arranged that day and tens of thousands of photos of Eva, complete with a mourning band on one corner, were distributed within hours in Buenos Aires. Eva died of uterine cancer on July 26, 1952. She had been ill for sometime and from 1949 onward she was subject to constant vaginal discharges which likely made sexual intercourse impossible.

The next year, 1953, Peron moved into his years of heaviest womanizing. The education minister came up with an idea to "Peronize" teenagers. To this end the Union of Secondary Students (UES) was created to foster sports oriented recreation. Peron had his summer residence at Olivos turned into an athletic facility. There were both a girls' branch and a boys' branch of the UES. Only girls used Olivos. Soon rumors spread that Juan and his cronies were having orgies with the girls. That the only function of UES was to satisfy the dictator's appetite for young girls.

After Peron's ouster, an investigating committee could find only one instance which may have been an orgy. That was at a 1953 Christmas party. Several UES girls testified they attended the affair with Peron and some of his associates. The girls stayed three days and received expensive presents. Peron then took them to his farm where they stayed with him for a few more days. The investigators also found that the dictator lavished gifts on UES girls in general and arranged plastic surgery for any that needed it.(11)

At Olivos, Peron was an almost daily visitor. He came to watch the hundreds of young girls out exercising on the fields in their shorts. Sometimes he rode through the streets of town on his motorcycle, followed closely by a horde of these teens on their bikes. Townspeople closed their curtains as they were loathe to see their president cavorting in such a fashion. Juan was neglecting affairs of state and Olivos would be one of the factors that led to his military ouster from power.

Olivos didn't take up all his time as he was able to squeeze in affairs with one of Argentina's best tennis players as well as with Edda Ciano, the daughter of Italy's Benito Mussolini. Lunch at Olivos was a regular affair in which the UES girls, in turn, would get to eat at their leader's table. In October, 1953, Nelly Rivas had her turn. She was a basketball playing daughter of a janitor. She was fourteen years old when she hooked up with the 58 year old dictator.

After the first meal, she became a regular at his table and then at his downtown residence. After a few such visits, she moved in with Juan and stayed until he was ousted. He took her to boxing matches and, in 1954, to an Argentinean film festival which attracted such international stars as Errol Flynn, Edward G. Robinson and Irene Dunne. The couple stayed in a hotel.

Nelly spent most of her days watching movies and resisting the efforts of teachers that Juan had sent to instruct her in the rudiments of culture. After a year, an exasperated Peron gave up and said to

149--Sex and Politicians

Rivas, "There won't be another teacher coming here. If you want to remain an ignoramus away with them."(12) He lived openly with Nelly as he did with all his females, making no effort to keep his affairs secret.

When Peron fled the country in exile, he wrote a note to Nelly - then back home with her parents. It read in part, "My dear baby girl... I miss you every day, as I do my little dogs... Many kisses and desires." It was signed "Daddykins." He said he would send for her but he didn't. Said Nelly, "He loved me. He could have been my grandfather, but he loved me."(13) The new regime sent Nelly to a reformatory for eight months. When she was released and she and her family tried to leave the country to join Peron, they were all turned back at the Argentinean border.

Once exiled, Juan lived in various South and Central American countries for a few years before beginning a longer period in Spain. Back in Argentina, a tribunal of five generals formally condemned him for a variety of misdeeds, including having sexual relations with a minor - a reference to Nelly.

A writer named Gwen Bagni observed him in Panama and said that he still had his sex appeal. Whenever a woman took his fancy his feelings were made known through a friend and the woman would be ushered into his presence. His tastes ran "from the sophisticated to the naive and unpolished." When asked about it, he replied simply, "I like women."(14)

One woman he picked up was a young American from Chicago who was on holiday from her job in a restaurant. Peron was apparently ready for her to live with him and several times this woman postponed her return to the US - much to the dismay of her parents. Finally, after much wavering, she decided in favor of Chicago and returned home.

Late in 1955, Peron met a member of a traveling dance troupe then in Panama. Her name was Maria Estela Martinez - known as Isabel - and within a few weeks they were living together. By 1960 Juan was in exile in Madrid with Isabel posing as his secretary. Spain was conservative and Catholic enough to look with much disfavor on open living arrangements such as displayed by Peron and Isabel.

Persuasion caused them to marry on November 15, 1961. Peron was 66 at the time while Isabel had just turned thirty.(15)

Finally Peron triumphantly returned to Buenos Aires in 1973. He was elected President again that year with Isabel as Vice-President. His health was poor though and he died the following year. Isabel succeeded to the presidency but was ousted by the military on March 25, 1976. Held under house arrest until July 6, 1981, she immediately left for Spain once freed. During her time in exile with Peron, Isabel had shown no interest in politics. Of all his women only Evita was obviously strong. And even Eva clearly deferred to Juan calling his acts and wisdom "God-like." She once said, "I am the little sparrow to Peron's eagle."(16)

When he was once asked about his womanizing, Peron replied, "I like women. I could never live without one. I have always needed a woman." It didn't seem to matter much which one - as long as she was young, usually very young. He didn't think it was immoral for a man to like women. "What would be immoral," he thought, "is to like other men."(17)

PHILANDERERS

This is a variable group for which little has been reported on a number of the men included. Just enough has been reported to indicate, however, that they have earned a place in this book. Romulo Betancourt, Salvador Allende, the Duvaliers' and Zulfiqar Ali Bhutto are men in this category. Jomo Kenyatta and King Hussein have a little more information available but it remains brief and sketchy.

Libya's Muammar Qaddafi appears to have become a womanizer later in life which would make him unique in this book. More likely he wasn't as pure as the one source on his early life indicates. Making passes at visiting journalists seems to be the Libyan strongman's specialty. Israeli's David Ben-Gurion was an active womanizer. Some blamed it on his bad marriage instead of considering that perhaps his philandering was a major cause of his bad marriage.

Anthony Eden and Nelson Rockefeller both faced the prospect of negative consequences in their political careers because of a divorce. Even though Eden's took place many years before Rocky's, and in a country regarded by some as more conservative, Eden came through it unscathed politically while Rocky was less fortunate. His divorce took him out of contention for a shot at the 1964 presidential nomination. Argentina's Carlos Menem is a new man on the world political scene but an old hand at philandering.

MUAMMAR QADDAFI

Libya's Muammar Qaddafi became well known in the 1980s for his penchant for making passes at visiting journalists who had come to interview him. He was born in June, 1942, and came to power as Libyan strongman in September, 1969, as the result of a military coup.

The only reference to his early sex life comes from a writer who claims that Qaddafi wasn't a womanizer in his youth like his fellow military officers and that his reputation for "purity" has rarely been questioned. Given that womanizers almost invariably take up the habit young, rarely starting out of the blue in middle age, this reference seems unlikely, but possible. Particularly since this same writer adds, "Arab culture would not generally condemn promiscuous behavior by a male; if anything, it would be somewhat inclined to consider sexual advances as evidence of virility and as a natural reaction to the presence of a female."(1)

Muammar's first marriage was to Fathia Khalid, the daughter of a general who was a senior officer in the old Libyan regime under King Idris. It was a short lived and rather cursory union which ended in divorce in 1970 after producing one child. Soon after Qaddafi came to power, he was in the hospital for treatment of appendicitis. One of his nurses was a woman named Safiya, who became his present wife. They married in 1970 and had six children. Safiya keeps very much in the background which is in keeping with Qaddafi's philosophy which places females in a secondary role in life - or, as the dictator liked to refer to it, "separate but equal."(2)

It has been reported that Muammar has a need to surround himself with adoring and strong but subordinate women. This began to manifest itself around 1980 when "Qaddhafi had been seen, though not photographed, with a partly feminine troop of bodyguards, apparently young women specially trained by East Germany."(3) Others have called them "female Amazon" soldiers and Qaddafi has jokingly referred to them as his "revolutionary nuns." Most observers express doubts about their chastity.

Another group of close companions are a team of three female partners in Tripoli. Two of them are Yugoslavs, a nurse and a masseuse, and the other is an East German. They are known simply as "the three." The Libyan leader is said to be not averse to enlarging this team.(4)

Qaddafi in now famous for his propositioning of female journalists. One such American protested too vigorously when she felt Muammar's hand on her thigh. She was bundled out of the barracks in the middle of the night and left to find her own way back to her hotel. Another was brought to his barracks one night to hear Qaddafi tell her, "You have brave eyes. Can you make me forget my troubles for a day. Or at least for an hour?" A third woman whom he asked to sleep with him refused saying she didn't know him well enough. Qaddafi replied, "I respect you."

In January, 1986, Muammar invited five female journalists from abroad to meet him and his wife and children at home. The reason for the conference was to try and ease tensions between Libya and the United States - then very high - and to erase speculation that he was a "mad dog" as he was frequently called in the western press. He said he invited female reporters instead of males for ideological reasons - to promote women's rights. The conference, and Qaddafi's image as a family man, was marred when he made passes at three of the five women.

Not every woman turned him down. One of these was Australian journalist Renate Possamig, who interviewed him in the mid 1980s and then had a brief fling with him. Before she left she was showered with clothes and jewelry and his request to become his wife. An American reporter also got a present from her host, after a bedroom wrestling match. It was the watch he was wearing at the time. Qaddafi took it off and gave it to the woman saying how much he admired her. The watch was seven minutes slow when she got it and later that night at her hotel it stopped completely. It was a cheap replica of a Rolex, made in Taiwan, with Qaddafi's picture stamped on the face.

One of his visitors was Imelda Marcos of the Philippines. She wanted him to stop funding Muslim rebels in her country. After her second visit he did stop the funding. Imelda was said to have been taken with Qaddafi, describing him as "macho." Later an acquaintance asked her if she'd slept with Qaddafi. Imelda replied shyly, "What a question to ask a girl."(5)

By the end of the 1980s, some of the western newspapers and TV networks recruited their youngest and prettiest journalists for Libya. They felt, and hoped, that this would be the fastest way to obtain an exclusive interview with the Libyan leader.

KING

HUSSEIN

Jordan's King Hussein was born on November 14, 1935 and proclaimed to the throne in 1952. His early sex life illustrates the all
too common themes of a dissolute playboy, the male searching for an
obedient and unintellectual female and the role of political concerns.

Educated in England, Hussein indulged in fast cars and girl friends
at Harrow in 1951-52. While on an outing form the school, he met
Dina Abdul Hamed, who was his distant cousin and seven years older
than him. Hussein fell in love with her right from the start, but Dina,
described as highly intelligent, said she never loved him but respected
his position and responded to his need for support and understanding.
The next year, he put Dina out of his mind while he continued his
education in England at Sandhurst where "he chased many girls" and
frequented night clubs and parties.

Back home in Jordan in 1954, Hussein continued to live the life
of a playboy as he spent time with many women. Gossip made the
rounds in the capital of Amman as his name was linked with a large
number of different women. On April 19, 1955, he married Dina but
the marriage didn't last and the couple divorced the following year.
Dina was an intellectual who wanted to be involved in politics and was
often out of the house working for one cause or another. Hussein
wanted a simple woman who stayed at home all the time and who
didn't mix in politics. Additional criticism came from Hussein's
mother, who resented Dina's increasingly prominent role.(1)

Dina went off for a short holiday to Egypt in the fall of 1956.
She left her baby daughter in Amman. When she arrived in Cairo, she
got a letter from Hussein in which he said it would be better if they
stayed apart permanently. Dina wrote back asking that her baby be
sent to her but Hussein refused. Over the next six years, she saw her

child only once before Hussein relented and allowed more generous visitation rights. That was said to have been at the urging of his second wife.

Divorced from Dina, Hussein reverted to the playboy life again. His name was once more linked with innumerable women and one of his favorite activities was to drive away from one of his palaces or embassies in one of his many expensive cars with a beautiful woman at his side. He gave frequent parties and many of these lasted through the night.

At one of his parties, he met Antoinette "Toni" Gardiner, the daughter of the number three man in the British Military Mission to Jordan. Soon they were a regular twosome. Toni was described as having no interest in politics, no ambitions and as unintellectual. Gossip about them started in the winter of 1960. The British ambassador to Jordan instructed the military mission to find out what was going on. Middle East tensions were high at the time and the British didn't want to inflame anything by being accused of engineering the marriage of Jordan's King to a British girl. The British were worried that such a union would be viewed in the Middle East as cementing the colonialist relationship between the two countries.(2)

The first reports back were that there was nothing to worry about - the affair was a passing thing only. The British still felt they had to do everything they could to discourage it. They also hoped that Hussein wouldn't "commit what looked to the British very much like political suicide." Suddenly though, he did. Hussein summoned the British ambassador to the palace in 1961 and told him he was going to marry Toni. The ambassador urged him not to do it as it might provoke a wave of propaganda against him from the Arab countries. A number of Hussein's government ministers also argued against the wedding.

It was all to no avail. Toni had agreed to become a Muslim and to take an Arabic name which they had jointly chosen. That was Muna al Hussein - "Hussein's wish." On May 1, 1961, Hussein announced his engagement over the radio describing Muna as "a Muslim but not an Arab." It was left to a later broadcast to explain her English background. The wedding took place on May 25, 1961. Hussein did receive some sharp criticism from the media - the

Egyptian media in particular. Crowds of ordinary citizens cheered the wedding motorcade through the streets of Amman and there was no storm of protest. Muna relinquishing all claim to the title of queen and settled down quietly in the background.(3)

The marriage lasted until 1972 when the couple divorced. Hussein's escapades, if any, have failed to attract any media attention for the last couple of decades. He married a Jordanian, Alia Toukan in 1972. She was killed in a helicopter crash in 1977. The year after that, Hussein married an American named Elizabeth Halaby, who became Queen Noor.

JOMO
KENYATTA

Jomo Kenyatta was born circa 1897-1898. Long involved in the politics of his native country, Kenya, he became that country's first president in 1963 when Kenya won its independence. It was a post he held until his death on August 22, 1978.

His first marriage took place in 1919 or 1920 when he wed Grace Wahu and installed her on his family's farm. The wedding was in accordance with Kikuyu custom and didn't please the Presbyterian Church, of which Jomo was a member. Kenyatta had to appear before a church court where it was charged he had "committed sin with the girl whom he is buying as wife, as the result of which she is with child." Jomo admitted guilt. As punishment Kenyatta was suspended from Holy Communion and other church privileges until he repented and made amends for his sins. The tribal Kikuyu ceremony wasn't acceptable and he was told to have a "proper" marriage performed. This he did in 1925. It was not till the end of that year that Jomo was restored to full church membership.(1)

By 1957 Jomo was in England for a long stay. That year in London he met 35 year old Dinah Stock. She was described as an intelligent woman who made a great impact on the African. Initially she helped him with a book he was working on but soon he moved into her apartment and the couple lived together for a few years.

At the start of the Second World War they moved out of London - for safety - and settled in Storrington. Stock took a teaching job in Yorkshire in 1940 sending money back to Jomo to keep the apartment. During this time Kenyatta saw other women. One of them was 31 year old Edna Grace Clarke, whom he met in 1941. They married on May 11, 1942 - Jomo was allowed more than one wife. On the marriage certificate Kenyatta claimed he was a 37 year old bachelor. Edna knew about Grace and about the two children back in Kenya.

Jomo did some traveling in Europe, and it was reported that he had much "amorous success in the different capitals of Europe. Kenyatta had a disarming openness about these relationships. He was an African; the monogamy of the West was an interesting anthropological phenomenon, no more."(2)

When Jomo returned to Kenya after the war, he married the daughter of a chief named Koinange after the chief offered him one of his daughters. This was mainly a political union to cement a tribal alliance. A few years after that he took a fourth wife. She was a young college girl named Ngina. It was she who became the Kenya First Lady.

After Jomo's 1946 departure from England, he didn't see Edna again - or their son Peter - until 1963. That year he had them flown out to Kenya for the celebrations marking the country's independence. It was reported that Edna had remained loyal to him - at least through the mid 1950s.(3)

FRANCOIS DUVALIER

Francois Duvalier was born in Haiti on April 14, 1907. Mrs. Duvalier was a madwoman locked up until she died when her son was 14. An aunt raised Francois. He graduated from medical school in 1934 but had been involved in politics from early on. Medicine was forgotten and Papa Doc, as he came to be known, was elected president of Haiti in 1957. The election was equal but unfair as both sides cheated liberally. One of Francois's first acts was to establish his own secret police, the dreaded Tonton Macoutes. Duvalier declared himself president for life in 1964 and ruled until his death on April 21, 1971.

When Francois was in his early thirties, some of his friends decided it was time that Duvalier got married. They introduced him to a nurse named Simone Ovide. At the urging of these friends the couple married on December 27, 1939. They would have four children. As Haiti's leader Duvalier had a private secretary, Francesca Foucard Saint-Victor, who wielded great influence. She was rumored to be more that a secretary and Simone was reportedly very jealous of her. So great was her influence that Saint-Victor was considered the "woman behind Papa Doc and the person most often mentioned as his successor."(1)

Francois' regime was brutal and ruthless from the beginning. All opposition was silenced. Bodies turned up everywhere in quantity. One of his enemies was Yvonne Hakime-Rimpel, who, along with her husband, refused to campaign for Papa Doc. One evening early in 1958, Francois and eight other men, all dressed in military uniforms, raided her house and beat up two of her eight children. They dragged Yvonne out of the house and drove her to a deserted spot where all nine raped her in turn. They then savagely beat her. When they were finished Duvalier said to the others, "Now finish her off."(2) The man who volunteered for that task deliberately fired his gun into the ground thus saving her life. While Yvonne survived, she never recovered her psychological health.

Francois' health was poor from the time he first took office. In 1959 he suffered a massive heart attack which left him, according to New York doctors, a "madman" from time to time. When JFK was murdered on November 22, Papa Doc celebrated in the palace with his cronies over the death of his enemy. Since he considered 22 to be his lucky number - his only election victory occurred on that date - Francois felt he had caused JFK's death through voodoo. Early in 1964, Duvalier sent an envoy to Arlington Cemetery to collect a vial of grave side air, a bit of earth and pieces of funeral flowers for further rituals.

One of Duvalier's daughters married Luc Albert Foucard - Saint-Victor's brother. Another daughter, Marie-Denise, married a man named Max Dominique. These two men jockeyed for power and favor with their father-in-law. Mrs. Duvalier sided with the Dominiques. Max fell from grace and was slated for execution. He was saved only by the intervention of his wife and mother-in-law with Papa Doc. Max was sent out of the country as Haitian ambassador to Spain. The dictator had a very sudden change of heart for almost as soon as Max's plane had left Duvalier had his Tonton Macoutes gun down Dominique's chauffeur and two bodyguards. Max was charged, in his absence, with treason, thrown out of the army and ordered to return to Haiti.

An irate Duvalier chastised his wife for taking Dominique's side. Simone refused to change her mind which further angered the dictator. Papa Doc began to beat his wife with his fists. Duvalier's son, Jean-Claude, broke up the altercation, pushed his father into another room and locked the door. Papa Doc fumed for three hours before he set off an alarm which brought the military who released him. Duvalier continued his tirade against Simone in front of the astonished military men and complained that Simone wasn't as helpful to him as Eva Peron had been to Juan Peron. All was soon forgiven and Max and his wife returned to Haiti and received a warm welcome from the Duvaliers. Simone, however, had had enough. She moved out of the palace at the end of the 1960s and thereafter lived separate from Papa

Doc.(3)   Marie-Denise fired Saint-Victor and became her father's secretary.

By November, 1970, Francois was close to death and pondered the question of a successor. Considering he only had one son, 18-year-old Jean-Claude, the choice should have been cut and dried. However, even Francois realized his son wasn't very swift. With some reservations, Jean-Claude was designated as Haiti's next president for life. The constitution required the president of Haiti to be at least 40 years old. Before he died, Francois fixed that so a teenager could hold the position.

JEAN-CLAUDE DUVALIER

Jean-Claude, who would quickly become known as Baby Doc, was a source of derision to all who knew him. He was immensely fat and immensely stupid. "Fat Potato" and "Baskethead" were two of his nicknames which paid homage to his bulk and brain. The boy had no interest whatsoever in politics. Nevertheless he was installed as president for life on April 22, 1971.

Doctors had shot him so full of drugs that he didn't go to his father's funeral. He didn't believe his father would really die. When Francois told his boy he would soon be president Jean-Claude tried to interest his father in appointing his sister instead saying, "What about Marie-Denise. She's so good at things like that."(4)

Motorcycle racing was one of his hobbies although he had trouble squeezing himself onto the machine. Other interests included sports, partying and watching movies. At school he failed everything but school officials, understandably, always promoted him. His laziness and lethargy were so profound as to inspire more wonder than contempt in beholders. Jean-Claude never did any presidential work. He never attended cabinet meetings. For years power rested unofficially with his mother. Simone had moved back into the palace.

The pursuit of girls was given as much devotion by Baby Doc as to his racing. Long haired girls were his favorites. Friends always obliged by bringing girls to his parties for him. One writer noted, "He had no trouble seducing them, for a favorite girl could expect not only jewelry and money but even a car in appreciation of her prowess in Jean-Claude's bed."(5)

Professors were summoned from the university to the palace to tutor the president but had little success. One such man recalled that when he showed up at the appointed time Jean-Claude would be found playing with toy cars on his bedroom floor. Fifteen minutes after the lesson started, Baby Doc would always be asleep. Initially the Haitians seemed to love him and cheered him for years even though his regime was as corrupt and violent as that of his father.

Jean-Claude liked to talk about girls with his friends. He also liked to drive from the palace to a nearby business school where he could sit and ogle the girls going in and out of the building. He took great care in going over the details for one of his parties such as adding or deleting names with a casual laugh saying, "I'm sleeping with his wife."(5)

During the summer of 1979, Simone married her son Jean-Claude in a voodoo ritual which was supposed to guarantee him another 22 years in power. It was a pact with the devil. The next year, in May, Baby Doc married Michele Bennett. Described as an unstable promiscuous young woman with a vulgar background, she fucked everybody. Her partners would rush back to their friends to report her prowess. It was agreed that she was hot in bed. For this reason she was introduced to Jean-Claude for casual sex. Baby Doc had almost exhausted the supply of available and willing women in Haiti.

When they met, they quickly retired to the bedroom from where Jean-Claude emerged several hours later to joke with his buddies. "Hey guys. Do you know what? I've finally met my match."(7) After a session in bed with her, Jean-Claude would have Michele's scratch marks over his mountain of fat. Michele became his steady, although he wasn't faithful. When she caught him cheating, she would throw a tantrum. Slowly she overcame opposition to her presence from Baby Doc's entourage and persuaded him to marry her.

Nobody wanted to see Baby Doc married to a "mulatto slut," especially Simone. Ultimately Simone gave up and went into voluntary exile when she realized she couldn't stop her son. Michele took revenge by exiling 96 of Simone's relatives - all she had in Haiti. The wedding was one of the most expensive the world has ever seen at an estimated cost of $3 million. Palace officials had to teach Michele a variety of social niceties such as sitting so her underpants didn't show, to not scratch her armpits in public, and to stop chewing on her sunglasses during long speeches. Baby Doc lived in fear of his wife and Michele often said to him, "If you're not a man like your father then I'll wear the pants."(8)

Corruption and violence continued apace in Haiti with the country being in full revolt by January, 1986. In February Jean-Claude, Michele, Simone, three bodyguards and 18 other relatives fled the country. The entourage left with champagne glasses in hands and smirks on their lips. They were flown out in a United States cargo plane and settled into opulent exile near Cannes, France where they rented a house from Mohamed Khashoggi. Jean-Claude spent most of his time there partying and chasing women. Many were introduced to him by Michele's brother who was grateful for the financial support Jean-Claude provided him. In an interview from his exile, Baby Doc said, "I never say myself as a dictator. I believe I was a well-loved President."(9)

DAVID BEN-GURION

In between his political work in forging the new state of Israel, David Ben-Gurion also found time to forge a number of sexual alliances. His marriage lasted until death but it was an unhappy and bitter one, the division exacerbated by his womanizing. He was born David Yosef Grun (Green) on October 10, 1886 - taking the Hebrew name "Ben-Gurion" in 1910. David was the Prime Minister of Israel from 1948 to 1953 and again from 1955 to 1963. Death came on December 1, 1973.

Rachel Nelkin had known David from childhood and she became his first real romance, around 1904. So attached were the couple that they committed a daring act for the times - she appeared unescorted with him in the street. Several families forbade their daughters to befriend Rachel because of this breach of etiquette. David recalled, "People were very conservative. A young man and a young woman just did not walk in the streets together. So when I walked out with her, there was a terrible uproar."(1)

Despite this love for Rachel, Ben-Gurion sought out other women. He had an affair with the daughter of the landlord of the apartment in which he lived. Her name was Genia Ferenbuk (Jenny Fernbuch). It was said that David's health began to decline as his anxieties grew and that he found relief with Genia.

David, Rachel, and some others arrived in Palestine around 1906 and it was here that he had a falling out with her a year later. The group had a reputation as hard workers. When Rachel was fired from her first job the group, fearing their reputation would be tarnished, ostracized her. As the criticism grew, David didn't defend her but sided with her critics. When it came to a choice between ideology and love, Ben-Gurion chose the former. One writer concluded that David's feelings for Rachel were probably the most profound love he would ever experience.(2)

In 1908 David had an affair with a 17 year old girl named Chana Anavi. She was engaged at the time and the couple had to arrange secret meetings. The affair lasted a couple of months. The following year he had another brief liaison. This time with a farmer's daughter. He was depressed at the time and, once again, found relief.(3)

Ben-Gurion was in New York City in 1916 - having been deported from Palestine for his Zionist activities - when he met Paulina "Paula" Monbaz. She was a nurse and not political. The couple fell in love and married on December 5, 1917. When David proposed he warned Paula she would have to leave the United States and go to "a small impoverished land, where there is no electricity or gas, or electric trolleys."(4)

Relations between them deteriorated almost immediately. The marriage would last until Paula's death in 1968 but it was never good. Paula was worried and jealous about her husband's affairs right back to 1918. She often expressed these fears in letters to him. As it turned out, her fears were well founded.

Paula was described, by one biographer, as being uncomplicated. Her tastes were domestic and not bookish. She couldn't speak Hebrew and had no particular interest in Zionism. Said this writer, "Her talents and inclinations were all built on the hope of a settled family life. For many years, her task was to wait at home while her dynamic husband travelled the world on difficult and sometimes dangerous missions."(5) Paula resented all the trips away from home that her husband took.

Early in the marriage there was little money and Paula often gave up a meal, surreptitiously, to leave enough food for her children and husband. Once she was diagnosed as suffering from chronic malnutrition. Throughout the marriage Ben-Gurion rarely talked or played with the children, leaving it all to Paula. He also rarely had any time for her - even when he wasn't away on trips. With the exception of state functions, the couple never spent a social evening together. However, he always found time to enjoy the transient company of other women.

Paula became bitter and took to nagging. They also apparently differed in terms of sexual desire, or, as one writer put it, "Ben-Gurion was still full of a tremendous spirit of romance. But his wife failed to provide an outlet for his romantic yearnings."(6) In December, 1923, Ben-Gurion made the following entry in his own diary: "What a wretched family life this man had." Ten years later he entered in his diary the birth dates of, in this order, his parents, children, and self. Paula's was omitted.(7)

David visited his old flame Rachel - then married - during the early 1930s but both other spouses were usually present. Paula was deeply jealous of Rachel and once called her a "vamp." Ben-Gurion once told Rachel, "if I had married you, I would not leave home as often as I do now." Rachel and David continued to meet occasionally and Paula's worries increased after Rachel's husband died in 1958. She feared they would draw closer.

As a Zionist Congress in 1929, David met Rega Klapholz. She was 22 and he was 42. They began an affair in 1930 or 1931. It started on a trip to Vienna where Rega was, by chance or design. Ben-Gurion had planned to stay just three days in Vienna and then proceed to Czechoslovakia. However, when he met Rega there, he stayed as long as he could in Vienna and forgot about Czechoslovakia.

The couple exchanged letters often and met when they could. Usually it was in Vienna but at least once it was in Prague. Once, to get some time with Rega, David left Paris - he was there with Paula on business - telling his wife he had some things to attend to and would then meet her in Warsaw. Originally he and Paula were to travel from Paris to Warsaw together. Ben-Gurion went to Vienna to liase with Rega. He dallied too long and Paula found no husband when she arrived in Warsaw. Recalled one of the delegates assigned to meet her "there was a perfect scandal... I went to greet her and she threatened suicide."(9)

Rega moved to Palestine in 1935 - David was there. Paula seemed to be aware of her rival by then. Once, when she visited the Ben-Gurion home, Rega was met by a hostile Paula, who gave her photos of herself and David together. From then on Paula kept a close eye on Rega's movements. She dropped in to Rega's apartment every now and then, ostensibly for a friendly chat. The affair between Rega and David soon petered out.

About the time he began his affair with Rega, Ben-Gurion started another one with Rivka Katznelson, who was also 22 at the time. This affair lasted two years. Rivka visited her lover at home in 1931 and described the 44 year old Paula as looking worn out and that "her expression was repulsive, primitive, bad." As for the meetings she and David had alone, Rivka said that Ben-Gurion showed up "hungry, harried, aggressive, hugging, kissing, undressing; like someone looking for release and nothing else."(10)

While David was in New York City in the early 1940s, he had an affair with Miriam Taub, an employee of the Zionist Organization of America. She chauffeured him around and did a lot of his secretarial work. Another liaison during this period - in Palestine - was with a "young new immigrant," Rachel found him with one day. Rachel bought the girl some clothes since she had found her "practically barefooted." Ruth Goldschmidt was another of Ben-Gurion's conquests. They first met in London in 1941. The affair began in 1947 when Ruth - in her twenties - came to Israel at Ben-Gurion's insistence. One of the most demanding periods of David's life was the 1948 war during which "Ruth served him well as a tranquilizing influence, usually in the home of an aide, Zeev Charef, where she lived."(11)

Ruth was close to David's daughter Renana. When Renana once brought Ruth home for a visit, Paula upbraided her daughter for bringing home a friend "who was father's mistress." David's relationship with Ruth ended in 1951. After that, there was an involvement with Yael Uzai, a secretary.

Paula was shocked and hurt by all of her husband's affairs and threatened to kill herself. Her friends counseled her to take more interest in David's activities in order to regain his love. It was too late for that, however.

One of Ben-Gurion's longest affairs - although sporadic - was with a Gentile, Doris May. She was an Anglo-Catholic from Lancing, a small town on the English channel. She was very British and described herself as "in a sense, an imperialist." David first met her in the 1930s when she worked as a secretary in the London Zionist

Office. They spent much time together in 1940-41 when Ben-Gurion was frequently in London. Their affair started then. He was 53; she was 41.

Over the years that followed, they kept in contact with discreetly forwarded letters and by short meetings - sometimes years apart. After the war they met in London once in a while and at least twice David visited her in Lancing. Letters were still exchanged. In the 1950s, Doris worked at the Israeli embassy in London. Ben-Gurion came to London and Doris made a couple of trips to Israel. There were rumors and gossip about them at the London embassy.(12)

Paula was jealous of Doris and suspecting, or knowing, of the affair she constantly reminded her husband that May was a "shisksa" (Gentile girl). She once asked Doris how she could "believe in all that Catholic rubbish." May had a slight hearing problem and once when David was on the phone with Doris, Paula yelled out to David, "Speak louder! She's deaf."(13)

In August, 1956, Doris came to Israel with the idea of staying permanently and working alongside David. Her hopes were soon dashed. She was given a job in an office but was constantly hounded by Paula, said one observer, because "almost every day she telephoned one of her husband's secretaries and insisted on knowing where Doris was and what she was doing." David had no time for her. After a few months, she returned to England. Correspondence between David and her came to a halt. They never met again except briefly, once in 1966, when Doris was in Israel. May spent her final years in Lancing and died in 1968(14)

When he was prime minister in the 1950s, he continued to have affairs. He would meet the women after hours in his office when all the other employees had gone home or in the home of accommodating friends. His aides jealously guarded his private life and nothing was ever published about these relationships. Some observers tried to explain these affairs by pointing out Ben-Gurion's "bitter disappointment in Paula, who did not fulfill his emotional needs."(15)

Something of Ben-Gurion's attitude to womanizing can be seen in his response to the publicity which surrounded the Israeli politico Moshe Dayan when his affairs became public knowledge. When an angry husband wrote to David, accusing Dayan of seducing his wife,

David responded by writing, "A man can be an escete and a saint all his life and be unfitted to public tasks; and the opposite is true." Dayan's wife Ruth complained to David about her husband's affairs to which Ben-Gurion said, "You have to get used to it. Great men's private lives and public lives are often conducted on parallel planes that never meet." Ben-Gurion held George Bernard Shaw in contempt when he heard that Shaw hadn't had sex until he was seduced by a woman when he was 29.(16)

ZULFIQAR ALI BHUTTO

Zulfiqar Ali Bhutto was born on January 5, 1928. He was president of Pakistan from 1971 to 1973 and then Prime Minister from 1973 until 1977 when he was overthrown. Despite world wide protests the new regime executed him on April 4, 1979.

When he was just thirteen years old and still at school, Bhutto's family arranged a marriage for him to one of the daughters of Sarder Ahmed Khan Bhutto. She was a distant cousin almost ten years older than him. Bhutto later recalled, "I didn't even know what it meant to have a wife, and when they tried to explain it to me I went out of my mind with rage, with fury. I didn't want a wife, I wanted to play cricket." He rarely ever saw this woman but in deference to his family's wishes, the union was never dissolved.(1)

By the end of his adolescence, he had developed what was termed an "early fondness for women." Around 1947, Bhutto had a crush on an Indian actress called Nargis. She remembered him as being "very charming and likable, but always reeking of gin and perfume." She also said, "Bhutto as I knew him was the feudal landlord with princely pleasures - drinks, shikar and dancing with a new girl every night."(2)

In the summer of 1951, he met Nusrat Sabunchi and married her on September 8, 1951. Bhutto had persuaded his parents to propose for him. As a cabinet minister in the late 1950s and early 1960s, under Ayub Khan, he maintained a reputation as a man with a quick eye for a pretty face. This got him into trouble on more than one occasion but didn't damage his political career. Some of his troubles took place at home with his wife complaining of his womanizing. It is believed that Khan himself had to intervene to patch up the difficulties. Bhutto's official biographies refer to Nusrat as his only wife but "Bhutto is believed to have another tucked away in his country seat." It was usual in big landlord families to have a "village wife" from within the clan to keep intact inherited properties.(3)

ANTHONY EDEN

Anthony Eden is most notable for showing the position of a divorced man making a run for higher office in post-war England. Eden was born on June 12, 1897 and died on January 14, 1977. He was Prime Minister of England from 1955 to 1957.

Eden was attending Oxford right after World War I and had, it was said, "developed a propensity for falling in love." Three women had rejected his marriage proposals by 1923. He also had engaged in a passionate affair with a singer/actress then appearing on the stage. Anthony became a regular patron at the theater until the affair, which wasn't serious, ran out of steam. While running in the 1923 general election, it was said of Eden that "he had already acquired that almost mesmeric hold over women audiences that was to be the wonder and despair of his envious colleagues and opponents for the rest of his career."(1)

That same year, on November 5, Eden married Beatrice Beckett, the daughter of a friend. She was described as unintellectual with no political interests. The marriage was rocky from the beginning and the couple spent less and less time together. One of the problems was Anthony's frequent absences from home which put added strain on the union.

Things came to a head in 1935 when Eden discovered that his wife was having affairs and had been since early in the marriage. Anthony was deeply wounded and distressed to discover this but they came to a tacit agreement that they would stay together until it became intolerable. Each would go their own way. Divorce then was thought to kill a political career.

Eden had been having affairs of his own during the same period as his wife, and he had entered into indiscreet correspondence with "numerous lady admirers." All of these affairs were casual except one potentially serious one. This woman had left one of Eden's letters on her dressing table which her mother had read. This prompted the woman to call off the affair. She wrote to Eden saying, it's "not worth risking my happiness and a lot of yours... I always knew something horrid would happen, but I've thought of every way, but I'm terrified... Please, Anthony dearest, don't let your love turn to real hate."(2)

The marriage formally ended in 1947. The couple had been on an extended trip visiting the United States. Beatrice stayed in the US while Eden continued on to other points alone. She had continued to have affairs. There was a man in America who wanted to marry her, she said. The divorce became final in 1950. Beatrice didn't marry a second time and died in 1957.

When they separated, Eden faced a dilemma for no divorced man, even a so-called innocent party, had ever been prime minister. He chose to gamble on a divorce perhaps because he was then seeing Clarissa Churchill, niece of Winston. He first met her in 1936. They began to see each other in 1947. She was 23 years his junior. They married on August 14, 1952.

Before he remarried, Eden's Conservative Party had some of its officials canvas constituency offices all over the country. The party also had its Public Opinion Research Department prepare a report. The conclusion was that "all the evidence obtained indicates the immense public approval of your marriage... I am afraid this all sounds very pompous but I really want you to know that there is absolutely nothing to worry about."(3)

When he did remarry, Eden received some criticism from the church but it was definitely a minority opinion. Within a few years, Eden became England's first divorced prime minister. The newspaper, *Church Times*, led a campaign of protest against Eden. They maintained that a generation previously a man in Eden's place - he was Foreign Minister - would have had to quit rather than be allowed to remarry while his first wife was still alive. The paper said, "Mr. Eden's action this week shows how far the climate of public opinion has changed for the worse... the world is openly rejecting the law of Christ as in so much else."(4)

ROMULO BETANCOURT

Romulo Betancourt was born on February 22, 1908. He was the president of Venezuela twice, from 1945 to 1948 and again from 1959 to 1964. He died on September 28, 1981. While he was in Costa Rica in 1934, Romulo married Carmen Valverde, a teacher.

From his adolescent years, Betancourt was much attracted to, and attractive to, women. It was reported that he felt more at ease and less on his guard with females than with members of his own sex. He had affairs. However, as his biographer noted, "to whatever degree he had tended to conform to the relatively relaxed Latin standards of male sexual morality, Romulo Betancourt had always been discreet. His private behavior has never been a subject of public gossip."(1)

In between his two terms as president, Betancourt went into self-imposed exile in New York City with Carmen. While there he had an affair with Renee Hartmann, also there in self-imposed exile. She was a psychiatrist and political activist. When the Perez-Jimenez regime fell in Venezuela, Romulo and Carmen returned to Caracas together, as did Hartmann. In Caracas, Romulo served his second term as president and arranged discreet meetings with Carmen.

Rumors about marital difficulties circulated during Betancourt's second term. However, they generally weren't public knowledge. Carmen continued as the official First Lady. Once Betancourt finished his second term in 1964, he again went into self-imposed exile - this time to Europe. Carmen didn't accompany him but soon after he departed, Renee joined him. Betancourt then got a divorce and married Hartmann.(2)

SALVADOR ALLENDE

Salvador Allende was born on July 26, 1908. In 1970 he was elected President of Chile becoming the first Marxist freely elected in the Western hemisphere. On September 11, 1973, he was killed by opposition forces during the bloody overthrow of his regime. In 1939 Allende married a teacher, Hortensia Bussi, in Valapariso. The couple was at least partially estranged, for Hortensia didn't regularly spend her nights at the president's residence.

One observer noted that "throughout Allende's four decades in politics he made no secret of the fact that he liked women." Famed writer Gabriel Garcia Marques called Allende a follower of the old school with "perfumed notes and furtive rendezvous." Politician Pedro Ibanez referred to his "licentious manner of living."

While president, Allende was having an affair with his personal secretary, Miriam Contreras Bell, nicknamed La Payita. He had bought a property for her, and in her name, in a suburb outside Santiago. Allegedly this estate was also used as "an intimate hideaway where sex films were shown and the president, his big wigs, and their girlfriends cavorted - and had themselves photographed as they did so."(1)

NELSON ROCKEFELLER

Nelson Rockefeller's affairs of the groin cost him dearly - an anomaly in itself - not once, but twice. His chances for a shot at the presidency were blown away and then his womanizing literally killed him. Perhaps, though, that's the way the true stud wants to go - pecker up. Nelson was born on July 8, 1908. He was governor of New York State from 1958 until 1973 and then Vice-President of the United States under Gerald Ford, from 1974 to 1977. Rocky died on January 26, 1979.

One writer has stated of Rockefeller's youth that he "never hankered after the fleshpots."(1) If brothels is what's meant by that, maybe so, but Nelson was no puritan. His brother Laurance borrowed Nelson's car in 1928 and when he returned it, Laurance joked, "I didn't know the road but I just turned your car loose on the highway and it headed for the nearest girls' college, you have it so well trained." Nelson summed up his own future by saying, "I had two choices. I could have become a gigolo or a governor."(2)

Nelson married Mary Todhunter Clark (Tod) on June 23, 1930, right after he graduated from Dartmouth. It didn't take long for rumors of her husband's womanizing to reach her ears, rumors which she found best to file and forget. Mary Clark had a sense of dignity that in time grew to become, wrote one biographer, "almost regal as she stoically suffered the scandal of her husband's extramarital affairs."(3)

In 1957, Nelson launched his first campaign for governor. Just before that he fell in love and decided he wanted a divorce. Rockefeller told his friend Francis Jamicson of the situation and his decision. Jamieson took Rocky out for a long car ride and convinced his friend that a divorce could be political suicide. By the end of the ride,

Nelson had dropped the idea and continued his affairs. On his estate there was a special "hideaway" where he could entertain his women. Rockefeller's marriage was essentially dead by 1961 but the couple had an arrangement whereby appearances would be maintained. Publicly Nelson would play the part of father and husband while Tod would cause no trouble. In private, each would go their own way.

Joseph Persico had worked for Nelson and said of his boss, "He was and remained throughout life a vigorous and virile man... He was attractive to and attracted by women. He began to display that paradox of a certain breed of man, of fanatical obsession with work that seemed only to generate excess energy to be exhausted elsewhere." Persico claimed that when these various affairs ended it was always with mutual respect and affection. He also found the various Rockefeller businesses dotted with employees who were women from Rocky's past. About his first marriage, Persico wrote, "The effect of his private behavior on his relationship with Tod was not immediately fatal, but it marked the beginning of a protracted death of the marriage."(4)

Public knowledge of Nelson's marital difficulties came the night of March 3, 1961, when the Executive Mansion in Albany caught fire. Newsmen on the scene noticed that firemen escorted Tod to safety from a wing of the building opposite to the one where her husband slept. Tod never again returned to Albany to live but no separation was announced at the time. Nelson was involved in the New York City election - jockeying for power and influence to boost his chances for the 1964 Republican presidential nomination - and didn't want any bad publicity. In November, 1961, after the New York City election, the separation was announced to the media.(5)

Tod went to Reno, Nevada in February, 1962 to file for divorce. Nelson adamantly denied he was involved with anybody else. He was saving that piece of news for after his re-election as governor that year. Rocky knew how dicey it was for a man in his position to leave a wife of over thirty years and the mother of his five children.

Of course he was involved with somebody else and that was Mrs. Margaretta Fitler Murphy (Happy), who was almost twenty years his junior. Their affair started in the mid 1950s. It intensified when she became a volunteer worker for his first gubernatorial campaign and

then stayed on as a paid member of his staff - in Albany. To facilitate
the affair Nelson, arranged a job transfer for Happy's husband, Robin,
from New York City to Albany.

Dr. James (Robin) Murphy had long been a part of the Rockefeller circle. Nelson had arranged several jobs for him at the Rockefeller
Medical Institute. A friend of Rocky's recalled that "Robin was the
chief force in courting Nelson. He truckled to him, laughed too hard
at his jokes, praised his art collection too unctuously. He was obvious.
Usually the Rockefellers saw through such fawning."(6)

When Nelson announced he would remarry, the family took it as
a body blow. Brother David was devastated and brother Winthrop
flew up from Arkansas to argue against it. David's daughter Abby said
of her father that "the remarriage was the most distressing thing to
him that ever happened in the world." Three of Nelson's four
brothers refused to attend the wedding nor did any of Rocky's four
surviving children attend. The ceremony took place on May 4, 1963.
He was 54; she was 36. Happy had obtained her divorce one month
previous and given up custody of her four children in the process.(7)

The Presbyterian minister who officiated got his "wrist slapped" for
not getting the approval of his superiors. Within the first week after
the marriage, clergymen from all three major faiths "rushed into print
with their condemnations." Religious criticism then quickly died.(8)

The general public was not so quick to forget. Prior to his
remarriage, Rocky was the clear front runner for the 1964 Republican
presidential nomination - it went to Barry Goldwater. But his divorce
and remarriage brought about a sharp decline in his popularity from
which he couldn't recover. A Gallup poll taken before the remarriage
had Rocky leading Goldwater by 45 percent to 26 percent. A Gallup
poll taken three weeks after the wedding saw the figures switch to 35
percent to 30 percent - in favor of Goldwater. As Stewart Alsop
wrote at the time "Nelson could have remarried or run for President,
but he couldn't do both."(9)

Nelson kept campaigning. During the crucial California primary
campaign the far right organized a mass call-in to radio talk shows
complaining that Rocky was morally unfit for the presidency. Through
hard campaigning, Rocky had taken a lead in the polls for that
primary with only a few days to go. However, three days before the

primary, Happy gave birth to a son. This reminder of Nelson's marital escapades lost him the California primary and his presidential run was over.(10) Even Russia's Premier Nikita Khrushchev got into the act. Referring to the Nelson/Happy marriage, he denounced "parasitic capitalists who live a life of luxury, drinking, carousing, and changing wives."(11)

It was back to womanizing as usual for Rocky. In the mid 1970s, one writer commented that while he had a young wife "even she had not been able to keep his amorous eye from wandering."(12)

Nelson's death set off a flurry of contradictory reports. He died on Friday night, January 26, at 10:15 PM of a heart attack. The first version given was that he had been in the company of his chauffeur and a security man when he died. This was quickly changed to a story that he had been alone in his office working on an art book at the time. When Persico heard that story on the news he said to his wife, "There is no way that Nelson Rockefeller was working at ten o'clock on a Friday night." Neighbors saw a woman in evening dress accompany the ambulance men as they carried the body to their vehicle. A Rockefeller aide, Hugh Morrow, said he knew of no such woman. At the hospital this woman, Megan Marshack, was there, among others. Morrow ushered Megan out of sight, told Happy, "Don't worry. She's not here," and, taking charge, told the office story.(13)

The New York Times started to dig and after a couple of days reported what really happened. Nelson had dined with his family and left home at 9:00 PM. He went to 13 West 54th Street - a town house connected to his offices on West 55th Street. He was not alone but with Megan. Rocky had a heart attack at 10:15 PM. Megan panicked and phoned her friend, Ponchitta Pierce, in desperation and asked her to come over. She did and it was Pierce, who phoned the emergency number, one hour after the heart attack.

Marshack was 25 years old and was employed as an aide to Rocky. Her salary was $60,000 a year which was four times the salary of her previous job. Megan also had received a $45,000 interest free loan from Nelson to buy her co-op apartment which was two doors from Nelson's town house. In Rocky's will this loan was forgiven.(14)

181--Sex and Politicians

At the time of his death, Nelson Rockefeller was engaged in, as one magazine coyly put it, "a pursuit other than the high-minded study of art that had been originally reported."(15)

CARLOS MENEM

When the mother of Carlos Menem gave birth to him, she insisted the Virgin put in an appearance. If so it may have been the only time a virgin came that close to Carlos and walked away in the same condition. For Menem, the President of Argentina, has a reputation as a serious philanderer. Only five feet four inches in height, Carlos fancies himself a macho stud, lying about his age, and doing booze, sports and broads in a big way. "His reputation as a night crawler," wrote one observer, "makes Gary Hart look like the pope."(1)

Menem was born on July 2, 1930, in the impoverished Argentinean province of La Rioja into a family who had immigrated there from Syria. By 1964, Carlos was a lawyer with an interest in Peronist politics. He also had an interest in Ana Maria Lujan, a divorced young mother. Mrs. Menem didn't think this woman was a suitable mate for her son so she took Carlos to Syria to find a more appropriate match. In Damascus, Carlos met Zulema, who was also born in La Rioja. She had temporarily gone to Syria with her father who wished to spend his last few years in his homeland.

The couple had a fast 20 day courtship before Carlos left for Spain. Two years later he proposed by mail and they married by proxy. Zulema returned to Argentina accompanied by her father who wanted to make sure his daughter had a proper Muslim ceremony. Which they did in October, 1966. Zulema remained a Muslim while Carlos converted to Catholicism. Argentina's Constitution requires that the president be a Catholic.

The marriage was rocky from the beginning. The couple had a son in 1968 and a year later, Zulema took the child and returned to Syria with him. It was a rift due to Carlos continuing his liaison with Lujan. "He continued to see her many times with the help of my sister-in-law, the wife of his brother, Senator Eduardo Menem," claimed Zulema. She returned to her husband in answer to his pleas. A daughter was born in 1970. Zulema had three miscarriages during the early years of the marriage saying "probably my marital insecurity had a lot to do with it."(2)

Menem was elected governor of La Rioja in 1973, remaining in that post until he became president with the exception of a seven year hiatus during which he was ousted by the military who were then running the country. During some of those years Menem was jailed while for others he was just under house arrest. For part of this period, he lived with the daughter of a former cell-mate. Toward the end of his house arrest period, Menem was transferred to a village near the border with Paraguay. He fathered a son by a local woman while there. This woman confronted him during the 1989 campaign by representing his opponent when Menem visited the area. Carlos took it all casually.

The on and off marriage to Zulema was on again when the couple reconciled just before Menem's 1983 election campaign for a second term as governor of La Rioja. Rumors were that he had to pay Zulema a substantial sum of money to return to him. Carlos was linked with a variety of women, many actresses, who passed through La Rioja as well as in Buenos Aires. The governor liked nothing better than to be seen in public with as many young women as possible. He was also partial to having his photo published with starlets in Argentinean celebrity type magazines. An observer of the scene in La Rioja commented on his governor's sexual habits: "He is famous for denying no one. He is always ready to be the conquistador. Actually, women like him for being macho like that." This commentator's wife was present and reportedly nodded her head in agreement.(3)

Zulema and Carlos soon split up again even going so far as to begin formal separation proceedings in 1987. However, Menem then began to covet the presidency of his country. Argentina's Catholic church made it plain they would not tolerate a candidate with an "irregular" relationship. The message was not lost on Menem and soon a reconciliation with Zulema was effected early in 1988. Zulema took out an ad in the newspaper to let everyone know that the couple were no longer separated. Carlos even campaigned against the Argentinean divorce law.

This truce was more political than personal. Some commentators believe that Zulema doesn't live with Carlos in the president's official residence. Menem is known to maintain a suite in a Buenos Aires hotel which he regularly uses. A waiter winked at a reporter and laughed, "We attend him well here."(4)

Zulema is said to be domineering, ambitious and tempestuous. She is said to see herself becoming another Eva Peron - Carlos is the candidate of the Peronist party. Menem is dead set against his wife attaining this much influence. The often public squabbles between the couple have left her with a reputation of being unstable, but not him. Zulema fears a conspiracy exists to have her declared insane. When asked if his wife had emotional problems, Carlos said, "I am not a doctor but I hope she gets better. She needs help, but more than I have done I cannot do, and I don't want to talk about it anymore."(5)

Shortly before the 1989 presidential election, the Menems and another couple were having dinner in a Buenos Aires restaurant. Around eleven PM, a car driven by a young blonde pulled up. The woman got out and beckoned to Menem, who left his table with no explanation and disappeared into the night. An infuriated Zulema, sick of his "exhibitionism," reportedly vowed that she would put a knife into his back one day.

Carlos took over Argentina as president in July, 1989. During the campaign, his age increased slowly from his preferred 54 to his actual age of 58. He has continued his pub crawling and philandering. Even in a macho Latin country like Argentina Menem's sex life is considered messy and outrageous. His sexual prowess is called legendary.

When questioned by reporters about his image, Carlos told one, "If with this lifestyle I have gotten to be president, I have no reason to change it." To another reporter posing the same query, he replied, "Why should I change? Maybe I couldn't be re-elected."(6)

An observer who has watched him work his way through the women of Argentina said, "He's insatiable. It's a sexual sickness." Menem's response to such criticism is, "I am a seducer, not a womanizer. I can't say I'm a saint, because I have no halo. Let's say I'm an ordinary man."(7)

SWINGING BACHELORS

It's still rare for a bachelor to work his way up to the position of leader of his country but a few made it there. Despite the similarities these men have the image of bachelor has been handled quite differently by them. Both Fidel Castro and Henry Kissinger are not actually bachelors - both being divorced men. However, both were unmarried during their years in power and thus their inclusion as bachelors.

Married men play down their womanizing, at least to the masses. Pierre Trudeau and Kissinger did the opposite. Both men enjoyed the image of being the swinging bachelor but the underlying reality was different. For both of them it was more important to be seen in public with a variety of young and beautiful women than it was to engage in a large number of sexual conquests. Trudeau had done it all of his life. For Kissinger the swinging lasted only for around five years but it was of enormous publicity value to him. Ghana's Kwame Nkrumah was the opposite. He put on the public face of an almost celibate, like Hitler, while the underlying reality for him was that he was something of a swinger.

Castro is the only one of these four men who didn't bother one way or another to cultivate an image based on his bachelorhood. After a few brief affairs, he settled into a long time relationship with a woman who was five years older than him, which makes Castro unique in that respect. The men in this book limit their womanizing to young, sometimes very young, women. Something which doesn't change as they age themselves. This quirk of society is definitely mirrored and reinforced by the political leaders.

The personalities of these men do have some similarities that may explain their long periods in an unmarried state. All are aloof, self-centered and very much solitary by nature. It is this solitary aspect of their nature which prevents them from ever moving across the line to become gross and compulsive womanizers.

PIERRE

TRUDEAU

Pierre Trudeau was swept into Canada's highest political office on a wave of charismatic appeal! - he was truly a swinger of the 1960s. It was more illusion than reality, however. A life long bachelor, he married for the first time when he was 51, and leader of Canada. Trudeau was born on October 18, 1919. He was Prime Minister of Canada from 1968 to 1979 and again from 1980 to 1984.

Pierre had only two serious involvements with women before his marriage. Both took place when he was in his twenties. Therese was one and Trudeau was briefly engaged to her. This engagement was broken by Therese, according to Pierre, because she was worried about all the time he spent away from home - dashing off around the world. Therese told a different story to her friends. To them she said she broke it off because she thought Pierre would be impossible to live with. Not long after that, Trudeau was working in Ottawa when he fell in love with the daughter of a Swedish diplomat. That ended when the woman went home.(1)

During his long bachelorhood, he had many affairs. He would inform his married friends that it was wrong to demand fidelity from their mates - an infringement of their freedom. When he married, however, he saw things differently. One other long term relationship he had was with university professor Madeleine Gobeil. She was a regular companion and his semi-official hostess during the 1960s. Trudeau didn't tell Gobeil of his wedding plans. Instead he left fellow politician Gerard Pelletier to tell her for him as he, Pierre, flew to Vancouver to marry Margaret.(2)

Trudeau began to date Margaret Sinclair in the late 1960s. While they eventually professed their love to each other, Pierre was full of doubts and kept telling Margaret, "I am simply too old. How can you take up with a man two years older than your mother?" During periods of his strongest doubts, Pierre went back to dating other women. These included Gobeil, a French-Canadian actress and Barbra Streisand. Pierre flew Streisand up to Ottawa to accompany him to a gala at the Arts Centre in Ottawa. They also had a candlelit supper at the Prime Minister's official residence - 24 Sussex Drive. The media widely reported this as a romance. All of this made Margaret jealous and for a few days, every time Pierre phoned her she answered by shouting, "Go back to your American actresses."(3)

After she got to know him, Margaret decided Pierre wasn't the playboy he was reputed to be - notwithstanding the media hype and reputation to the contrary. He didn't, Margaret thought, take his affairs lightly and didn't want to hurt anybody. In addition, he had a strong Jesuit influence in his background which would have worked against one night stands.

The Streisand story is an example. Before he invited her to Ottawa for the weekend - in 1970 - he had seen here a few times in New York. Barbra's mother came along as a chaperon. Streisand was into color psychology at the time and kept telling Trudeau about his blue aura or red aura. Pierre was happy to be photographed with her but, "found her conversationally a bit of a bore."(4)

When Margaret and Pierre dined out together and photographers caught them, they just assumed she was one of his many girl friends, not thinking there was anything serious. To be seen with young and pretty women seemed to be the main thing. He was always charming and complimentary with females. One author wrote, "Within five minutes of arriving at a party, Trudeau seeks out the prettiest girl in the room and stays with her for the rest of the party. Aboard planes, he chats up the prettiest stewardesses. And so on and so on, whenever the women are pretty and young." He added further about women that Pierre "adores having them around but misses no woman in particular when she's no longer around."(5)

It has also been reported that Trudeau made just one demand on women - that they make no demands on him. They must be young and beautiful. Even when Pierre passed sixty, it made no difference. A friend of Pierre's thought he was "incapable of a relationship with a mature woman." Beyond first youth these women might make demands, or refuse to "sink into sycophancy."(6)

When Pierre was dating Margaret, they sometimes spent weekends alone together at his country residence at Harrington Lake. The pair would go around and mess up all the beds in the house. This was done to try and fool the Monday morning maids into thinking many house guests had been present.

Margaret also had doubts about the relationship. Early in 1970, she began to date a divinity student during a rocky period with Trudeau. To make the Prime Minister jealous, she even agreed to an engagement. It was quickly broken off by Margaret to go back to Pierre. Her mother warned her, "Don't be the mistress of a politician twice your age. Pierre will never marry you." During one of their arguments, Pierre said, "I don't believe you would be faithful." When he did propose to her he said, "I'm fifty years old, I have never lived with any woman for long, and I'm extremely solitary by nature."(7)

In September, 1970, Trudeau sent Margaret away to her home city of Vancouver - 3,000 miles from Ottawa. He wanted her to demonstrate her ability to be faithful amongst her own friends of her own age. A second task for her was to give up marijuana smoking. Margaret claimed to have accomplished both. Pierre and Margaret married on March 4, 1971. He was 51 while she was 22. Within four and a half years, they would have three children. She was back to smoking the odd joint by then as well. When fellow politician Jean Marchard learned of the marriage, he commented, "Thank God she's twenty-two." Even so, the marriage was doomed.

Once in a while Margaret took a trip alone to get away from things. She called such vacations "freedom" trips. On one such trip in 1974, she went to Paris for two weeks and then met Trudeau in New York City. It was there she said she "fell in love" with an American - over the course of an afternoon. The next day, Trudeau caught her drunk and kept asking, "Have you been unfaithful to me in Paris? Have you? Have you?" After a bad weekend, Margaret finally admitted she'd fallen in love. To which Trudeau replied, "You're sick."(8)

The end of the marriage came on a weekend in March, 1977. Margaret flew to Toronto to party with the Rolling Stones, spent a few days there with them and then flew to New York City with the rock group to party some more. They took separate planes. In Toronto Margaret stayed in the same hotel as the Stones. The group was up most of the night drinking and Margaret was seen wandering around in her pajamas. It was of course a huge scandal. Newspapers in countries other than Canada, such as England, covered the affair in much greater, and more lurid, detail. Canadian media people gave it much less coverage out of respect to the Prime Minister and his office.

It must have been tremendously humiliating to Trudeau but he never publicly discussed the matter. The Prime Minister was razzed in the streets by people who yelled, "cuckold" when they saw him pass. Margaret returned home to 24 Sussex Drive after her infamous weekend but by the summer of that year, 1977, an official separation was announced. Pierre got custody of the children. The Stones affair did boost Pierre's popularity in the public opinion polls. Often viewed by the voters as aloof and arrogant, sympathy had come his way after Margaret's scandalous departure to the tune of anywhere from a five to a seventeen point increase in his score in the polls.(9)

Trudeau has always been attractive to women. One writer summed up his appeal by saying, "His allure for women has existed all his life and is undiminished by age. The hint of the farouche Peter Pan. The hint of cruelty. The hint of ambivalence. Beyond all of this, a quality Trudeau possessed even before he became prime Minister, the aphrodisiac aura of a powerful man."(10)

KWAME NKRUMAH

As a bachelor world leader, Kwame Nkrumah liked to present an image of himself as a purist. The image of a swinging bachelor was one he felt to be not suitable for the head of a country. Nkrumah was born on September 21, 1909 and died on April 27, 1972. He was the Prime Minister of Ghana from 1957 until 1966 when he was ousted in a coup.

For a long time the belief was held in Ghana that Kwame would never marry because he "hated women." Many of those who said this did so with a sense of admiration. It was just a political myth as was the idea, also widespread, that he was a teetotaller. There was never any hint that he was involved with women. It was all part of the image of political purity that Nkrumah favored. He liked to say that because he had no time for romance he was the husband of all Ghanaian women. In reality he had "had a number of girl friends and some children." One of those out of wedlock children became a doctor who practiced in Ghana.(1)

A long involvement and one of the women closest to him was Genoveva Marais. Though Nkrumah lashed out publicly at South Africa, Marais was born in that country. They met in 1957 after Marais was appointed an inspector of schools in Ghana. Later he proposed to her but was turned down, Marais said, because she wished to remain independent and devote herself to her career. The couple remained close until Kwame's ouster from power.

According to Genoveva, the Ghanaian "liked women." Females wrote to him from all over the world and often addressed him in their letters as "Dear Mr. Charm." When he replied to these letters, he usually didn't sign his full name in the belief that "Far too many men have suffered because of writing to women." Nkrumah had a constant need for female companionship and, wrote Marais, "He liked women to be feminine, commenting on what they wore, even making his criticisms... As he drew away from his male friends, his female entourage assumed an importance which sometimes verged on the fanatic."(2)

Nkrumah finally decided to marry even though he disliked the idea. He came to feel it was expected of him - for so-called respectability. Young women were said to revere him as "some kind of God" and his political associates hoped a marriage would end this type of idolatry. A marriage would show his humility. Some of his fellow politicians were also of the opinion that marriage was necessary for all heads of state.

To find a wife, Nkrumah turned to his oracle consultant, Kankan of Guinea, who advised him to marry a woman from Egypt. Kwame sent off a letter to Nasser of Egypt explaining his intentions. In reply Nasser sent the pictures of a few women. From these photos, Kwame picked out Fathia Helim Rizik. He had considered marrying Fathia's sister but the family followed the tradition of not letting the younger daughter marry first, so Fathia it was.

Arrangements were made for her to come to the capital of Ghana, Accra. When she arrived, Fathia was so confused that when she was met at the airport by an aide, she thought the aide was her future husband. While the couple didn't speak a common language, they were wed on the day, in 1963, that Fathia arrived in Accra.(3)

The couple had three children but Marais considered the union to be a failure in that they had nothing in common, did little together and Nkrumah never confided in her. She wrote, "he needed a quiet, calm woman who would not challenge his dictates or interfere in his politics. Fathia certainly did neither... She was nothing special to him." Toward the end of his reign, Marais said, "He was almost celibate." After the coup, Marais was first jailed and then deported. Fathia left the country for Egypt.(4)

Nkrumah once said, "Women are strange creatures, moody." He also declared that, "A great man ought to have more than one woman to cater for his various needs and moods."(5)

FIDEL CASTRO

Fidel Castro's first and only marriage was a brief union which was ultimately sacrificed to his political goals. Since his early days and early affairs, Castro has settled into a long run as an unmarried head of state devoting less and less time to women - or perhaps its just guarded more closely and effectively. Fidel was born on August 15, 1926 and took power in Cuba in 1959.

Thanks to his Jesuit education, Fidel had been kept pretty much cloistered with regard to women until he arrived at university. While there, he was reported as very shy around girls. His political activities also left him little time for a normal social life. One woman he did become involved with was Mirta Diaz-Balart. Some accounts claim Mirta was his only involvement while he was at university while others claim there were other liaisons. One source claims, "he had a certain promiscuity when it came to women." Mostly likely Mirta was his only involvement.(1)

Fidel met Mirta, a philosophy student, early in 1948 and the couple, both 22, married on October 12, 1948. It was a match that wasn't approved by the Castro family as Mirta's father and brother both worked in high level positions for the Batista government - which Fidel was working against. The wedding was lavish and was followed by a three month long honeymoon in the United States - Miami and New York City. Angel Castro, Fidel's father, paid for everything. The couple's only child, Fidelito, was born on September 14, 1949.

By the early 1950s the marriage was under a strain. One reason was that Fidel was so busy with politics that he had little time to spend with his wife and son. A second reason was a woman named Naty Revuelta. She was the wife of a doctor and she helped raise money for Castro's political movement when Fidel met her in

November, 1952. Soon they began an affair which would last through his time in prison and his divorce. Mirta likely knew of Naty.(2)

His political agitation landed Castro in jail on the Isle of Pines where Mirta and his sister Lidia both visited him regularly. Working as intermediaries, they helped to keep his political network going. On July 17, 1954, while in jail, Castro heard a radio report that shocked and stunned him. The report said that the Ministry of the Interior had dismissed Mirta. It was a vile blow to Fidel intended to destroy him. It implied that his wife worked for the Batista regime - the very one he was sworn to overthrow.

Publicly, Mirta had always supported Castro and his cause. However, while he was in jail, Mirta had become desperate for money. She went to see her brother Rafael - a Ministry of the Interior Subsecretary - and asked him for some financial assistance. Rafael gave her $100 a month but took it out of his Ministry's funds by entering Mirta on the books as an employee. Batista's Minister of the Interior eventually learned about it and happily announced that Castro's wife was on his Ministry's payroll.(3)

Refusing to believe the report, Fidel wrote to Mirta immediately, affirmed complete faith in her and urged her to start a libel suit against the Ministry. He thought somebody might be forging her name to collect money. So furious was Fidel that he was ready to challenge his brother-in-law and the Minister to a duel. Fidel thought that his own family, who had money, was supporting his wife.

Lidia visited him in prison on July 21 to tell her brother that the report was true. According to one source, once he learned this, Castro immediately started divorce proceedings while another source states that Mirta initiated the divorce. The couple was divorced in 1954 with Fidel taking custody of his son. Mirta never publicly spoke about the incident - whether or not she knew where her brother got the money he was giving her. Three decades later, a member of Mirta's family said, "I think she was the only woman he ever truly loved." Several other people also thought that was true.(4)

Released from prison in 1955, Fidel soon left for Mexico. Naty was then pregnant by him. He told her he would marry her if she went to Mexico with him. Naty declined. Later, when he was criticized for his treatment of her, Castro told his detractors, "She had her chance but she missed the train."(5) Today it is said to be an open secret in Havana that Fidel has at least one adult child - other than Fidelito - and a grandchild from a romantic liaison. Presumably this would be the child from Revuelta.

While he was in Mexico in the summer of 1956, Castro had a liaison with an eighteen year old named Isabelle Custodio, whom he met through a mutual friend. Shortly thereafter, he proposed to her and was accepted. The intention was that she would accompany him on his return to Cuba. Isabelle quit her job in a record store to prepare for the wedding. Fidel had, in the traditional manner, obtained her parents' consent. Fidel bought some new clothes for his future wife and a one-piece bathing suit to replace her bikini "which offended his Puritan sensibilities."

That September and October, Fidel was deeply involved in plans to invade Cuba, and Isabelle felt abandoned. She suggested he give up the revolution and settle down in Mexico with her. Other strains between them developed. Some of his rich Mexican backers called her, in her presence, the "future First Lady of Cuba." Castro thought it went to her head. Not long after that the couple split up with Isabelle returning to an old fiance who had just returned to town. This almost wife was forgotten in short order by Castro, who remarked to a comrade that he had only one fiancee - the revolution.

Just before he met Isabelle, Castro had learned Mirta was going to marry a wealthy businessman. Friends speculated his involvement with Isabelle had been a reaction to this news more than any feelings for Isabelle. The involvement with Naty had no deep emotional ties. One of Fidel's friends said, "I am convinced that one hundred percent of the time that he was in Mexico he was still in love with Mirta."(6)

Fidel's most important involvement with a woman began early in 1957 in the mountains of Cuba as he began his final push to oust Batista. Celia Sanchez, a doctor's daughter, met Castro at that time and later in 1957, she moved to the mountains for good. Five years older than Castro, she soon became his most trusted aide. They became inseparable companions and remained so for 23 years until her death from cancer in 1980. Celia maintained her own apartment, where Fidel often slept.

Early in 1959, just one month after he took power, the German cruise ship "Berlin" visited Havana. Castro and some others went on board where he was strongly attracted to Marie (Marita) Lorenz, the nineteen year old daughter of the ship's captain. The Cuban leader was enamored enough to try and convince Marie to stay in Havana. He offered her a job as his secretary. Lorenz declined. Two weeks later when the ship was docked in New York, it was boarded by Cuban officials with a message from Castro. The message begged her to reconsider and that Fidel desperately needed her as an interpreter. This time Marie agreed. She was flown in a government plane to Havana where she was installed in Castro's suite at the Habana Libre.(7)

Later in 1959 Castro was in New York on an official visit to the United States, accompanied by Marie. At an embassy reception, he met Dr. Lidia Vexel-Robertson who was a child psychiatry fellow at Mount Sinai Hospital. She pursued him aggressively and even followed him back to Havana. It is not known if Castro encouraged her or not but he did tell her that Marie was his bodyguard's girlfriend. The romance, according to Lidia, was intense but "proper."

When the group returned to Cuba, Marie claimed she was placed under what amounted to virtual house arrest at the hotel and then confined for a week to the Isle of Pines. Speculation increased, said Lidia, that she and Fidel would marry. It all came to an end when Celia intervened. Up to then Celia had shown no interest in Castro's occasional dalliances with women like Marie, perhaps viewing them as harmless. But she did draw the line at anything "serious" which might lead to Castro remarrying or to her position being usurped.

According to Lidia, "Celia made implied threats to her and told Fidel that if he continued the relationship she would take drastic measures." Lidia eventually learned of Fidel's involvement with Marie and the romance cooled and ended. Lidia married a member of Castro's entourage. The involvement with Marie also ended and she did, in fact, become the girlfriend of a Castro bodyguard.(8)

During the early 1960s, Fidel had become, wrote a biographer, a sex symbol of "astonishing proportions, even to ordinary Cuban women." There was at least one other affair during this period. Castro invited the widow of a former Colombian presidential candidate, and her daughter, to visit Cuba as his guests. Gloria Gaitan, the daughter, and Fidel were rumored to have had an affair during the few weeks she was in Cuba.(9)

Celia Sanchez, however, intensified her grip on Fidel to make sure no one else would become the number one female in his life. "She continued to serve as manager, wife, secretary, confidant, adviser, and protector rolled into one." She was with him almost constantly and controlled access to the Cuban leader."(10) Since Celia's death, no other woman has had her name publicly linked to Castro.

HENRY KISSINGER

As chief henchman to Richard Nixon, Henry Kissinger was an unlikely swinger. And he wasn't, at least until 1969. Then he was suddenly one of the biggest swingers around - or so he was portrayed. Henry was more interested, however, in being seen around town with beautiful and young females than in actually swinging. Just as quickly as this image was turned on it was turned off, in less than five years. Even so, in the annals of womanizing, Henry will always be remembered for his oft quoted remark as to why women are drawn to politicians.

Heinz Alfred Kissinger was born on May 27, 1923 in Germany - he took the name Henry only when he came to the United States, which he did in 1938 after fleeing from the Nazis. From 1968, Nixon named him Assistant for National Security Affairs. In 1973, he was named Secretary of State under Nixon, a position he continued to hold under Gerald Ford.

Like Kissinger, Ann Fleischer was a Jewish refugee from Hitler's Germany. The couple met in the US and married in February, 1949, while Henry was still a Harvard undergraduate. The marriage which lasted fifteen years was best described as stormy. Sometime in the 1950s, things were not well at home. One of Ann's friends commented that she was almost "oriental" in her devotion to Kissinger. Another observed that, "Ann was a European wife, solicitous, ever at her husband's service but never his equal." Henry always held center stage and was not one to make Ann feel self confident. Henry was described as "very self-centered." Kissinger could be brusque to Ann. It would be noticed by those around them and it would make them uncomfortable. A neighbor said that he "wasn't very nice to his wife."

A mutual friend commented that "Ann lived her life according to Kissinger's needs. He was the boss who laid down the law."(1)

By the time he was forty, the Kissinger marriage was on the verge of breaking up. A friend once visited Henry in his study. Ann joined the pair but her husband asked her to leave. During an address he delivered to the Military Intelligence Association of New England in Boston at a hotel, Henry made his wife sit in the lobby even though some military wives were inside the auditorium. A psychiatrist in Boston reportedly said, "Henry made Ann feel inadequate not only as an intellectual but as a woman... She was not perceived by her husband as a suitable consort." Ann got a divorce in Reno in 1964. There was no third party involved."(2)

The year of his divorce, Kissinger met Nancy Sharon Maginnes, a 30 year old graduate student, at the Republican Convention in San Francisco. Ten years later, on March 30, 1974, the couple married in a secret ceremony. When the news was announced, it made the front pages of newspapers around the world. Henry would often slip away from Washington to spend a weekend in New York with Nancy. And while they dated over that decade, Nancy was never mentioned in the media linked with Henry. Before she wed Henry, Nancy had to put up with Henry's swinging macho escapades - and that's what the media covered.

After his divorce, Henry spent several years working his way up as a colorless White House adviser. As a plain and portly intellectual over forty, he was unlikely material for a swinger. The transformation can be dated to October, 1969, when he attended a fashionable cocktail party at the home of Washington's Barbara Howar, in honor of writer Gloria Steinem. Kissinger was alone in a corner when reporter Sally Quinn spotted him and asked him to pose for a photo with Steinem. Quinn joked, "You really are a swinger underneath it all, aren't you?" To which Henry replied, "Why don't you just assume I'm a secret swinger." It all started then. His picture with Gloria, and his quote, appeared around the country and changed him totally. NBC's Barbara Walters called him, "the Jackie Onasis of the Nixon administration."(3)

Soon Henry was a fixture on the party circuit in Washington. He loved the attention and was linked in columns with various females -

"a cast of dolls from coast to coast." At function after function, he showed up with a beautiful woman, some were famous and some weren't. Usually it was a different woman each time. Photos would be taken and published in papers the next day which further enhanced his reputation as a swinger. Henry was not unaware of the publicity value of this new image - to himself and the Nixon administration. A friend told him that he'd gone too far but Kissinger replied, "I know what I'm doing."(4)

Through Frank Sinatra, he met Jill St. John and then Hollywood gossip columnist Joyce Haber, who later arranged more dates for him with Hollywood women when he was in California. Amongst the Hollywood stars he dated and was photographed with were: Samantha Egger, Joanna Barnes, Marlo Thomas, Hope Lange, Candice Bergen, Jill St. John, Liv Ullmann, Ann Miller, Susan Oliver, and Judy Brown. Zsa Zsa Gabor was another and after she met him said, "He is not much to look at first; after he opens his mouth, he's Cary Grant... He's everything a woman could want." Zsa Zsa gave Kissinger advice on his wardrobe - advice he didn't take. They dated a few times.(5)

That he was suddenly so in demand was a puzzle to Henry. He still found it hard to believe he might be appealing. Growing up he had thought of himself as a grind, as hopelessly asexual. It all changed when he got power. So, Kissinger ascribed all of his appeal to that source. From this came his own assessment of his success with women. "They are women attracted only to my power. But what happens when my power is gone? They're not going to sit around and play chess with me... Power is the ultimate aphrodisiac." Another time he joked, "Now when I bore people, they think it's their fault."(6)

This reputation as a swinger was also a puzzle to those who knew him in his younger days. One professor friend from Kissinger's Harvard days commented, "I'm baffled and stunned. It is not the Henry we knew here." Most believed it though. At the White House, Alexander Haig stood to Henry as Kissinger did to Nixon. While Haig was deferential to Kissinger to his face, behind his back was a different story. According to Kissinger aide Laurence Lynn Jr., "Haig called him pussy-whipped and cock-crazy. He would always say that Henry's got his mind in his pants - talk about him beating off in the privacy of his office."(8)

If Henry used some of his actresses for publicity purposes, they sometimes returned the favor. Kissinger dated St. John for several months and enjoyed being seen all over Washington with her - she had a penchant for low cut dresses. When Mexico City staged the World Cup soccer tournament, Kissinger attended as both a fan and a Presidential delegate. A press agent for Jill jumped the gun by announcing she would journey to Mexico with him. Quickly and emphatically, Henry denied it.

More lurid was Kissinger's involvement with actress Judy Brown, who had starred in an X-rated Danish film. Kissinger said their affair was limited to three dinner dates while Judy insisted it lasted over a year and included gifts and promises. Brown issued a press release about their dating, but when it didn't boost her career as expected, she went further. Brown charged that Henry kept her "in a closet" while he dated more "acceptable" women. According to Brown, they were once having dinner in a restaurant when Henry learned photographers were out front. He rushed Judy out the back door. Back at her apartment, Judy told Henry that that sort of behavior was unacceptable and he couldn't have his cake and eat it too. Kissinger left and said, reported Judy, "Well then, I guess I won't have my cake." Brown went public about this "incident" the next day.(9)

Danielle Hunebelle was a French reporter who also fell under the Kissinger spell. Reportedly, she fell madly in love with Henry and when he came to Paris and dated another woman instead of her, she ran her car off the road. Danielle next recounted her experiences with the swinger in a book *Dear Henry* in which Kissinger was described as having dirty laundry all over his disorganized bedroom and poor table manners. Danielle wrote, "We were two romantics, made for passion like Tristan and Isolde." When a visitor quizzed Kissinger about this woman, he replied, "If you speak with me three times, our relationship will be deeper than mine was with Hunebelle."(10)

Even when he wasn't with one of his starlets, Henry liked to keep his swinger image alive. A friend, Peter Peterson, asked him once: "Tell me, Henry, when you go out with girls..." Kissinger interrupted him and laughed. "Eat your heart out, Peterson." He was fond of pulling off mysterious disappearing acts for a couple of days at a time. Once after one such absence, reporters questioned him about his whereabouts. They were skeptical about the official story that he had been in Acapulco for four days. Henry said, "I've got four witnesses to prove I was there - all girls."(11)

Actresses held a special fascination for Henry but he didn't hold them in high esteem. He said, "I go out with actresses because I'm not very apt to marry one." Later he said, "These starlets I go out with aren't very sexy." By the few reports available, Kissinger was no firecracker himself. One of his regular dates commented, "Henry is very old-fashioned. He has old-fashioned virtues, and a strong belief in family life. He is a very moral man. The 'swinger' is as square as he can be." Another regular, when asked what they did, said, "Mostly we ate." A third joked that, "Henry's idea of sex is to slow the car down to 30 m.p.h. when he drops you off at the door."(12)

When Ann Miller was dating Henry, she chided him for having been seen in Trader Vic's snuggling and kissing a young woman. Miller told him it was an unpleasant sight while servicemen were being killed in Vietnam. Kissinger got angry and replied, "You don't know anything about me. I was miserable in a marriage most of my life. I never had any fun. Now is my time to enjoy myself. When this Administration goes out, I'm going back to being a professor at $1.95 a week. But while I'm in the position I'm in, I'm damn well going to make it count."(13)

Kissinger was said to have shied away from intelligent women, with one writer noting that, "His tastes run to big bosoms." White House dinner partners were chosen by social secretary Lucy Winchester by what she jokingly called "the Cleavage Factor." If someone less than amply endowed was seated next to him, he would go to Lucy and complain, "You seated me next to a 98-year old crone last night!" Another writer noted of Kissinger's women: "his dates' boobs got bigger and their brains got smaller." Someone at the State Department also seemed to notice this because a protocol officer there suggested to his counterpart in Henry's office that Kissinger would be better off with a "higher-class date at certain diplomatic affairs." Henry took the hint and usually used one of two "legitimate ladies" as needed. One was Nancy Maginnis.(14)

Just as quickly as he became a swinger, he ceased to be one. After he became Secretary of State, the starlets and the others disappeared. Shortly after that, he married. Henry once told journalist Oriana Fallaci his views on women: "What counts is not how much time I devote to women. What counts is to what extent women are part of my life, a central pre-occupation. Well, they aren't that at all. To me women are no more than a pastime, a hobby. Nobody devotes too much time to a hobby."(15)

ONCE
WAS ENOUGH

The *once was enough* men are those who have limited themselves to just one adulterous - but well publicized - affair or who have suffered consequences as a direct result of one affair. Dwight Eisenhower engaged in only one liaison as did, most probably, FDR. By the time Ike's came to light, he was long dead and it became an historical footnote, albeit an interesting one. He had a few hassles with his wife and some difficulty ending the affair but it had no effect on his career. Roosevelt as well came through his liaison with no career damage. However, it had an enormous impact on his marriage which was reduced to a joyless union for the rest of their lives. A bitter Eleanor would never forgive her husband's transgressions.

Four other men in this section were all caught quite literally in the act. Politicians in this kind of trouble must all refer to the same manual for guidance for these four men responded as one. Each straight out lied and denied every thing which only made it more difficult for them as the days passed and evidence mounted up. Ultimately they had to admit the affair and also to justify all the lies they had told.

All four of these men come across as the kind of sleazy characters that politics can well do without. Whether they engaged in more than one affair is unclear. There are stories that Wayne Hays did and certainly Gary Hart did. Hart would belong more properly in the *Macho Men* section were it not for the direct career damage he suffered from his affair. That is what sets these men apart. Others, like Rockefeller and Ted Kennedy have lost shots at the presidency due to womanizing, at least as one factor. The tie-in isn't direct and can't be "proven" in a rigorous sense. But for these four, the link is obvious. When Congressman Wilbur Mills was caught boozing, brawling, and frolicking with his stripper girlfriend, he first lost his prized committee chairmanship and then declined to run again for his Congressional seat. He knew what was coming. Congressman Wayne Hays was even more blatant and placed his mistress on the government payroll. Despite such gross acts, Hays wouldn't go quietly and had to be forced out one step at a time - from his committees, no re-election bid, and then resignation. Hays was an unpleasant man who was not loved by his colleagues in Congress, yet he was able to cut a deal. Shed no tears for Wayne for he walked away with no charges of any kind laid against him. He also walked away with a fat pension for life which was far more than the average wage-earner made at the time. All this for a man whom it was rumored, was maybe a hitter of women. Over in England, Cecil Parkinson was in an even bigger mess. Not only did he have an affair but he got the woman pregnant. He wouldn't come clean until the woman forced him to. As an up and comer in the Conservative Party, Cecil was a member of Thatcher's cabinet, and one of her favorites. Cecil's punishment was direct but brief and mild. He never lost his Commons seat but he did resign his cabinet post only to be given one back by Thatcher in a few years after another election. It helps when a powerful one is on one's side.

Most of the men in this book have been involved with what can best be described as bimbos. Cecil's woman wasn't, however. She was intelligent and sought justice and her own political career. And, for having the gall to do that, the powers that be whipped her ass.

Gary Hart, the joke of 1988, rose to new heights in the whining and self-pity derby. Hays showed more than a little of that himself but couldn't match Gary. When caught with his hand in the cookie jar, Gary was outraged that anyone could have that much effrontery and then to go on and report him. He forgot that he had dared people to tail him to the cookie jar. Some thought it might he a sort of death wish on his part, a desire to be caught - unconscious religious guilt driving him toward capture, confession and redemption? What it was, instead, was simple arrogance - the arrogance of being above the rules, over the law. However, arrogance, when combined with stupidity, can be a deadly combination - especially to the holder.

Greece's Andreas Papandreou, dumped a long term wife to dally with a woman half his age. The physical contrast between them was so extreme that Andreas soon became a European joke. It cost him an election. The last man here, Japan's Sousuke Uno also lost an election, and was forced to resign due to his affair. Arrogance did in Uno as he refused to discuss the allegations. The women of Japan also did him in as they rose above their image of being particularly obsequious to males to put extreme pressure on Uno.

Some of the women involved with the *once was enough* boys were able to get some rewards - financial - out of their situation. FDR'S woman was dead but Ike's wrote a book, although she was terminally ill at the time. Mills's friend got a flurry of bookings and saw her salary as a stripper rise to never before attained heights. The women with Hays and Parkinson both wrote books. Hart's Donna Rice received a number of financial offers to exploit her affair. Uno's *geisha* was paid monthly in a straight money for sex deal.

DWIGHT EISENHOWER

Dwight D. Eisenhower presided over the United States during the sleepy 1950s and it seemed a most appropriate pairing. Surprisingly, even Ike engaged in an affair - just one. And, perhaps in keeping with his image, he had troubles with that one.

Ike was born on October 14, 1890 and died on March 28, 1969. On July 1, 1916, he married Mary Geneva Doud (Mamie). He was president of the United States from 1953 to 1961.

While his one fling took place during the Second World War, it didn't become public knowledge until thirty years later when the man in the White House before him, Harry Truman, mentioned it in a book about himself. That was in late 1973. At about the same time, the woman involved learned she was terminally ill and she went public as well.

According to Truman, right after the war ended, Eisenhower wrote to General George Marshall and said he wanted to divorce Mamie Eisenhower when he returned to the United States so that he "could marry this Englishwoman." Truman said, "It was a very, very shocking thing to have done, for a man who was a general in the Army of the United States." Marshall was furious and he wrote back to Ike and said, "if Eisenhower even came close to doing such a thing, he'd not only bust him out of the Army, he'd see to it that never for the rest of his life would he be able to draw a peaceful breath." Marshall would hound him in or out of the forces, in any country, and make his life a "living hell." Truman added, "I don't like Eisenhower; I never have, but one of the last things I did as President, I got those letters from his file in the Pentagon and I destroyed them." At least that's what Harry Truman remembers.(1)

Rumors about these mysterious letters were said to have surfaced as early as 1952, before that year's Republican National Convention. Robert Taft was Ike's main opposition and Taft's people wanted to get hold of the letters to use against Dwight at the convention. Major General Harry Vaughan, an aide to Truman, recalled that Truman didn't want the story spreading all over the country so, "I think he sent them to General Marshall with a covering note that said, 'These belong in your personal files. I don't think they should be used for dirty politics.'"(2)

This idea of wanting a divorce would not have been unusual. One of Dwight's closest war time companions had done just what Ike supposedly wanted to do. As well, there were a couple of high ranking generals under Eisenhower's command who had been "persistently and notoriously faithless" to their wives at home, according to author Peter Lyon. This author contacted the executive director of the George C. Marshall Research Foundation in Arlington, Virginia, who said there was no material corresponding to that mentioned by Truman in the Marshall papers. The director added that over the course of the many interviews he held with Marshall the subject was never mentioned.(3) The woman involved was unaware of such a letter. Truman was very old when he was interviewed and his version of the story is most probably incorrect. However, Ike did have an affair.

Kay Summersby was the woman involved. She was born in Ireland in 1908 and died in 1975. By 1939 Kay was separated from her husband Gordon Summersby and was living in London where she was working as a model when the war broke out. Immediately she joined a volunteer corps, Britain's Motor Transport Corps. Although America was not in the war early in 1941, many of its military brass were in England and drivers were needed to ferry these men around. What with the fog, no street signs, no highway markers, nightly blackouts and only minimal headlights allowed, locals were used as drivers. Kay became one of the drivers assigned to the Americans.

The fateful assignment was made in May, 1942, when Summersby was assigned to the sole task of driving Eisenhower, then a two-star general. The man giving out these assignments said to her, "Kay, you don't mind, I hope. This Eisenhower? He's the only one left." Kay responded, "He knew I wanted a crack at the top general, not a two-star nonentity. I made a face and said, 'Okay.'"(4)

War work kept them together working long hours every day, sometimes even seven days a week. Gossip that there was something going on between them was making the rounds by the summer of 1942, but it was then baseless. Even so, Ike wrote to Mamie in October of that year that, "I've like some - been somewhat intrigued by others - but haven't been in love with anyone else and don't want any other wife."(5) Kay was engaged to an American airman at this time. One writer has described Summersby as a "flighty and impulsive" and "coquettish" woman who admired Ike to the point of hero worship.(6)

It was around the summer of 1943 that Ike suddenly professed his love for Kay - which was reciprocated. They were working out of Algiers then. Eisenhower told her, "We have to be very careful. I don't want you to be hurt. I don't want people to gossip about you. God, I wish things were different... Goddamnit, can't you tell I'm crazy about you."(7) The airman Kay was engaged to had recently been killed in action. She had rarely seen him since he was away most of the time and Summersby worked long hours. When he died, she admitted she hardly knew him.

Eisenhower liked to show Kay off and to become himself "show-offish" in her presence. According to General Patton, Ike found excuses for touching her hand or brushing her knee. Gossip intensified. The couple frequently went out horseback riding together. When they were seen out together by military personnel, they often were the focus of suggestive catcalls from soldiers, which invariably left the general "rigid and red." Ike discussed Kay with an old friend named Everett Hughes. This man wrote in his diary, summer of 1943: "I don't know whether Ike is alibi-ing or not. Says he wants to hold her hand, accompanies her to house, doesn't sleep with her. He doth protest too much, especially in view of the gal's reputation in London."(8)

Meanwhile back home in the United States, Mamie was getting suspicious and jealous. She saw many, many news photos of her famous husband and in the background of a lot of these photos kept recurring the face of Kay. Ike had to write and reassure Mamie there was nobody else but her. He also said he was too busy to have an "emotional involvement" and he was also "too old for romance." Other military aides and colleagues, including General Bradley, were aware of the rumored affair but the thinking had been "leave Ike and Kay alone. She's helping him win the war. Correspondents covering the general had cooperated" in keeping the involvement quiet.(9)

The general got a couple of weeks furlough early in 1944 and spent them at home with Mamie. They argued over Kay. When Eisenhower returned to London, he told Kay about the reunion. "The big trouble was... I kept calling her Kay. That tore it... Every time I opened my mouth to say something to Mamie, I'd call her Kay. She was furious." Kay herself spent a short holiday in New York City and Washington in the summer of 1944 while Ike was tied up in France. The general's son, John, escorted her around and Kay also met Mamie and a few of her friends over drinks. She found her reception to be decidedly chilly. Summersby became aware that gossip about herself and the general was active in America and not just limited to the UK. Kay was informed of "several gossip column mentions of the General's glamorous driver and nastily-pointed insinuations about our relationship."(10)

Kay had been the only civilian on the general's staff until October, 1944, when she became a WAC. Eisenhower had pulled strings to get her in since she was a British citizen. Ike told her, "I'm not going to be in Europe forever. I told you once that I was never going to let you go. If you're a WAC I can keep you on my staff later on." Summersby still spent all of her time working with Dwight but no longer had to drive. Instead, she rode in the back with him. Her hopes were that she would be able to become a US citizen in order to continue to work with Ike back in the US. Kay knew it was ridiculous to expect the American chief-of-staff at the Pentagon would be able to have a British subject as a personal aide.(11)

According to Kay, the couple had occasional necking sessions and the general spoke to her about having a baby if she wanted to. However, the relationship remained nonsexual for almost a year - which would make it spring or summer of 1944 - before they tried to have sex. When they did, Eisenhower couldn't get an erection. Later he explained his failure by saying there was a deep hurt on both sides between himself and Mamie. "Kay, I guess I'm telling you that I'm not the lover you should have," he told her. "It killed something in me. Not all at once, but little by little. For years I never thought of making love. And then when I did... When it had been on my mind for weeks, I failed. I failed with you, my dearest. Didn't I?" They tried again about a year later. Once again Ike couldn't get an erection. Kay told him, "Wait, you're too excited. It will be all right." Ike replied, "No, it won't. It's too late. I can't." He was described as bitter.(12)

With the advent of peace Ike knew, regardless of what he may or may not have told her, that the connection had to be broken. At first he tried to arrange a job for her in Germany, with his successor General Lucius Clay, but Kay wouldn't take it. Towards the end of 1945, Eisenhower permanently departed for the US. Kay was still expecting to follow and work with him in America. Then a telex message was received advising the general's personal staff to prepare to follow to America in ten days. Shortly after that a second telex was received which dropped Summersby from the list of those scheduled to leave for Washington. No explanation or reason was given. Kay then received an impersonal and dictated letter from Ike which said it was impossible for him to keep her as a member of his personal staff.

The excuse Ike used to terminate Kay was that she could not retain her commission as a WAC without becoming an American citizen - which was a five year process. And that he couldn't have a civilian employee working for him in the War Department.(13) Undaunted, Kay journeyed to Washington on her own and in that city dropped into the Pentagon to see some old friends - and Ike. She found him polite but distant. Then she got her new WAC orders which sent her to California. Unhappy there, she took her discharge and moved to New York City. While there, she managed to bump into Ike on purpose at Columbia University while he was President of that institution. He told her, "Kay, it's impossible. There's nothing I can do."(14)

Periodically Kay tried to re-establish contact with Ike. He avoided those meetings when he could and was very formal when he couldn't. Finally he just refused to see her. When she once tried to arrange a meeting by letter, Ike wrote back, "I can scarcely estimate when there might arise an opportunity for you to come past the office. The days are an unending series of conferences and work... My time is practically solidly booked."(15)

The affair was over. Kay authored a book in 1948, *Eisenhower Was My Boss* which did well and gave her an author's tour around the United States. It was a book very favorable to the general and didn't even remotely hint at their affair. However, Ike was embarrassed when a copy was sent to him. Field Marshall Montgomery was aware of the affair - he and Eisenhower didn't get along and strongly disliked each other - and maliciously asked Ike for a copy of the book. Eisenhower claimed that he hadn't even seen the book.(16)

Kay returned to the UK and later married a man named Reginald Morgan. There are still those who don't accept the affair. David Eisenhower, Ike's grandson, in his book on his grandfather's war years acknowledged Kay's contribution as a member of Ike's staff but said that she "exaggerated the tale of romance."(17)

WILBUR MILLS

Wilbur Mills shot himself in the foot. Finding it left him virtually unharmed, the surprised Wilbur, now perhaps feeling somewhat invulnerable and definitely emboldened, shot himself again. Not so lucky this time, it was goodbye Wilbur as his career was blown away. Mills was born in 1909 and was first elected to the House of Congress in 1938 - a Democrat representing Arkansas. Wilbur became the Chairman of the House Ways and Means Committee in 1958. This chairmanship gave him great power over tax legislation. Sometimes he was called the most powerful person in the House. In 1974, he was still chairman of that committee and was returned to his House seat faithfully by the electorate every two years. He was 65 years old and had been married for forty years.

In the Washington area on October 7, 1974, the authorities stopped a car which was being driven with its lights off at 2 AM, erratically, and at an "unreasonable rate of speed." Several people were in the car. One was a 38 year old woman named Annabella Battistella, originally from Argentina but then living in the United States. She ran from the car and jumped fully clothed into the Tidal Basin, a backwater of the Potomac River. She was quickly rescued. Whether she was trying to do harm to herself or was just a somewhat disoriented drunk is not clear. A second occupant of the car was Congressman Mills, who was reported to be bleeding from the face and intoxicated.

A witness to the incident reported he saw a fight in the car just before it was stopped. Wilbur was bleeding from the nose and from scratches on his cheeks. Some of the newsmen covering the incident said that the police directed one of the car's occupants away from a photographer saying to the occupant, "Come on Congressman, you don't need this kind of publicity." The first statement from Mills's office about this affair was delivered by Gene Goss, an aide to the Congressman. Goss related that Wilbur had told him he was "not in the car at that time and knew nothing about the incident."(1)

A couple of days later, on October 10, Mills acknowledged he was in the car. Previous denials he attributed to a misunderstanding with his aides. Wilbur referred to Battistella, who lived in the same apartment complex as he did, as a close friend. What happened that day was that Mrs. Battistella was ill, related Wilbur, and he and some others were taking her home. On the way, she tried to leave the car. He had to restrain her and in doing so her elbow bumped his glasses which broke. That was the cause of the few small cuts on his face. Wilbur claimed to be "embarrassed and humiliated" by the whole incident. Asked if there was anything between himself and the woman, Mills replied "no."(2)

The timing couldn't have been worse for Wilbur. He was coming up for re-election in less than one month. Speculation was that winning might not be so easy. Mills had spent almost no time campaigning in his district and very little money. His excuse was that he was too busy in Washington. One supporter said, "The stuff about being too busy up there obviously won't go over very well after Sunday night." Another Arkansas friend said, "I always thought of him as pretty much of a square. I thought it was a little out of character for him to be running around that time of night with a go-go dancer."(3)

Fence mending seemed in order, or at least a token effort, so Mills went home to Arkansas to campaign. His first public appearance anywhere since his trouble was on October 17, when he addressed the Little Rock Jaycees where he admitted he had been drinking on the day in question and that he was "high." After apologizing to his constituents and family for the embarrassment, the Jaycees rewarded their Congressman with prolonged cheers and applause. He fared less well when he addressed a high school audience and was hit with hostile questions. Mills complained because he'd heard that a newsman had "passed out $5 bills" to bribe students to ask those hostile questions. Wilbur was also denounced from the pulpit by a minister in a small town.(4)

By then Annabella's history was generally well known. A former stripper she had once been billed as the "Argentine Firecracker," although she was better known under the alias of *Fanne Foxe*. As Foxe she was stripping at a sleazy Washington nightclub called the Silver Slipper in July, 1973, when Wilbur met her in the club. Just a month after that, Mills and his wife moved into an apartment in the same building as Fanne. About twice a month, Fanne and Wilbur would visit the Silver Slipper where he would sometimes order magnums of champagne for Fanne and drinks for the house. Rarely did he spend less than $100 a night and once he went through $1,700 in a night - all paid in cash. The fight in the car wasn't the first because one night at the Silver Slipper the pair had a loud fight after Foxe thought Wilbur was paying too much attention to a stripper by the name of Vegas Vixen. Foxe was separated from her husband but he occasionally stayed in her apartment. Sometime after Fanne met Mills, and before the car incident, she quit her job as a stripper and had no visible means of support.(5)

Wilbur won his re-election comfortably. It was closer than any of his past races but still was no contest. The Congressman had fallen into shit but landed on his feet. Fanne reported that her marriage had permanently broken up as her husband, living in Argentina, was "very uncomfortable" with all the publicity she had received. She did admit her marriage hadn't been all that stable before the incident.

Career-wise, though, things were looking up for Foxe. By the middle of November, she landed a two week stripping job which paid her $3,000 a week. Previously, she had made a maximum of $700 a week stripping. The venue was Boston's Pilgrim Theater where she was billed as the "Washington Tidal Basin Bombshell." Fanne had spoken to Mills about her new job but he was perturbed and told her, "Anna, I don't like what you're doing. I don't like what you're doing." When she had left the Silver Slipper, Mills had made her promise that she would never go back to show business.(6)

November 31, 1974, was closing night for Foxe after her two week run. At the final curtain Fanne said to the audience, "I'd like you to meet somebody. Mr. Mills, Mr. Mills, where are you?" Wilbur was led on stage, acknowledged the crowd, called Foxe "my little Argentine hillbilly," and minutes later strolled off the stage arm in arm with the

stripper. Back stage when reporters spoke to him, Mills was staggering and had to lean on a chair for support. He claimed it was
medication for his heart which made him "drunk."

About his appearance on stage, the Congressman said, "This won't
ruin me. Nothing can ruin me. I've been an angel to a lot of people.
I'm going to make a movie star out of her." Wilbur went on to say
he had started the stage careers of fourteen or so other performers but
he wouldn't name them. One he did mention by name was Shirley
MacLaine, who, he said, "just flopped." When contacted later,
MacLaine just laughed and said she had no connection with Mills.(7)

This time there was an uproar over Mills's antics. House
colleagues scorned him. Some of his powers were stripped away and
the question of censure was raised. The *Arkansas Gazette*, a newspaper published in Little Rock and the state's biggest paper, called on
him to give up "his public indiscretions" with the stripper or resign.
Only a month previously this paper had endorsed Wilbur for re-election. Regarding his appearance on stage, Fanne commented, "I didn't
invite Mr. Mills. He said he wanted to come out on the stage because
he had nothing to hide." She also added that, "I love Mr. Mills and
he loves me, but we're not lovers, just friends - very close friends."
Another time she coyly referred to Mills as "a young man in an old
body." Mills claimed he made his stage appearance to stop "innuen-
dos" about his relationship with the stripper. He said, "I think I was
right. Of course, I could be wrong." Foxe had several more stripping
jobs lined up.(8)

More pressure was applied from the House. First Wilbur lost the
right to assign committee memberships. Then he was given the
ultimatum of entering a hospital or of being replaced as chairman of
his committee. His House colleagues were shocked, it was said, not
by the damage he was doing to himself but by the damage he was
doing to them. Wilbur did check into a hospital. The reason given
was that Mills was said to be exhausted. Complaints also came from
his constituents. The Arkansas governor received phone calls wanting
to know if something could be done to remove Mills from office.
Also, several nasty calls were received at the Little Rock office Mills
maintained. On December 10, 1974, Wilbur gave up the chairmanship
of the Ways and Means Committee. On December 30, 1974, he

attributed all of his recent erratic behavior to alcoholism. In the future he pledged total abstinence. He also declared that he would retain his seat in Congress.

Wilbur took treatment for alcoholism and didn't return to Congress until May, 1975. Foxe had hinted by then that she and the Congressman might marry. Mills scoffed at such an idea by saying, "Well, I am married. I am not going to commit bigamy." Fanne had also written a book about the affair and when Wilbur was asked if he had any resentment about what she wrote, he replied, "No, not a bit. The only time anything happened was when I was drinking and I just have to live with it. I don't even know where she is today. I didn't read her book. She did call me before it came out and told me they made her put a lot of things in there that weren't true."(9)

Wilbur didn't run for Congress again and ended his career in the House in December, 1976, after 37 years.

CECIL
PARKINSON

The indiscretions of Cecil Parkinson brought about his resignation from Thatcher's cabinet. However, rehabilitation was swift. He was back in the cabinet in short order. The woman involved got the shaft, literally and figuratively. She illustrates what can happen to a woman who tries to obtain justice, who makes too much noise, and disturbs the "natural order" of things.

Parkinson was born in 1931 and first entered Britain's House of Commons in 1970 as a Conservative MP. As one of the party's bright lights and a member of Prime Minister Margaret Thatcher's inner circle, his future looked promising. In 1983, he was a member of the cabinet - Secretary of State for Trade and Industry. Cecil married his wife Ann in 1957. The couple had three daughters.

Private Eye, the UK's muckraking journal, got the ball rolling in the fall of 1983 when they printed a short item suggesting that a woman named Sara Keays was involved with a politician. Mistakenly, they named as the man, not Parkinson, but another Conservative MP. This confusion was cleared up on October 5, 1983, when lawyers for Cecil issued a statement on his behalf admitting their client had had an affair with his former secretary - Sara Keays - and that she was expecting his child in January. According to the statement, Cecil had wished to marry Sara but was now going to stay with his wife. The relationship had lasted a number of years and Parkinson was in the process of making financial arrangements for both mother and child. Through her spokesman, Thatcher said she was aware of her minister's statement and the question of his resignation "does not and will not arise."(1)

Initially, it was thought that Cecil's chances of political survival were poor given Thatcher's well-known distaste for scandal or even a hint of sexual transgression. It was also felt Thatcher may have known of the affair as early as April, 1982 - she didn't - when Parkinson was included in the Falkland Islands war cabinet. That he hadn't had to resign immediately was a sign of the PM's respect and liking for one of the inner circle of her cabinet. Thatcher continued to call the whole thing a "private matter."(2)

Two days after his statement, Cecil made his first public appearance when he gave a speech to the Eastbourne Parliamentary Club. He won applause when he arrived and a standing ovation when he left. The local MP praised the "notable courage of Cecil." Not everyone felt that way. The Conservative Party Central Office received a "significant number of protest calls" which complained of the minister's treatment of Sara and his wife. Hastings Keays, Sara's father, said it was around 1980 that Parkinson told him he was going to marry Sara. Said Hastings, "I feel let down by him, bitterly let down."(3)

By October 10, only the PM had made a public statement of support for her minister - all other prominent Conservatives maintained a discreet silence. Privately, many were critical and wanted him out. Said one senior party official, "I admire the Prime Minister's courage... But I do believe his days are numbered, for the sake of her rather than anyone else." A poll taken of 580 adults found 62 percent saying he shouldn't resign with 32 percent saying that he should.(4)

A few more days after that, the Conservative Party gathered at Blackpool for their Conference where a strong display of solidarity was mounted. A couple of speakers mentioned Cecil's name favorably and this drew prolonged applause from the majority. Cecil made his entrance on stage with Thatcher so he could share her applause. Ministerial colleagues were also on hand and over half the cabinet stood beside and behind him on the platform. Again he got prolonged applause from the majority of the 5,000 delegates. The minority, who didn't applaud, or booed, were drowned out. One person in the minority was outspoken Conservative MP Ivor Stanbrook, who called Cecil a "self-confessed adulterer and a damned fool." Ivor was provoked by what he saw as the determination of the party elite to pretend nothing was wrong. He thought Cecil should resign.(5)

The *Times* (London) newspaper was confused by the whole issue and wrote a puzzled editorial. They felt Cecil should have stood on the principle that his private life was nobody's business. The *Times* felt this was a position to command respect. After pondering whether it was necessary to reveal the story, and if necessary, did he do the right thing by not resigning, the paper decided they could legitimately comment now because Parkinson had made it legitimate by going public. They concluded that Cecil "had made a sad and silly blunder." It is not clear whether the blunder, in their eyes, lay in the action or the revelation of that action. What the *Times* didn't know then was that Cecil had gone public not by free choice, but under duress.(6)

After his October 13 appearance at the Blackpool Conference, Parkinson looked like he would weather the storm and come through it without his career skipping so much as a beat. The press was mildly rebuked by the party for overstating Cecil's problems with the Conservatives, phone calls to the party were now reported to be 90 percent in Cecil's favor and Parkinson himself said he wouldn't resign unless he "ceased to be an asset to the government." Things were looking up. Until 2 AM on October 14 when he read at Blackpool, as did Thatcher, the advance copy of an article to be published in that day's edition of the *Times*. The article was a long statement by Sara Keays giving the whole story about what had been going on. Later that morning as people all over the UK were reading the article, Parkinson handed in his resignation from the Cabinet. Thatcher accepted it. Cecil kept his seat in the House of Commons and didn't intend to resign it. Sara was born in 1947. At the age of 25, she got a job as secretary for the newly elected MP Parkinson. They began an affair around 1973 which continued for ten years. Said one observer, "One always thought of them as a pair, as political colleagues. She was a sounding board to him - more like a PA than secretary - and she worked 12 to 14 hours a day." Cecil first proposed to her in 1979 but then quickly withdrew it on the grounds that one of his daughters was going through the difficulties of drug addiction. The relationship cooled and Sara worked abroad for a year, 1980, as a secretary at the European Commission in Brussels. Indications are that Sara tried to break off the affair that year but Parkinson wanted to continue and persuaded her to return and resume her job as his secretary. She did so in 1981. The couple still planned to marry and, according to Sara's father, Cecil told him June 1983 was the target date.(7)

In the *Times* article, Keays said she only allowed the long standing affair to continue because she felt they would ultimately marry. One of her reasons for revealing the story was that she felt the media implied she tried to trap Cecil into marriage and he only proposed after she became pregnant.

Sara learned she was pregnant in May, 1983. Cecil then decided he no longer wanted to marry her. Sara said she could accept that but could not deny her baby the right to know the identity of its father. During May and June, Keays repeatedly urged Parkinson to tell the PM. A general election was held that year and on polling day, June 9, Cecil sought a reconciliation. He asked her to marry him and she accepted. Parkinson told her he would inform Thatcher of the relationship and get a divorce. That night he said he did tell Thatcher and told members of Sara's family of his plans. Sara was asked to leave her job as his employee, and give him time to arrange matters. Keays quit her post at the end of June. Cecil went on holiday abroad with his wife and children on August 5, first reassuring Sara of his intention to marry her. Toward the end of that month Sara informed the still vacationing Parkinson that the press had got wind of the story and were pressing her for details but she had said nothing. The minister advised her to leave London - she did - and he would talk to her when he returned. On September 1, the couple met at an office in London where he told her he had changed his mind yet again and he wasn't going to marry her.(8)

Cecil did tell Thatcher on election night of his involvement with Keays. A little before that the PM had given Parkinson positive indications that he would be named Foreign Secretary after the election. It was the post he most coveted. That ended with the revelation of his affair. Thatcher did tell him he would still get a cabinet post and some days after the election he was appointed to Trade and Industry. When Thatcher learned of her minister's intention to marry Sara, she advised caution and further consideration. A friend of Cecil's, and the parliamentary private secretary to Thatcher, Ian Gow "became active in reinforcing that strong and influential advice." Thatcher's concern was for the wife, Ann, and to keep the scandal quiet. Apparently during his August holiday, Cecil confessed to his wife and obtained her forgiveness for his sins. This would explain his rejection of Sara on September 1. This decision pleased and delighted Thatcher. Ann Parkinson now also wanted the affair kept quiet. Thatcher's work behind the scenes is one of the reasons why she publicly supported Parkinson and didn't request his resignation when the story first broke. The PM also felt Cecil had been at least partly punished by being denied his favored cabinet post.(9)

The September 1 meeting ended the affair between Keays and Cecil but it still was the subject of gossip in political circles. The rumors were leaked by a Labour Party politician to the *Daily Mirror*, a Labour supporting paper. The paper held off publishing believing "a private life should be private." From there, a garbled account moved on to, and was published by, *Private Eye*. Between September 1 and that day, Sara had continually asked Parkinson to issue a statement on the affair to clear the air and set the record straight. If he didn't issue a statement she would, she said, be forced to defend herself. Cecil only agreed to publicly admit he was the father of the baby, through his October 5 statement, after Keays threatened to reveal the truth herself.(10)

Following his resignation, the *Times* claimed to have interviewed a random sample of Cecil's constituents and found that he had the support and sympathy of a majority of them. However, a poll by the *Sunday Times* showed that 59 percent agreed with the minister's decision to resign while 37 percent thought he should have stayed. By a margin of 55 percent to 42 percent those polled felt the affair was a private matter which had nothing to do with his political career. Extramarital sex was thought morally wrong by a margin of 71 percent to 23 percent. Forty percent thought Ann would suffer the most, 26 percent said it would be the baby while Sara and Cecil tied at 14 percent each. Another poll found females more sympathetic to Parkinson than men. Thirty-four percent of males thought he should not have resigned while 42 percent of females felt that way.

The *Times* published many photos of Cecil, and of Cecil and his family - all happy and smiling - over the course of the scandal while very few photos of Sara ever appeared. This newspaper "apportioned blame for his embarrassment equally between the media and Miss Sara Keays." One voter they polled said, "his private life had nothing to do with his public life." Another was quoted as saying, "It was unfortunate that he said he would marry her, but it was very naive of her to think she could have taken any real hold of him."(11)

Friends of Cecil turned on Keays and "accused her of a wilful campaign to destroy the career of her former lover." A government minister commented: "It's remarkable that he kept going through the election campaign with that woman ringing him up twice a day and asking about the divorce. We should be grateful that he kept the flag flying."(12)

Sara was active herself in the Conservative Party and saw a possible career for herself as a politician. Sara had sought the Conservative nomination for the riding of Bermondsey but lost by one vote to Peter Davis - this was in 1982. Unexpectedly, just one week later, the sitting Labour MP for the riding resigned his seat suddenly, necessitating a by-election. Davis decided it was all too sudden. His business commitments prevented him from campaigning so he withdrew. Some of the local party executive, some say a majority, wanted Keays to assume the candidature. However, national party executives entered the riding and intervened. They decided to open a full selection process. A short list of three names was drawn up - all men. Sara was interviewed only after thirty to forty men had been interviewed. One reason given for not choosing her was that the party didn't "want a woman to stand against Mr. Peter Tatchell, the Labour candidate."(13)

Cecil had told Sara she would be wasted in Bermondsey where the Conservatives would be beaten and she should apply for other seats even though she lived in Bermondsey. After their affair ended, Keays claimed her former lover had intervened and blocked her chances fearing that media attention she might attract as a candidate could link her name with his. After Parkinson resigned from the cabinet, Sara's name was removed from the list of approved Conservative candidates. The party would not discuss the matter with her nor give her any reason for their action. She also claimed pressure from high places was applied to members of her family to keep them from speaking out in her defence. An angry Sara said, "The Conservative Party was quite determined to turn me out and to do so in the most underhand and cowardly way possible. They have continued to apply blatant double standards in their judgements of Cecil and myself." In 1987, she announced she would not support the Conservatives in that year's election.(14)

Keays gave birth to a daughter on December 31, 1983. The newspapers had often mentioned that the settlement on Sara by Parkinson was as large as 100,000 pounds. In fact no settlement had been reached then and by the summer of 1984, Sara had received a total of 5,000 pounds from the minister. Speaking of the much larger sums of money mentioned in the media, Sara said "no doubt that the talk of money came from Cecil or someone very close to him indeed, and that it was designed to swing opinion against me."

The house Sara was staying in was broken into in 1985. Sara said that an investigating officer told her, "10 Downing Street had been informed and had ordered a news blackout" of the burglary. Nothing was taken from the ransacked house except for one or two of Sara's personal diaries. Sara had stated that Parkinson told her some of the secrets of the inner cabinet during the Falkland Islands war. Scotland Yard questioned both of the ex-lovers for possible security breaches. After she was interviewed, the Yard gave her a copy of the transcript of the interview for her to sign. She refused to sign because she had never made some of the statements in the transcript including one that she was "never made privy to any information that might remotely be described as secret." It was a statement that would have effectively cleared Cecil. Not long after, Scotland Yard did just that. In 1987, Sara's home was broken into. This time she received a warning from the police about a possible raid on her father's house. It didn't occur.(15)

Parkinson played a key role in the UK's general election in 1987. He was one of half a dozen senior Tories chosen to argue the party's case on radio and TV. He won his own riding handily with 51.8 percent of the vote. In 1983, he had obtained 54.1 percent. After the 1987 election, Thatcher named Parkinson to her cabinet as Secretary of State for Energy.

In August, 1986, Keays confirmed that her daughter, Flora, was being treated for epilepsy. Cecil had seen neither the child nor the mother since birth. Flora underwent a brain operation in July, 1988. A month following that, Cecil agreed, in court, to increase the maintenance payments for his daughter to 10,000 pounds a year from the 3,000 a year granted in a court order when she was born. Magistrates allowed the new amount on the grounds that the child's expenses had "substantially increased."(16)

WAYNE HAYS

When Wayne Hays was caught with his pants down, he did what so many others do - he issued barefaced lies - which only made matters worse. So appalling were his actions, and so blatant, that his political colleagues were forced to move to oust him. While he left in disgrace he went unpunished, for he was able to cut a deal for himself.

Wayne Hays was first elected to the US House of Representatives as a Democrat representing Ohio in 1948. Every two years over thirteen more elections, he was returned to the House, sometimes with 70 to 80 percent of the vote. By the spring of 1976, he was the chairman of four committees with the House Administration Committee being the most important one. Hays was born in 1911. He married his first wife Martha in 1937. The couple divorced in 1975. On April 13, 1976, he married Patricia Peak - in her 40s - who had been employed as his administrative secretary in his Ohio office.

Elizabeth Ray was a 27 year old - later changed to 33 - member of the House Administration Committee staff, who went to the *Washington Post* with a story late in May, 1976. Ray told the newspaper she was the mistress of Hays and had been for about two years. While she was paid $14,000 a year, Elizabeth said, "I can't type, I can't file, I can't even answer the phone." She was revealing the relationship because she said she was afraid of Hays. These allegations were adamantly denied by the chairman who explained he was a happily married man. Wayne told the *Post* he thought Ray worked on the staff of another Administration Committee member, Mendel J. Davis (Dem - S.C.). Ray was listed in the Congressional Staff Directory as a member of the Administration staff. Said Hays about the whole story: "It's not true; it's just not true. The girl is under psychiatric care. This is my reward for trying to help somebody who's sick." When questioned, Davis said that Elizabeth had worked for him for one month in the summer of 1975 and of her working abilities said, "She's not an expert 300-words-per-minute typist, but she could have addressed envelopes."(1)

The next day, Wayne continued his denials but implicitly acknowledged her as a staff member of his committee when he said she was "never on the payroll to do anything else but work eight hours a day for the committee like everybody else." He denied so much as taking Ray to dinner. However, two reporters had seen the pair in a restaurant just a week previously. This forced Wayne to backtrack. It was only twenty minutes he spent with her there he said. And that was only after she'd called him to say she had no money and was hungry. Wayne bought her a sandwich in the restaurant, gave her $5 for breakfast, and then left. An angry Hays blamed everything on the *Post* whom he accused of "carrying on a political vendetta against me for a long time." Another member of his committee, Rep. Frank Thompson Jr., was asked about Ray's description of her office skills and thought it was "pretty accurate."(2)

Another day passed and the Department of Justice announced it would investigate charges that the Congressman had placed Ray in her government job in return for sexual favors. Ray elaborated a little more. She had been provided with a private office on Capitol Hill but claimed she rarely went there. On average, Wayne took her to dinner twice a week in Arlington restaurants after which they returned to her apartment for sex. She reiterated she went public because of threatening remarks by Hays and because she was anxious about accepting her government salary.(3)

Meanwhile, Hays continued to deny allegations of sex. "I never had a relationship with her," he said. "My relationship with her was a business relationship." As far as her working ability he said, "She was all right as a worker under close supervision. She did typing, filing and the phones. She was quite good on the phones." Hays fired Ray shortly after the story broke, not because of the sex charges he said, but because she wasn't showing up for work. Still angry he blamed the *Post* for trying "to trap me" and Ray by whom he'd been "suckered... But I won't be again. I'm not too old to learn." Wayne's claim that Ray was seeing a psychiatrist was backed up by Rep.

Kenneth L. Gray (Dem -Ill) - a one time employer of Elizabeth - who thought she had been under treatment for five or six years and said, "she had an extreme mental problem, Jekyll-Hyde." Ray acknowledged being under a psychiatrist's care but that it was due to anxiety over her relationship with the Congressman.(4)

Elizabeth Ray had at one time worked as a waitress, rental car clerk, and stewardess. Her first job on Capitol Hill was with Rep. Gray sometime in the period 1970 to 1972. A spokesman for Gray said she did her work fairly well but was a "known troublemaker." Sometime before the end of 1974, Ray was working on Hays's House Administration staff as an $11,000 a year clerk. Early in 1975, she left to try her luck at an acting career in Hollywood. Back in Washington in July, 1975, Wayne arranged to have her placed on the staff of Rep. Davis. The following month, Hays transferred her back to the House Administration staff at $14,000 per year. Some speculated she was angry when her boss married Peak and that this may have been the real reason for her going public with her story.(5)

After a few days, Hays finally came clean. In a speech to the House of Representatives on May 25 he admitted to having had a "personal relationship" with his former employee for an extended period of time. The relationship was, he said, "voluntary on her part and on mine." He maintained she wasn't hired to be his mistress but admitted he had "committed a grievous error in not presenting all the facts" of the case. The Congressman claimed he told Ray their relationship would have to end when he proposed to Patricia Peak. Upon hearing this, Ray became hysterical and threatened suicide - as she had done in the past. She also threatened blackmail and to destroy his engagement, related Wayne. All his previous denials were due to his first overwhelming reaction "to protect my marriage and my new bride."(6)

Newspaper columnist Jack Anderson spoke out to say that Ray had gone to him some two and a half years previously with the Hays story. Anderson had her interviewed by two of his people but concluded she was "strange and cold... We never wrote the Hays sex story because the gal was so erratic." Sometime in 1974, Ray was dating a Washington restaurant owner and vandalized a car belonging to a woman she thought had designs on her boyfriend. She received a suspended sentence of six months' probation.(7)

In Hays's background lay a couple of rumored incidents. A source reported to the FBI about a woman who had once worked for the Congressman. According to this source, she got the job only after consenting to have sex with him several times a week. She finally quit the job when Hays suggested they fuck on his desk at lunchtime. In January, 1975, *The New York Times* investigated an allegation that Hays had struck Peak - then his secretary - in his Ohio office. Hays wouldn't answer the charge but referred all queries to Peak's doctor. The doctor said that Peak was in the hospital not because Wayne had hit her but because "she has lots of problems, emotional problems."(8)

Many took delight in Hays's difficulties. He was not a well loved figure in the House and was often described as "autocratic" and "punitive" in his conduct as a committee chairman. When he took the chair of his Administration committee in 1971, it had 28 employees. When the scandal broke, it had 274 people on staff - the largest staff of any House Committee. It was a clear case of empire building, some thought. Hays had in the past often brought down his considerable wrath on those he criticized for questionable work and payroll practices. He headed a 1966 investigation into payroll abuses by Rep. Adam Clayton Powell, which led to Powell's exclusion from the House. In 1972, Hays announced he had formed a special committee on superfluous employees to find out how many unnecessary employees there were. When he wanted something done, it had to be immediate and he freely criticized inferiors who didn't jump to his dictatorial rule. On his way into the House to deliver his confession he told colleagues, "I'm in deep trouble. I need all the help I can get." Surprisingly, he got it.(9)

The day after his confession, Wayne asserted that Elizabeth had extorted $1,000 from him in the past month with the threat to go public. Hays said he had documentary evidence to support just $325 of that amount. Asked if he had reported this extortion to the authorities, the Congressman said, it "wouldn't do any good. The F.B.I. is out to get me anyway." Moves were then afoot by some members of the House of Representatives to strip him of his committee chairmanships. This was said to have the tacit approval of the

Democratic leadership. Within a week of the scandal breaking, Ray announced she would publish her account of her adventures on Capitol Hill in the form of a novel. Ghosted for half the royalties, this paperback was out instantly for on July 4 it was reported to have 1.6 million copies in print one month after publication. July 4 was just six weeks after the scandal broke. The book was on the bestseller list.(10)

Public opinion seemed to be mostly running in his favor back in his home riding in Ohio where calls to his constituency office reportedly ran 95 percent in his favor. Some even admired that a 65 year old could "go with those young girls." Samuel Lofton, mayor of the small town of Bridgeport, commented, "The people are not mad about him having a girl friend. They're upset about using Federal money to keep her." Nobody in his district seemed very upset.(11)

If Ohio's voters didn't care, those in other places did. By the beginning of June, Congressmen were mounting pressure to force Hays to resign from his seat. The 75 freshmen representatives were virtually unanimous in this view. They were getting pressure to force Hays to resign from their constituents. Wayne tried to deal by offering to temporarily vacate his chairmanship of one committee, the Democratic National Congressional Committee, until the charges against him were resolved. This wasn't enough and on June 9 he was permanently ousted from the chair of that committee. Two nights later, on June 11, Wayne went into a coma after taking ten times the prescribed amount of a sleeping medication. It was considered a possible suicide attempt. Hays denied this when he addressed a July 4 crowd in Ohio. Only an accident, he said. His audience of 200 gave him a pair of standing ovations.(12)

Pressure continued and on June 18 Wayne announced his resignation as chairman of his prized Administration Committee. On August 13 he announced he would not seek another term in Congress - elections were that November. Ill health was the reason he cited, along with "the harassment my family and I have taken from the *Washington Post*. And on September 1, he announced his resignation from his House seat, effective immediately.

During the two months between his overdose and resignation, Wayne claimed both mental depression and physical impairment. Yet he was able to wage a two month long battle all the way to cut a deal and save his ass. Before his resignation letter went in, Hays and his friends tried to gain a concession - assurance from the House that it would take no further action against him after his departure. Officially, a House leader said, "It's a guarantee we couldn't give." However, the very evening of his resignation, the House Ethics Committee voted 12 to 0 to end its three month investigation of Hays. They denied a deal had been struck. They dropped the investigation because the resignation made the matter moot. The Justice Department dropped its investigation. Wayne was eligible for a pension of approximately $30,000 a year.(13)

One member of the Ethics Committee said he didn't think the Hays affair was worth the time spent on it. During the deal making, Hays told friends he intended to be re-elected and try to regain the chair of Administration. He told Rep. Frank Thompson Jr. - who replaced him as Chairman of Administration - that he wouldn't run against him next year if Thompson would stop auditing the Committee's financial records. Thompson refused to agree and the fresh evidence of "cronyism" uncovered further undermined Hays's support. During all this a Congressional friend of Wayne's had been spreading the word that Hays was very depressed and all the stress had left him with a slight impairment in the use of his right hand.(14)

In November, 1978, Hays won election as a state representative to the Ohio legislature. His Republican opponent had said he wouldn't use the scandal in his campaign ads but then did - a technique that backfired on the Republican. Two years later, in the election of November, 1980 Hays lost that seat to a 26 year old making his first try for state office. Never say die, Hays ran again and in November, 1981, he won a seat on the Belmont County Board of Education in Ohio. In February, 1989, Wayne Hays passed away.

One House colleague summed Wayne up as "the meanest man in Congress." Someone else called him a "petty dictator." And one writer concluded of the scandal that, "It is not Hays's personal morals that are offensive, from the public point of view. These, however unappealing, are his own business."(15)

FRANKLIN ROOSEVELT

Like Eisenhower, Franklin Delano Roosevelt's extramarital affair didn't emerge for many decades after the fact. And like Ike, FDR limited himself to just one affair - although there is some dispute on this point. The affair turned a shaky marriage into a joyless and sexless one, while maintaining a happy front. Franklin was born on January 30, 1882 and died April 12, 1945. He married his wife Eleanor on March 17, 1905. FDR served as President of the United States from 1933 until his death.

The seeds for FDR's affair may have lain in the prudish attitude toward sex and birth control prevalent at the time. Eleanor's last baby was born in March, 1916. It was her sixth since 1905. She wanted no more but didn't know anything about contraception or even how to suggest the subject. From 1915 onward, the couple always maintained separate bedrooms. Son Elliott Roosevelt said that "Eleanor's blank ignorance about how to ward off pregnancy left her no choice other than abstinence." Her pride and shyness also prevented her from seeking any such advice from a female friend or a doctor. There was more to it though, than fear of pregnancy. Eleanor simply didn't like sex. Years later, she told her daughter Anna that sex "was an ordeal to be borne."(1)

Lucy Page Mercer was hired by Eleanor in early 1914 or thereabouts to work as her social secretary for three mornings a week. She was 22 and was paid $25 a week. Lucy made a good impression on the family and Eleanor would sometimes invite her employee to parties and dinners where an extra female was wanted. FDR's mother, Sara, wrote, "Miss Mercer is here, she is so sweet and attentive and adores you, Eleanor." Described as pretty, vivacious, charming, and with a talent for putting men at ease, Mercer contrasted sharply with her boss who was termed then as serious and somewhat humorless. Mercer came from a "good" family which had fallen on hard times. As a result she had been brought up to be able to earn a living as a social secretary. In April, 1917, Lucy left the employ of the Roosevelts to volunteer as a yeomanette in the Navy. She was released from the service in October of that year. During her stint in the Navy, she lived just around the corner from the Roosevelts in Washington."(2)

Just when the affair started is unclear - certainly by the summer of 1916 or 1917 at the latest. During the summer of 1916, Eleanor spent the whole period at their summer residence at Campobello. In his letters to her, Franklin cast himself as being virtually a wallflower - busy all the time with work. It was the custom then for everyone who could escape Washington to do so for the entire summer, to escape the capital's oppressive heat and humidity.

By the summer of 1917, Eleanor was clearly uneasy and suspicious as gossip was making the rounds. While Eleanor was away, Franklin was sometimes seen on outings with a group of people which included Lucy. Usually Mercer's name was linked with that of Nigel Law, a friend of FDR. This was probably an attempt to divert any suspicion. Sometimes Lucy and FDR were spotted out alone together.

Eleanor's departure for Campobello in the summer of 1917 was delayed until July 15 and only then after an open quarrel with her husband. FDR urged her to go to get away from the stifling weather. The quarrel likely related to the affair. Later that summer, she wrote her husband making a pointed demand to show up at Campobello. "Remember I count on seeing you on the 26th. My threat was no idle one." The threat was that she would leave him.(3) FDR did go up and Eleanor probably tried to put an end to the affair. She enlisted the help of his mother, Sara. FDR denied any affair.

One source of gossip about the affair, and encouragement of it, was the couple's cousin, Alice Roosevelt. Alice would invite Lucy and FDR to dinner. Later she was anxious to let Eleanor in on a "secret" but Eleanor wouldn't listen. She related to FDR that Alice "inquired if you had told me and I said no and that I did not believe in knowing things which your husband did not wish you to know so that I think I will be spared any further secrets." When asked why she invited

Lucy and FDR to dinner, Alice replied, "It was good for Franklin. He deserved a good time. He was married to Eleanor."(4)

Everything came out into the open on September 20, 1918. FDR had just returned from Europe stricken with pneumonia. As he lay sick in bed, Eleanor unpacked for her husband and found incriminating letters to him from Lucy. FDR admitted the affair to her, for the first time. Eleanor was bitter at the thought of being discarded after thirteen years of marriage and so many children for a younger woman. Armed with the hard evidence she needed, Eleanor enlisted Sara as her ally.

Initially Eleanor wanted a divorce - and offered one. Sara threatened to cut Franklin off from the family money. Discussion ensued and presumably tempers eased. Divorce and/or separation were ruled out for their effect on the children, the threat from Sara, the likely negative impact on his political career and the fact that Mercer, a Catholic, might not want to marry a divorced man. FDR promised to sever his "romantic relationship" with Lucy and never see her again. One of Lucy's relatives said that Lucy told her the main factor was that "Eleanor was not willing to stand aside." This may have been Roosevelt's way of getting out of a tight situation.(5)

Eleanor was deeply hurt by the affair to the extent that she never mentioned it in any of the books she wrote. It would be many years before she would even discuss it with a few close friends. Years later, speaking of the affair, she said, "I have the memory of an elephant. I can forgive, but I cannot forget." A quarter of a century after the fact, she told a writer, "The bottom dropped out of my own particular world. I faced myself, my surroundings, my world, honestly for the first time." After the affair, she went on to carve out a life of her own - independent from that of her husband.(6)

The Roosevelts reconciled, at least publicly, but the hurt remained for the rest of their lives. Son Elliott recalled, "My mother had an iron stubbornness of her own and she was bound and determined that she would have nothing to do with my father, even though he was quite abject in seeking to rehabilitate himself in her eyes... Through the rest of their lives, they never did have a husband-and-wife relationship... there were few light moments... They never enjoyed anything in the way of lightheartedness in their lives."(7)

Lucy went on to a job as governess for a wealthy, and recently widowed, dog breeder and sportsman named Winthrop Rutherfurd. They married in 1920 when she was 29 and he was 58. Over the years, FDR kept in loose contact with her - behind Eleanor's back. Lucy got tickets to his first inauguration and was present for his acceptance speech at the 1936 Democratic Convention. When the elderly Rutherfurd was slowly dying from a 1941 stroke, FDR and Lucy would meet regularly in Washington. Secret Service agents drove Franklin out to a rendezvous on Canal Road outside of Georgetown where Lucy was waiting in her car. The pair then drove around and talked for an hour or so. After her husband died in 1944, Lucy visited the White House several times when Eleanor was away. Usually she was accompanied by a daughter or one of her step-children. These meetings were not clandestine, just a meeting of old friends.(8)

Roosevelt's daughter, Anna, after moving into the White House to assist her father, recalled she helped to arrange and presided over dinners with Lucy present and her mother absent. It has also been reported that when Franklin journeyed to his retreat at Warm Springs, Georgia, he sometimes took a side trip to meet Lucy. These meetings were arranged by, and took place at the South Carolina estate of Bernard Baruch, near the Rutherfurd place at Aiken, North Carolina.(9)

The day Franklin collapsed and died, a few people were present - Lucy was one. This caused more anguish for Eleanor when she learned this and that FDR had seen Lucy over the years and even had her to dinner at the White House. While she displayed little outward signs of anger or hurt, to those close to her "she was furious over the fact that Lucy was present when her husband died." When she learned everything, she was "even angrier... She confronted Anna with this information, and an ugly scene ensued."(10)

Anna recalled, "Mother was so upset about everything, though so cool on the exterior, and now so upset about me. I was upset enough to wonder whether it would make my relationship with Mother difficult. It did, for two or three days. That was all. She never spoke about it again." However, Anna would always wonder if her mother ever fully forgave her.(11)

After her husband's death, Eleanor told friends she hadn't been in love with FDR since the affair but that "she had given her husband a service of love because of her respect for his leadership and faith in his goals."(12)

It has been suggested by son Elliott that FDR also had an involvement with Marguerite "Missy" LeHand, a long time employee of FDR, who worked at his aide for extremely long hours from 1920 to 1941. She did fill in for some of the duties a wife is expected to perform - such as hostess at functions - but that was because Eleanor was absent so much. Missy never married and her own health was ruined in the service of her boss. She suffered a heart attack in 1927, then a stroke in 1941, and then she died from a cerebral embolism in 1944. Most writers, including son James, dispute the idea that FDR had an affair with LeHand. Most likely she was simply one of those super dedicated and self sacrificing employees that one sometimes finds. A recent biography of FDR mentions Livingston Davis, a college friend of FDR, who became one of his employees in 1917. Davis claims FDR was an ardent ladies' man, a man of many affairs and that Mercer wasn't his only mistress. According to this, he also had affairs well after Lucy.(13)

The information is vague and unsubstantiated. There is no evidence that FDR was anything like a ladies' man in his youth, before he married. Womanizing is a trait that doesn't change over time. Womanizers start young and tend to stay that way. Nor is the habit usually taken up late. FDR seemed to suffer real guilt over his affair with Lucy, to be genuinely sorry and went out of his way to make it up with Eleanor - although he never could. He had jeopardized his political career and brought down the wrath of his mother over the affair. In the summer of 1921, he contracted polio and perhaps even looked upon that as a form of divine punishment. Franklin made a remarkable recovery from the disease but he would never again walk unaided using either braces or canes. While doctors today say that medically he could have engaged in sex - he would have had to lay on his back - what would doctors in the 1920s have said? Ideas about sex by the disabled were likely none too progressive. It seems unlikely that Roosevelt had any affairs except with Lucy.

GARY HART

Gary Hart was considered to be the front runner for the 1988 Democratic presidential nomination until he blew himself out of the race with his sleazy antics. But then anybody who openly admires the Kennedys - as Hart does - should be automatically suspect. After he was caught and had reduced himself to the level of a bad joke, he engaged in more than the usual fits of public whining and self-pity.

He was born in 1936 as Gary Hartpence later changing his name to the more euphonious Hart. A former Democratic Senator from Colorado, he had been married to Lee Hart since about 1959. The couple had been briefly separated twice, once in 1979 and once in 1981. Gary had taken his first run at the presidency during the 1984 campaign. It was an effort that left him deeply in debt. Hart got an early start in the 1988 campaign when he formally announced his candidacy for president on April 13, 1987.

Soon after this announcement, the candidate was interviewed in depth by a reporter who noted, "no candidate suffers as much from scurrilous talk as Hart - about his relations with his wife and other women, about his own psychological make-up." Responding to these charges of womanizing, Hart said, "Follow me around. I don't care. I'm serious. If anybody wants to put a tail on me, go ahead. They'd be very bored."(1)

That interview was published in *The New York Times Magazine* on May 3. Unbeknownst to Hart, somebody had taken him up on his challenge and on the very day that New Yorkers were reading about the man from Colorado, Miamians were reading a different story about the same man. A group of reporters from the *Miami Herald* had followed Hart and they weren't bored. After receiving a tip, staff from the paper staked out Hart's town house in Washington on the night of Friday, May 1, 1987 and most of the next day, Saturday. The paper reported a young woman flew up from Miami and then spent the night with him. While the woman was unnamed, the newspaper said he'd carried on a relationship with her for at least two months, that on or about March 1, Hart had met the woman aboard a yacht in Miami where he was staying for the weekend. According to the *Herald*, Hart admitted phoning this woman several times for "casual" conversations but described her merely as an "acquaintance" a "friend of a friend of mine."(2)

William Dixon, Hart's campaign manager, identified the woman as Donna Rice and denounced the *Herald* for what he considered to be "outrageous" conduct in tailing his candidate. Donna had been a house guest of Hart friend and advisor William Broadhurst on the night in question, stated Dixon. Gary admitted to being on the yacht but couldn't remember when. The events of the night of May 1 he did remember and was adamant: "No one was staying in my apartment. I have no personal relationship with the individual you are following." In answer to a flurry of charges aimed at the *Herald* for its "questionable" tactics, executive editor Heath Meriwether said, "Mr. Hart has not denied that he met this woman in south Florida several weeks ago and that he made several long distance phone calls to her since that time... We observed Mr. Hart's town house for more than 24 hours from a respectful distance and we conducted ourselves in a professional manner throughout."

Donna Rice was 29 to Gary's 50. She was a part-time model and actress. Dixon claimed Donna and his client had first met at a party in Aspen, Colorado on New Year's Eve in 1986. Gary said he had phoned Rice several times about the possibility of her working on his campaign. All who knew Rice agreed that she had absolutely no political interests. Donna denied all the allegations which had surfaced and backed Hart. Providing details about the yachting story, Donna said she and her friend Lynn Armandt had been aboard for a weekend in March. Also on the ship were Hart, Broadhurst, and the crew. The group sailed to Bimini in the Bahamas. Not planning to stay overnight they were forced to when they found the customs office closed. For appearance sake, Rice explained, the men slept on a different boat.(3)

The New York Times had as much trouble editorializing about this subject as their English namesake did over the Parkinson affair. The paper couldn't decide if it was fair or not fair to judge a person on his private morality. Everything about the candidate should be known by the public, but not beyond the bounds of privacy. *The New York Times* released itself from the horns of this dilemma by deciding it was definitely fair to judge a candidate on the basis of his judgment and then proceeded to stomp Hart with both feet for his lack of that.(4)

For a couple of days, controversy swirled over the *Herald*'s stakeout coverage. Those in Hart's camp argued that the back door of the town house hadn't been fully covered the whole time. The paper, according to Hart, did acknowledge gaps in its surveillance. The candidate remained steadfast in his denials but did concede that he made a mistake by "putting myself in circumstances that could be misconstrued... Did I do anything immoral? I absolutely did not." In a Kennedyesque move, Gary ordered the wagons to circle but, unlike Kennedy, Gary only had one. Lee Hart flew up to join her husband in New Hampshire where he was campaigning. She said she loved her husband and believed him when he said nothing happened. When a reporter asked Gary if he'd ever committed adultery and if he had a monogamous relationship with his wife, the candidate refused to answer either question.(5)

The story was already damaging Hart's presidential bid. In March, his support among the Democratic candidates was 46 percent. A poll taken just after the story broke showed his support down to 36 percent, although he was still the front runner. Another poll quizzed respondents on what would happen if a candidate with whom them agreed on most issues was unfaithful to his wife. For 36 percent of those voters, the candidate would then lose their vote. However, this was the lowest vice; for drunk driving it was 39 percent, 55 percent for psychiatric care in a hospital, 65 percent if he cheated on his income tax, 46 percent if he lied about his war record, and 91 percent of those polled would not vote for a candidate even if they agreed with him on most issues if they discovered he used cocaine.(6) The *Washington Post* hammered in the final nail on May 8 when it reported it had what was called "documentary evidence" of a liaison between Hart and an unidentified woman - not Rice - on December 20, 1986. The *Post* claimed this relationship had gone on for some time. The Hart camp had been appraised of this story about a day before it was published. Within two hours, Gary decided to suspend further campaigning. First though, friends of Hart tried to persuade the *Post* not to run the story saying that Gary was withdrawing. There was no reason to report on a man, they argued, about to become a non-candidate. The information had come to the paper anonymously and then been confirmed by the *Post*. During a period of separation from his wife in 1981, Gary moved into Bob Woodward's apartment. Woodward and some of Hart's senate aides were "disturbed that Hart had implied to reporters and others that he was staying at Woodward's when more often he was staying with another woman."(7)

On May 8, Hart formally withdrew from the presidential race. A few days before that, on May 5, he addressed the American Newspaper Publishers Association and told them the reporters on the stakeout refused to interview the people involved. This prompted the *Herald*, in an editorial, to call him a liar. The reporters had repeatedly asked Hart to let them interview the woman they saw him with on Friday and Saturday. The paper also called Hart a liar for saying the newsmen conceded there may have been gaps in their stakeout. Gary was in a bitter mood when he withdrew and attacked the press for being more interested in his personal life than with his public agenda. In his farewell, Gary decided that he was a wonderful man, would have made a great president and, in spasms of self-pity, blamed just about everybody for his downfall - except Gary Hart.(8)

All was quiet then until May 31 when the *National Enquirer* published a cover photo of Rice sitting on Hart's lap with her arm around his shoulder. The photo had been taken on the Bimini trip and was sold to the paper for a reported $25,000 by Lynn Armandt. The paper wouldn't confirm the amount but said copies had been sold to several European publications and they expected revenue from secondary rights to reach $100,000 within a month.(9)

Lynn was a Miami boutique owner and early in June she went public with the whole story. According to her, Hart and Rice had slept together on the yacht during the trip to Bimini and that she had spent the night at Hart's town house on May 1 as the *Post* had said. The next morning, Saturday, Gary called William Broadhurst - at whose house Lynn had stayed - and asked the two of them to come over. He had discovered the reporters on stakeout. Said Lynn, "He looked pretty shaken - he was white... From then on Mr. Hart and Ms. Rice were *finito*. The mission was just to get her out of there. It was very cold - not even a kiss on the cheek, which really upset Donna." When the four got back to Broadhurst's, Lynn stated he didn't exactly tell people what to say, rather he told them "This is what happened."(10)

That should have been all for Hart and it was - until December 15. Gary then re-entered the presidential race to the surprise of most. And the laughter of many as he was the butt of a lot of jokes. Many felt he made this move to be eligible to receive government matching funds for his campaign expenses. It was money he was denied when he dropped out in May. His 1984 debt was some $1.3 million and he did get matching funds of over $1 million after he re-entered the race. Finances for his 1988 campaign also came under scrutiny for alleged irregularities. Some Democrats greeted his re-entry with fury and dismay. They thought he treated the Democratic Party as he treated his wife - as a personal convenience. Others considered him just a political oddity and not a serious contender.(11)

At the end of December, Hart complained he had been singled out by critics and had become a special target of the press because "my candidacy is different and it is the fact of that difference that threatens the defenders of the status quo." In the New Hampshire primary held in February, 1988, Hart managed only four percent of the vote and came last in a field of seven Democratic candidates. Early in March, a number of primaries were held on "Super Tuesday" with Hart receiving about three percent of the vote. On March 11, 1988, Gary Hart withdrew from the race again - this time for good - saying his political messages and not his personal mistakes turned off the voters.(12)

Way back in 1974, *The Christian Century* had discovered Gary when he was running for the Senate in Colorado. After noting his church background and activities, this magazine gushed over the candidate as a "moral" man. Said the writer, "I am going to be after him in a few months to tell me if it is possible for moral man to operate successfully in immoral politics." They had the wrong man.(13)

ANDREAS PAPANDREOU

Greek Prime Minister Andreas Papandreou's extramarital affair which started in 1987 was reportedly not his first. However, it did become a huge scandal in his country and threatened his political career. He was born on February 5, 1919 and spent much of his life out of his native country. While he was lecturing at the University of Minnesota, he met Margaret Chant, of Elmhurst, Illinois, in 1948. The couple married in 1951 and spent much of that decade in Berkeley, California. The couple and their four children moved to Athens in the early 1960s where Andreas entered politics. His growing popularity was nipped by the 1967 Colonels' Coup which jailed him and threatened him with death. Margaret organized an international campaign of protest which got her husband released in 1968 and given safe passage to exile. After the colonels fell in 1974, the Papandreous returned to Athens where Andreas became the country's first socialist Prime Minister in 1981. He served another four year term which began in 1985.(1)

Stories about the affair started in August, 1987, when Andreas failed to attend ceremonies in the town of Kalamata marking the first anniversary of an earthquake there that killed 22 people. His office said his work load was too heavy for him to attend yet he was spotted during this time on an Aegean cruise with Dimitra Liani, a 35 year old former flight attendant with Olympic Airways. Andreas was 68 and looked it. Soon the story was a scandal which hit all the papers and constantly dogged the Greek leader. A conservative opposition paper, *Kathimereni*, charged Andreas "abandoned his wife after 36 years of marriage" and "abandoned earthquake-stricken Kalamata for the sake of a private cruise and private pleasure that might cost him his leadership." *Eleftherotypia* was a largely pro-government paper which warned that his government might fall if the problem wasn't solved and urged him to "finish with this business anyway you like, but make it clean and straight."(2)

While such affairs are said to not usually cause problems this one did because Andreas broke unwritten rules in that he showed contempt for his family, contempt for the public and caused Greece to be the subject of international ridicule. Papandreou got Liani a job as an interviewer on a state-run TV program. Also given a job on the same show, as co-producer, was Liani's husband. Neither had any television experience. One of the first people interviewed by Dimitra was Papandreou(3) At the time the scandal first broke, Margaret acknowledged there was some truth to the rumors but said of her relationship to Andreas that, "We intend to remain together as... man and wife." She added that a strong relationship "cannot be shaken by certain events that most every woman experiences in her life. At any rate, this is not rare... There has been no talk of divorce."(4)

More attention was drawn to the affair in the fall of 1988 when Andreas went to London for open heart surgery. While he was in London waiting for surgery, he allowed photographers to take pictures of himself and Liani walking hand-in-hand around the hospital grounds. Mrs. Papandreou refused to visit her husband in the hospital because of the presence of Liani but, in a clear reference to her rival, said, "Future historians will shed light on all these immoral things going on, and will clarify which persons living next to him in these recent times bear primary responsibilities for the unforgiveable negligence or guilt for the Prime Minister's health." This statement profoundly embarrassed Andreas and prompted such jokes as "Papandreou has added a new position to the Kama Sutra - one foot in the grave."(5)

It was all too much for Andreas, who announced his intentions of getting a divorce. Liani was also getting a divorce. Papandreou hosted a European Community summit meeting on the island of Rhodes in December, 1988, where he flaunted his young mistress and earned more ridicule. Photos of the grandfatherly PM and his young, mini-skirted mistress were published in papers throughout Europe while much of the area snickered. The Turkish daily paper *Hurriyet* called him an "international laughingstock." Public opinion polls taken a few months before the June 18, 1989, election cited Papandreou's personal life as a major reason for his rapidly declining popularity and predicted defeat for him on election day.(6)

By the time of the election, Andreas and Liani, or Mimi as he called her, had been openly living together for over a year and Liani had taken over the role of first lady. Photos had been published showing her greeting heads of state as well as shots of her in the nude. The popular press portrayed her as everything from a Playboy centerfold to a gold digger to a Mata Hari. A popular show in Greece prior to the election was a satirical review titled "Greece is Looted While Mimi Pretties Herself." Margaret was accorded respect in the media for the humiliation she had undergone. Papandreou got his divorce a week or so before the voting with Margaret receiving an estimated settlement of $1 million for allowing it to go through quietly.(7)

The polls were right for Andreas lost the election. Other scandals, some major, had also plagued his administration but his affair with Liani was an important part of his downfall. Like they say, there's no fool like an old fool.

SOUSUKE UNO

Sex scandals involving Japanese politicos are rarely reported by the media. It seems to be understood that many of these politicians are involved in extra-marital liaison for which they will not be censured. To form such liaisons is almost a matter of right and that Japanese women - trained to be more subservient than North American females - will tolerate such affairs without protest. All these assumptions failed when 66 year old Sousuke Uno became Prime Minister of Japan early in June, 1989. Women banded together and, perhaps displaying a fury that had smoldered for centuries, were the main reason for Uno being forced from his post less than eight weeks after taking office.

When Uno was named PM he replaced Noboru Takeshita as head of the Liberal Democratic Party (LDP) which had ruled Japan for decades. Takeshita had himself been forced to resign because of a large and wide ranging scandal over allegations of influence-peddling and bribery which came to be called the Recruit affair. The LDP was then at a low ebb, divided and held in low esteem by the general public.

Uno had only been Prime Minister for a week when a popular Japanese Sunday magazine ran a story that the Prime Minister had had an affair of some four or five months duration with a geisha back in 1985-1986. The woman, who was not identified by name in the story claimed Uno paid her approximately $2,300 a month for the right to sleep with her at any time on short notice. When the affair ended, Uno, said the article, "apparently did not offer the woman consolation money when he severed the relationship, thus ignoring an age-old unspoken rule between geisha and patron." The geisha went on to describe Uno as a vain, pompous and sometimes crude man. She said, "I don't want him to use politics in the same way as he treated me."

This revelation by the woman identified as forty year old geisha Mitsuko Nakanishi, broke a long standing taboo in Japanese society about not discussing such matters in public. Usually geishas are trained from childhood up in the art of pleasing and pampering men, but Nakanishi came to the field late, in her mid 30s. By then she had been married, borne a child, divorced, and was working in an office for about $900 a month. Mitsuko turned to the occupation of geisha solely for the money thinking she could earn several times her office salary. Regarding the servility required of a geisha and the contradictions with her instincts as a modern woman, she said, "I made up my mind that this was business... I made up my mind to just cut it from my thoughts."

Uno first noticed her in October, 1985, when he was a prominent member of Parliament. He arranged to meet her in a fashionable restaurant. After a bit of small talk, Uno got down to business and settled on the monthly fee. Also fixed was the "start-up" fee for the affair, with Mitsuko receiving around $13,000. However, when Uno then commanded her to "lie down" right there on the straw mat in the restaurant, she refused. According to her, they didn't fuck until December when Uno spoiled the occasion by harping on the money he was paying her. The sums received by Mitsuko are reportedly meager by geisha standards. Typically Uno would call her early in the morning to boast about the newspaper coverage he was receiving as a rising politician. He promised her many gifts - also considered standard in a geisha relationship - but apparently never delivered. The future PM broke off the affair in March, 1986, saying only that he was under a doctor's order to abstain from sex.

Nakanishi maintained that it wasn't wounded pride that caused her to go public but that she believed a man who treated women so shabbily shouldn't be allowed to lead a country. Other than the magazine story, almost no Japanese mainstream press mentioned the issue at all as the media closed ranks around one of their own. It was left to another female to bring the story out fully into Japanese society. A female member of the Japanese Socialist Party, Manae Kubota, raised the matter in Parliament by carefully focusing on the effect of the affair on international perceptions of Japan and thus avoided the proscription on bringing "personal matters" to the floor of Parliament.

Kubota said, "the public, especially women, are looking at this situation with shame and grief" and demanded that the Prime Minister respond to the charges. Uno stonewalled completely and replied, "I would like to refrain from commenting on these reports in public." All this was reported on all the nightly news programs.

The scandal was compared to the one involving Gary Hart in 1987. Uno's wife, Chiyo, responded in true Lee Hart fashion, at least in public, when she said she continued to trust her husband and "anyway this is a story of the past." Initially, it was hoped the scandal would simply blow over. The general male view was that Uno's greatest embarrassment lay not in the fact that he was exposed as a man unfaithful to his wife but that he was exposed as a man who didn't pay enough to keep his mistress quiet. One observer noted "Mr. Uno seems to have acquired a reputation for doing things on the cheap, and it has not done him much good." A prominent industrialist with links to the LDP said, "It shows that he simply does not have things very much under control. If he knew what he was doing, he might have gotten the story killed or paid off the poor woman and kept it from embarrassing him. It was considered a poor performance for the leader of a party whose founder, Bukichi Miki, once yelled at a heckler when accused of keeping seven women, "Yes, it is true, but I take good care of all of them."

Women refused to let the issue die though. Stories about other alleged affairs by Uno surfaced including some that involved minor females. Uno continued to stonewall completely and his stubborn refusal to discuss the matter at all began to turn some media supporters against him. A coalition of women's groups began to picket all of Uno's public appearances and to demand that he resign. One of the groups, the Housewives Association, received almost continuous phone calls at their office, most of which condemned the PM. The vice president of that group, Kii Nakamura, said, "It has suddenly become clear that someone who does not respect women is not fit to be Prime Minister of Japan." The LDP suffered election losses first at the local and then at the national level. After watching his LDP lose an upper house Diet election - and its majority there for the first time in 34 years - Uno announced his resignation as Prime Minister on July 24, 1989. Uno admitted the sex scandal was one factor in the LDP's defeat saying, "I already said I would assume full responsibility for the defeat."

In the February 1990 elections, Uno was voted back in with an overwhelming vote of public confidence.

OF SPIES
WHORES
AND GAYS

The scandals in this section all turned out to be "bigger" than the man involved. In some cases the government of the day was dragged in by the participant. In others it was the opposition party which kicked the government in. While the issue of national security would often loom large and be endlessly bandied about, the real issue was political power and whether or not the opposition could gain political points out of publicizing the story. Some of these scandals lay dormant for years before emerging.

Jeremy Thorpe's past lay buried for nearly twenty years before it caught up with him. It finished him off permanently as a politician - to this date - and did major damage to his party in England, the Liberals. His homosexual paramour attempted for years to go public before he was successful. Another major party had a chance to make use of the story but refused to use it - perhaps finding it even too seedy for them.

Things livened up in Canada for many months when the Munsinger shit hit the fan. A cabinet member of the Conservative government had had a fling with an East German woman reputed to be a spy. The story lay dead for half a dozen years until the Liberal party had taken power with the Conservatives in opposition. The Liberal PM chanced on the story quite by accident but didn't use it for another fifteen months. They were saving it for a time when their own misconduct had given the Opposition so many weak spots to hit that they needed an ace in the hole. Then out popped the old scandal and cries of a national security breach were heard all over the land.

Back in England, the Conservatives had the equivalent of a bag-man extraordinaire in the person of famous novelist Jeffrey Archer. Until Archer did a really dumb thing. In general politicians kept hands off of this one. The few comments made by Conservatives were that he had to go for what had happened. Observers also agreed that he would never be rehabilitated politically - that remains to be seen. There seems to be a variation of severity depending on what type of woman is involved. Involvement with an "ordinary" woman, outside the politician's marriage, is seen as not as had as involvement with a prostitute: for example Parkinson and Archer. Involvement with a prostitute is not as bad as involvement with a prostitute who is also a spy, or suspected one: for example Archer and Profumo. That brings us to England's best known sex and politics scandal, that of John Profumo and Christine Keeler, and a vast supporting company. It had everything needed for high drama: commies, whores, aristocrats, spies, and so on. It too was brought to light, in part, by the opposition party and featured a government banding together to support Profumo in a series of statements they all knew were lies to the House of Commons. Then the powers that be arranged a whitewash inquiry and had the police set-up the major non-political figure in the story to take the blame and the fall, saving themselves. All in all it was a particularly vicious series of moves by the Conservatives as they circled their wagons. So popular and enduring has been the Profumo affair that a big budget Hollywood type film about it was released over twenty-five years after it had ended. The only story in this section that wasn't bigger than the man involved is that involving America's Barney Frank. Caught consorting with a male prostitute, Frank saved his ass with a judicious campaign of manipulation.

JEREMY THORPE

Jeremy Thorpe led England's Liberal Party to a postwar high of 19.3 percent of the votes cast in the general election of 1974. A few years later, Thorpe was forced to resign in disgrace. He would never recover politically, nor would the Liberal Party. The story took a long and tortuous path requiring almost two decades to completely unfold. It reached all the way to the British PM.

John Jeremy Thorpe was born on April 29, 1929 and educated at Eton and Oxford. First elected to the House of Commons in 1959 as an MP for North Devon, he quickly rose in the ranks of his party becoming leader in 1967 - a post he held until he resigned in 1976. He has been described as nakedly ambitious, politically, from the start. The story begins in 1960. Early that year it was rumored that Jeremy might be the best man at Princess Margaret's wedding to Anthony Armstrong Jones. Due to this possibility, the authorities subjected him to a background check. One conclusion of this investigation was that "many people believed that Thorpe had homosexual tendencies." At the time, homosexual activity was a criminal offence in Great Britain.(1)

Sometime during that same year, Jeremy met twenty year old Norman Josiffe - who soon took to calling himself Norman Scott - who worked as a stable boy. Scott was said to be then having mental problems and Thorpe offered to help him. This offer was taken up but not until November, 1961, when Scott came to see Jeremy at the House of Common. Later that day, Norman went home with his new mentor - Thorpe lived with his mother - and the pair began a homosexual affair that night, according to Norman. Thorpe always denied this allegation. However, as later evidence would show, they did have an affair which ended by the spring of 1963.(2)

The MP helped the stable boy to find a job and a place to stay but the relationship must have gone badly, for Norman went to the police on December 19, 1962. He told them, "I have come to the police to tell you about my homosexual relations with Jeremy Thorpe, who is a Liberal MP, because these relations have caused me so much purgatory and I am afraid it might happen to someone else." The police took control of a couple of letters from Thorpe to Scott but never interviewed the MP.(3)

Mental problems continued to plague Scott, who also couldn't hold down a job. He was generally regarded as a liar. Though the affair had ended, Norman still referred to Thorpe as his "guardian." In 1965 he wrote directly to Thorpe's mother detailing the affair he had with her son and asking her for money. The whole situation had become enough of a problem that Jeremy turned to a friend and fellow MP, Peter Bessell, for help. During a talk together, Bessell admitted he'd had homosexual tendencies as a youth. Thorpe made the same admission but later claimed he had never meant it seriously. Bessell took on the task of dealing with Scott.

Throughout 1967, Norman wrote to Bessell now and then asking for help in the form of money, a job, and so on. Bessell's solution was to put Scott on a "retainer" which varied from 5 to 10 pounds a week, until something more permanent could be found. In a fit of temper, Norman had destroyed his old passport and wanted Peter to help him to get a new one - with his new name. Scott wanted to go to the USA. While Bessell said he would help with this, he actually worked to see Norman didn't get a US visa. Peter was worried that Norman would tell his story in the US where less protection was offered against libel than under English law. The resultant publicity could be bad for himself, worried Peter, as he often did business there. By May, 1968 weekly payments were still made to Scott and would, in all, total some 600 to 700 pounds.(4)

The leader of the Liberal Party had decided it was time for a person in his position to be married; so, on May 30, 1968, Jeremy married Caroline Allpass. They had a son in 1969. Still worried about Norman and in particular about any letters he had from Thorpe, the MP and Bessell discussed and then unsuccessfully tried the ruse of Bessell pretending to be a reporter in order to question Scott and get any letters back. This is Bessell's version. David Holmes was best man at Thorpe's wedding and then he took over the function of monitoring Scott as Bessell had other interests to pursue.

Married by then as well, and desperate for money, Norman phoned the Thorpe residence in the summer of 1969. Caroline answered the phone and Norman told her everything. This was the first that she knew about it. The next year Caroline was killed in a car crash when she allowed her auto to drift across the center line into the path of an oncoming truck. A passenger in the truck said she looked like she was daydreaming. Other reports were that she may have been on sedatives. No satisfactory explanation for the accident was ever made and there was speculation that Caroline's behavior may have been the result of the Scott situation.

A friend of Norman made an appeal for money directly to Jeremy in 1971 but it was rejected by Jeremy, who said he was under no obligation. Gwen Paray-Jones was a woman who befriended Scott and believed his story that Thorpe had ruined his life. In 1972 she outlined the story in a letter to a Liberal MP. She and Scott then met with Liberal chief whip David Steel to whom they revealed Thorpe's name. The Liberal Party, aided by the police, conducted their own inquiry into the matter. Believing Thorpe's denials, they let the issue drop.(5)

Norman grew increasingly resentful at the way he was being treated and told his story to various friends. One passed it on to a reporter, Gordon Winter, who spent two weeks interviewing Scott. Winter, a Britisher, had lived in South Africa from the late 1950s until he was deported in 1966 due to reputed involvement with gangsters. Working out of London, Winter wrote stories for papers in South Africa which specialized in covering the anti-apartheid movement. The Liberal Party was an enemy of apartheid and Winter - who later said he was an agent of South Africa's bureau of State Security - held back the story until he thought it would do the greatest damage to the Liberals. Actually, Winter found no takers when he tried to sell the story to British newspapers. In 1973 Thorpe married Marion, Countess of Harewood.

Meanwhile, Norman was telling his story to anyone who would listen. It reached, in November, 1973, Tim Keigwan, who was the

Conservative opponent of Thorpe in North Devon. Up the ranks of the party it went until its use was forbidden by party chairman Lord Carrington and PM Edward Heath.(6)

Dr. Gleadle had Scott under psychiatric care in 1975 and he contacted Jeremy's lawyer to say that Scott had letters Thorpe might be interested in. David Holmes was dispatched and bought them for 2,500 pounds. He promptly burned them. Later, Holmes would say he had operated without consulting Thorpe.

Things came to a head and got rougher in 1975. Norman made an appointment with a reporter named Steiner to tell his story to the German magazine *Der Spiegel*. When he arrived at the hotel at the appointed hour with his briefcase full of material, the receptionist told him Steiner had been delayed but would arrive shortly. Later he was called to the phone where Steiner told him he couldn't make the appointment due to an urgent story but would see him another day. Norman then found his briefcase missing. It turned out that the magazine had no reporter named Steiner. About a week later, Scott was beaten up in the street by two men. He got strange phone calls. One was from a man claiming he had been authorized by Gordon Winter to set up an appointment. Norman didn't go. Winter was out of the country at the time and when he got back said he had made no such authorization. Then a man named Andrew Newton - using an alias and a ruse - got Scott to go for a drive with him out into the country. Norman had his dog with him. Out in the country, Newton shot the dog dead and then aimed the gun at Scott. It jammed and Newton drove off saying, "I'll get you." Newton, it seems, had no intention of killing Norman. He just wanted to scare him, he said.

The police were more actively involved by then because of the possibility of blackmail - the purchase of the letters. Newton was arrested and rumors grew there was more to it than an inexplicable dog shooting. David Holmes was sent to California - Bessell was living there - to persuade Peter to write a letter that could help establish Scott as a blackmailer. Holmes said Norman had blackmailed an airline pilot named Newton over a nude photo and in the course of an argument the dog was shot. Bessell didn't want to write the letter but did after Holmes assured him it wouldn't be used.(7)

January, 1976, saw everything come out when Scott was in court on a minor matter. Norman used that occasion to make his allegations against the Liberal leader public. Thorpe issued a statement which said, "It is well over twelve years since I last saw or spoke to Mr. Scott. There is no truth in Mr. Scott's allegations." Bessell's letter was used immediately and an angry Peter told the press that Norman had never blackmailed him and the money he sent to Scott - the "retainer" - was just charity. Thorpe had a private meeting with Prime Minister Harold Wilson, who promptly took his side. After the meeting, Thorpe said of the session, "It's good - it will be pushed on to the South Africans." At the meeting, Wilson suggested the Scott allegations were encouraged and exploited by South African agents to try and discredit the Liberals, who had been consistent critics of South Africa's racial policies. Winter was part of the evidence for this. In the House of Commons, Wilson stated, "I have no doubt at all there is a strong South African participation in recent activities relating to the leader of the Liberal Party."(8)

Jeremy continued to deny any homosexual relationship and, in regard to the letters, said there might have been one or two "formal letters, but that was all." Bessell's credibility was slammed in an article in the press and Peter knew the source had to be Thorpe himself. Outraged over this, he began to relate his version of the full story to the press. By May, 1976, a fuller - and more harmful to Thorpe - account of the story had emerged. Thorpe resigned as Liberal leader in that month. Harold Wilson had resigned as PM shortly before.

Finally, in 1978, Jeremy Thorpe was arrested. He and three other men were charged with conspiracy to murder. The other men were David Holmes, John Le Mesurier, and George Deakin. The latter two were friends of Holmes. The trial was originally set for May 1, 1979 hut was postponed to May 8 so that Thorpe could campaign for his seat in the general election which was held on May 3. He lost.

At the trial, the prosecution alleged the homosexual affair continued after the first night through 1962 and into the spring of 1963. Sometimes the pair liased at Thorpe's mother's house and sometimes at Scott's apartment. It was David Holmes, who pretended to be Steiner. Thorpe first thought of killing Scott late in 1968 when he told Bessell, according to Peter, that the affair loomed over him "like a black cloud." Peter said he thought it was impossible to get Scott a job in the US. Jeremy then said, "In that case we have got to get rid of him." Bessell said, "Are you suggesting killing him off?" Thorpe replied, "Yes." At a later meeting between them, Thorpe suggested they get Holmes to do the murder. The plan was put off when Scott married in May, 1969 - they hoped he would "settle down" - and then revived when he didn't. The others were then recruited. The defence concentrated on the unreliability of the witnesses. Peter had received a reported advance from a paper of 17,000 pounds for his story. He would get 8,000 pounds more in the event of an acquittal but 50,000 pounds more in the event of a Thorpe conviction.(9)

Of the four defendants, only Deakin testified. He said there was a conspiracy to frighten Scott - he agreed he had a part in that and would have pled guilty to such a charge - but not to murder him. Newton had turned and testified for the prosecution. At the trial, the judge summed up some of the principals for the benefit of the jury. Of Newton he said, "a highly incompetent performer. A chump... I doubt whether he has paid any income tax." Of Bessell he commented, "a humbug... You must look at Bessell's evidence with suspicion." About Scott the Judge stated, "A hysterical, warped personality, accomplished sponger... He is a fraud; he is a sponger; he is a whiner. He is a parasite. But, of course, he could still be telling the truth. It is a question of belief... I am not expressing any opinion."(10)

The judge described Deakin as being "of unblemished record." He termed Thorpe "a national figure with a very distinguished record." The judge added that even though Jeremy hadn't testified, it didn't mean his good character should be ignored. Jeremy's letters to Scott indicated an affectionate relationship, but, the judge warned, "you must not assume that mere affection necessarily implies buggery." On June 22, 1979, all four men were acquitted. There was no South African involvement.(11)

Generally, the media lauded Jeremy after his acquittal. One exception was the irreverent *Private Eye* - one of the few papers to deal with the Thorpe story in its early years. Most papers had ignored it. *Private Eye* produced a special issue devoted to the acquittal with a photo of Thorpe under the bubble "Buggers can't be losers."(12)

Lauded or not most political observers agreed that on the uncontested evidence alone Jeremy's political career was finished. His own lawyer had admitted, in court his client's homosexual tendencies. Thorpe had said, in the 1970s, "There are things that one passionately wants to keep private. Things that are no one's business. What isn't realized is how professionally I don't expose what I don't want to." He was appointed a director of Amnesty International in 1982 but a public furor erupted and he resigned. In 1987, Thorpe was elected president of the North Devon Liberal Association.(13)

PIERRE SEVIGNY

Canada's major sex scandal came to be known as the Munsinger affair, named after the woman involved. It didn't surface publicly for many years until the man involved had left politics and the woman involved had left Canada. And when the affair did come to light the reasons were political rather than the oft cited security breach possibility.

Joseph Pierre Albert Sevigny was born on September 17, 1917. First elected to Canada's House of Commons as a Conservative MP in 1958, he was named Deputy Speaker of the House that year. Prime Minister John Diefenbaker appointed him to the Cabinet as Associate Minister of National Defence. Dissatisfied with Diefenbaker politics, Pierre resigned from the cabinet in February, 1963 and was then defeated in the general election later that same year. Sevigny never returned to national politics.

The woman involved was Gerda Munsinger. She was born Gerda Hessler in 1929 in East Germany and fled that country in 1949 as a refugee. Gerda had tried to enter Canada in 1952 but had been refused admission based on security information. According to an RCMP report, she "engaged in espionage and conducted an immoral life." Both in East Germany and West Germany, she had been jailed for petty thievery and for prostitution. A West Germany arrest in 1949 led her to admit committing espionage for the Soviet Union.(1)

Still in Germany, Gerda married an American GI named Mike Munsinger, perhaps in 1952 or 1953. A dozen or so years after this marriage, Mike Munsinger - then a Brooklyn policeman - recalled that after the wedding he filed papers to bring his new wife to the US but that "I received a notice from the State Department that she was... under a certain law... for some reason she was a security risk and they would not allow her in this country." This notice was received in

1953. The marriage was annulled that same year. Gerda always denied she was refused admission to America. The US State Department later passed on to Canadian authorities confidential information on why she was rejected. This was never made public. One reason may have been because her father - who stayed on in East Germany - was a functionary in the Communist party.(2)

Munsinger worked in Europe in 1954 as a secretary for NATO. The next year, 1955, she was admitted to Canada. Why she was allowed in remains a mystery. The RCMP have never offered any explanation other than "unexplained error." Once in Canada, Gerda worked at a variety of jobs including secretary and waitress in Montreal. According to Gerda, she met Pierre Sevigny in 1958 when he came into a cocktail bar, where she worked as a hostess, for a drink. Then they went on to become "frequent companions" during 1958, 1959, and 1960. She traveled with him in a government plane to Boston "for the races." Gerda also claimed to know another Conservative cabinet minister, George Hees, "very well."

Davie Fulton was the Conservative Justice Minister in 1960 when the RCMP alerted him to the liaison between Sevigny and Munsinger toward the end of that year. They warned Fulton she was a prostitute and a security risk. It isn't clear how they became aware of the situation. Fulton passed on to Diefenbaker what he had just learned. The PM immediately called in Sevigny. When confronted with the facts, Sevigny stalled around a bit but "after some delay" did admit "I did know her. I did see her. I did meet her a few times. What happened between us is what happens between a beautiful woman who likes a man and a man who likes a beautiful woman, and that's all."(3)

The Prime Minister told Sevigny an investigation was underway and that Gerda had a record of theft in Germany and that she knew a Russian major in Berlin. The PM told his minister, "You realize that if the investigation reveals that she was a security risk that you will have to go." Pierre assured Diefenbaker there was nothing that could remotely involve a security breach. He also undertook to end the liaison right away and apparently did. The police met a few more times with Fulton but found, he claimed, no evidence of a security breach. The PM and Fulton had more discussions before Diefenbaker decided "We had the assurance that there had been no breach of security and that no further disciplinary action, as it were, needed to be taken." Fulton favored removing Sevigny from his cabinet post. The PM then phoned Pierre to tell him that security had not been breached. Diefenbaker asked Pierre if Munsinger was involved with others. He mentioned "George Hees?" to which Pierre replied "Yes." Pierre recalled, "Then he gave me hell again and I felt that I was duly and properly reprimanded and chastised. And he was right after all, let's face it."(4)

As far as Diefenbaker and his Conservative government were concerned, that was the end of the matter. It would not be made public. Gerda Munsinger had left Canada for her native Germany in February, 1961. During the last three months of her stay in Canada, the RCMP had her under close surveillance. They claimed the apartment house in which she lived was frequented by Russian agents though there was no evidence any had been in her apartment. Just before she left she was arrested in Montreal for cashing a bad cheque.(5)

Things remained dormant until November, 1964 when Prime Minister Lester Pearson sent a blanket request to the RCMP asking for any material the agency had on cases involving members of Parliament. It was at a time when Canada was excessively worried about the possible influence of mobsters in high places. The political regime in Canada had changed. The Liberal party, under Pearson, had come to power while the Conservatives, still led by Diefenbaker, had been reduced to the Opposition. All Pearson got from the police agency was the Munsinger file. On December 4, 1964, Pearson wrote a letter to Diefenbaker saying he was "greatly disturbed by the lack of attention" the matter had received. He asked the former PM to clarify the situation for him. He expected a letter but instead received a personal visit from Diefenbaker. These two politicians didn't like each other and had an "angry confrontation." Diefenbaker had done nothing, he said, because he had satisfied himself the case was only a personal indiscretion and there had been no security breach. Pearson said that was what he wanted to hear. The PM expected his political foe to put this in writing but Diefenbaker never did. Sevigny was out of politics by then. Rumor had it that Munsinger had died in Germany. Pearson did nothing more.(6)

The scandal finally erupted into public view, surrounded by a media blitz, in March, 1966. What had happened was that all through 1965 and the first two months of 1966, the Liberals had been taking a ferocious beating in Parliament. The assault was led by John Diefenbaker, who was taking a delight in tormenting the hated Liberals. The party in power was being pummelled over two incidents. One was the defection of six MPs from another party to the Liberals. The second, and major, item was an unfolding spy scandal - a man named Spencer. It was unrelated to Munsinger. In Parliament one of those subjected to particularly bitter attacks, some personal, was Justice Minister Lucien Cardin. The opposition demanded an inquiry on the spy story. Cardin rejected the demand but was overruled when Pearson bowed to the pressure and ordered one.

Finally, on March 4, in the House, Cardin could stand it no more. He turned on his tormentors and lashed out at Diefenbaker for his participation in the "Monsignor" case. The minister had never seen the name spelled out and had mispronounced it. Nor had he ever seen the file. By that stage, Lucien was on the verge of resigning from the Cabinet. Pearson knew all too well what his man meant and he was stunned. Pearson wanted the issue to stay dead and he was said to have also been on the verge of resigning over its revelation.(7)

The PM hoped the "Monsignor" reference would be forgotten. But of course the press gallery was frantic to know what it was all about. Cardin called a press conference for March 10. Pearson didn't become aware of this until ten minutes before it was scheduled to start - too late to cancel it. The PM did, however, warn his minister "To be even more careful not to get involved in any questions about Munsinger." The questions came immediately and Lucien explained the name of Munsinger was "provoked out of me."(8)

At the conference, Cardin laid out the facts of the case and explained his reasons for bringing the matter out into the public arena. "I knew that Mr. Pearson did not want the Munsinger case to be divulged, and, believe me, I had the greatest esteem and admiration for Mr. Pearson. And I didn't want to hurt him. On the other hand, I didn't believe that it was right for the party or right for Parliament or right for anybody that, after having been accused of all sorts of things and having again capitulated on the Spencer thing, we should sort of lie down and die. So I came to a compromise with myself, that I would not say anything about the Munsinger case unless I was asked a direct question, and then I would not shun the question nor try to go around it. I would answer it." He argued that Sevigny was not his concern - he just wanted to expose Diefenhaker's inept handling of a security case when he was PM. However, it was Sevigny who took most of the public scrutiny.(9)

Pierre did have some advance warning that trouble might be brewing. Back in November, 1965, shortly after a general election, Pierre had a private meeting with a wealthy Montreal financier who had, said Sevigny, inside information. This man told Sevigny that the Liberals felt it was essential to attack Diefenbaker with force - to take the heat off unfolding Liberal scandals - and direct attention onto Conservative misdemeanors. The financier said what the Liberals had was "the fact that at some point while you were a minister you were severely chastised by Diefenbaker for having known a woman who was supposed to have a record in Germany, a security record." The Liberals were going to break this and build it into a sex and security scandal. It was going to save the Liberals, involve George Hees and work up to "something similar to the Profumo-Christine Keeler story."(10)

Claiming to have been at the planning session, the financier remarked it could destroy Sevigny and his family. One of those present replied, "It's his skin, let him take care of himself." Pierre ignored this warning even though at Christmas and again in January, 1966, his friend warned him again that the Liberals were going through with it. Sevigny felt they wouldn't pursue it as he was out of politics. When it did break, Sevigny got mad and made angry declarations on TV and radio that he would fight. He recalled "The more I fought, the worse I made it for myself. All that the press was interested in was the sex angle. And all of a sudden I realized that I was fighting the prime minister of Canada, the minister of justice, the RCMP, the full weight of the Liberal party."(11)

The charges resulted in an inquiry being ordered - conducted by one man, Mr. Justice Wishart Spence of the Supreme Court of Canada. Davie Fulton insisted that Sevigny was not a security risk although he did admit "there was a security situation" in that the woman had a "murky background" and there was an illicit liaison and the possibility of blackmail. Previously, Diefenbaker had tried to hide everything. Only he and Fulton knew anything. No other cabinet minister, including the Minister of Defence, had been made aware back in 1960. Originally, the inquiry was to be held totally in camera but Diefenbaker insisted it be held totally in public. He apparently hoped this would put the focus on Pierre and his sexual activities and away from his own handling of the matter. In the event some of the inquiry was held in camera and some of it was open. When the affair broke, Sevigny tried to see Diefenbaker but the former PM would not agree to a meeting. Diefenbaker did advise him to stay at home and not appear at the inquiry. Advice which Pierre didn't take. Cardin thought that Diefenbaker was sacrificing Sevigny instead of protecting him.(12)

Of the relationship with Gerda, Pierre said in public, "I met Mrs. Munsinger during the month of August, 1959. I saw her socially a few times during the next few months and our relationship was just that, a social one." He claimed that when Gerda returned to Germany she was hired as a secretary in Munich, by the Intelligence section of the US Army. Pierre had a letter to that effect - from Gerda to a girlfriend. Presumably this was brought up to show the woman couldn't have been a spy. While the letter was introduced to the inquiry, Spence made no mention of it in his report because, Pierre said, the judge had to vindicate the Liberals and damn Diefenbaker. The letter may have been real but its contents weren't.(13)

Munsinger wasn't dead at all but alive and well and living in Munich in 1966 where enterprising reporters found her managing a coffee shop. She reiterated that she and Pierre had had a liaison while Pierre maintained it was only a social relationship. Gerda said she wasn't a spy and had left Canada in 1961 not under suspicion but because she was homesick.

The RCMP said, at the inquiry, that they were convinced the Soviet Embassy in Ottawa knew of her activities after her arrival in Canada in 1955. They also maintained that Munsinger worked as a prostitute after her admission to Canada and paid Montreal racketeers protection money.

The RCMP claimed that Gerda knew MP and former cabinet minister George Hees. At first Hees admitted that he may have had lunch with her once or twice while she was in Canada. Later he decided it was definitely two lunches and one dinner. While Hees resigned from the Diefenbaker cabinet around the same time as Sevigny there is nothing to indicate the Munsinger affair had anything to do with it. Hees didn't run in the 1963 election but was elected in the 1965 election.(14)

When the inquiry report was released in September, 1966, Spence found the relationship between Sevigny and Gerda had constituted a "security risk requiring his retirement from the Cabinet." The report called Munsinger a minor espionage agent for Russia, a prostitute, smuggler and petty thief while in Europe and an active prostitute who consorted with racketeers. Spence did conclude there was no evidence of a security breach but that regarding national security "the Munsinger case might well be worse than the Profumo case." Diefenbaker was "harshly criticized" for mishandling the affair. The former PM dismissed it all as a "political hatchet job - a political trial."(15)

John Diefenbaker was replaced - against his will and after a fight - as the Conservative leader in 1967. There were many reasons for his ouster. Munsinger was one. Sevigny once commented, "I knew this Gerda Munsinger. She was a pleasant beautiful girl. How many men would have done the same as I did? But that's beside the point."(16)

JEFFREY ARCHER

Riding high as a fund raiser for England's Conservative party best selling author Jeffrey Archer came a cropper for paying money to a prostitute whom he'd never met before to go away for a while and not talk about something the two of them had never done together.

Jeffrey Archer was born in 1940. He first entered politics in 1969 as an MP in the House of Commons. His political future looked bright but he resigned his seat in 1974 after losing some 400,000 pounds in a fraudulent share scheme. Close to bankruptcy, Archer resigned to save his Conservative party from any embarrassment. Jeffrey turned his hand to writing, penned a series of best sellers and became world famous in the process. One of his novels, *First Among Equals*, was being televised in Britain when the Archer scandal broke. Ironically, the plot included a prostitute who tries to blackmail an MP.

Jeffrey married his wife Mary in 1966. The couple have two children. Prime Minister Margaret Thatcher appointed the multimillionaire novelist to the post of Deputy Chairman of the Conservative party in 1985. He was charged with reviving morale among the Tories across the country - and raising money. In his travels throughout Britain, Archer was reported to have raised hundreds of thousands of pounds for his party in just one year - a result of his speeches. On Friday, October 24, 1986, Jeffrey had an intermediary meet with a prostitute at London's Victoria Station. On Archer's behalf the man handed the woman an envelope stuffed with 2,000 pounds. The money was for the woman to go abroad for a period of time and thus avoid the press. Unbeknownst to Jeffrey, others were aware of this transaction. The story made the Sunday papers that week and Archer resigned.(1)

The prostitute was 35 year old Monica Coghlan, who worked under the name of Debbie. According to Monica, she was working on the night of September 8-9, 1986 in London. Around midnight a man approached her and the pair fixed a fee for sex. Before commencing though, the man had to go and attend to his car. He was longer coming back than she thought reasonable and Monica assumed he wouldn't return. She went with another of her clients, Labour supporter and solicitor Aziz Kurtha, to the Albion Hotel. When they came out of the hotel, Archer was waiting. Kurtha took Coghlan aside and told her who her famous client was. Monica and Archer went into room 6A of the hotel and had sex for the agreed upon fee. At one point, Monica asked her client what he did for a living. The man said he sold cars. He left right after sex.(2)

A week later Kurtha contacted Monica and suggested she get in touch with reporters. He mentioned the sum of 700 or 800 pounds. Monica said she wasn't interested but that same night she was approached by a journalist from the *News of the World*. Later this paper would say that Kurtha came to it with the story and asked for money. Kurtha claimed he didn't demand money. Eddie Jones of the *News of the World* first talked to Coghlan and he didn't believe that Jeffrey had gone to a prostitute. Becoming convinced that she was telling the truth, Jones told her they needed more concrete evidence. A plan was hatched whereby phone calls would be made to Archer by Monica. They would be recorded by the *News of the World* without Archer's knowledge.(3)

On the night of September 25, Jeffrey received his first phone call from Debbie. She told him she was a prostitute and that a client of hers had associated with Archer earlier that month. Jeffrey denied any such association and said he didn't know what the woman was talking about and told her to go to the police. However, the woman kept calling and Jeffrey finally agreed to pay the caller 2,000 pounds after she said the press was pursuing her. He explained his actions later by saying, "Foolishly, as I now realize, I allowed myself to fall into what I can only call a trap in which a newspaper, in my view, played a reprehensible part. In the belief that this woman genuinely wanted to be out of the way of the press, and realizing that for my part any publicity of this kind would be extremely harmful to me, and for which a libel action would be no adequate remedy. I offered to pay her money so that she could go abroad for a short period and arranged for this money to be paid over to her."(4)

The day after the payoff was made, Jeffrey got a phone call from the Conservative party chief of staff who alerted him to the fact that a very damaging story about him would he published the next day, Sunday, October 26, in the *News of the World*. Jeffrey got in touch with David Montgomery, the paper's editor, and denied he had paid any money to Monica. It was then he was shocked to find out the paper had recorded the events. The novelist explained he feared a false story would hurt his chances in a general election to help his party and that's why he wanted the prostitute out of the way. According to Montgomery, Jeffrey told him, "A lot of what you have got is true. I don't know how to answer you. I will admit to you now that if the article goes in I'm going to tell the Prime Minister it's true, I'm going to resign and I'm not going to sue you... it's the end of all I want to do in life. It was very foolish of me, very foolish indeed. If my career is to be ruined by one mistake then so be it. I beg you not to put it in." The plea got nowhere and at a meeting with Montgomery, in the presence of political editor Grania Forbes, it was alleged that Archer threatened to use his influence with Thatcher to bring Montgomery into discredit.(5)

The story went in and Archer resigned for being foolish enough to pay money to a woman he didn't know. He said, "For that lack of judgment and that alone I have tendered my resignation... I have never, repeat never, met Monica Coghlan nor have I ever had an association of any kind with a prostitute." Wife Mary stood by her husband calling his resignation as deputy chairman of the Conservatives a "monstrous miscarriage of justice" and labelling the conduct of Monica as "despicable."(6)

Politically, he was considered dead. One observer said, "Not even he can hope to make a second comeback in the political field." The *Times* (London) editorialized that, "it is right that he is no longer the deputy chairman of Britain's governing party." Tory MP Peter Bruinvels stated his departure was inevitable because, "As a Conservative party we don't deal with prostitutes. We are a party of the highest morals and no deals must ever he done with people of dubious character."(7)   According to Tory party officials, Jeffrey was still a popular speaker. Calls poured into their office but not a single one requested a date be cancelled. Between the time the scandal broke and the following July, Archer had 130 speaking engagements lined up.

Lawsuits for libel were launched by Archer against the *News of the World* and *The Star* in November, 1986. The latter paper had also covered the story in detail and its case was heard first. In court, Monica said she had been paid 6,000 pounds by the *News of the World* for her story. *The Star* had run a long article purporting to contain conversations between her and her family. She admitted this was "sheer fantasy" but she stood by her allegations that she had sex with Archer on the night in question."(8)

On that night, Jeffrey told the court, he had been at a restaurant most of the evening with his book editor and his agent. The editor left at 10:30 and Archer drove his agent home at 12:45 AM. Then he returned to his apartment and went to bed alone - his wife being away. He was shocked to get a phone call from Debbie two weeks later. A major witness for Archer was Terence Baker the friend in the restaurant he had spoken to until 12:45 AM. Baker couldn't answer questions about the car Jeffrey was driving that night, the clothes he wore or the weather conditions. Baker said he was asked to testify on October 27, while Jeffrey said he didn't ask Baker until the middle of November.(9)

Counsel for the newspaper claimed that Archer used two different alibis for the night in question, different from the one he used in court. Before the trial he had told a reporter he had been at a meeting with fifty other people. A second reporter was told he had been at a function with forty other people and then privately met the Government Chief Whip. While Jeffrey claimed in court that he had never met Monica, two reporters had a different story. On the eve of the publication of the original story, Adam Raphael, then of *The Observer*, said Archer told him he had met Monica "very casually" six months previously. He is alleged to have told the same story, separately, to Rupert Morris, then of *Sunday Today*.(10)

The trial against *The Star* concluded in July, 1987. The judge summed up Mary Archer by saying, "Your vision of her will probably never disappear. Has she elegance? Has she fragrance? Would she have - without the strain of this trial - a radiance?" About Jeffrey the judge noted, "His history... is worthy and healthy and sporting... Is he in need of cold, unloving, rubber-insulated sex in a seedy hotel round about a quarter to one on a Tuesday morning?" The jury took only a little over four hours to reach a decision and award Archer 500,000 pounds in damages against *The Star*. No trial was held against *The News of the World* as an out of court settlement was reached. The sum settled for was reported as 50,000 pounds. Most of the money from these awards was said to have been given to charity.(11)

Even after the lawsuits were over, it was felt by political observers that Archer's lack of judgment still precluded him from ever again holding an official Conservative post. The jury had reached a very speedy decision in the libel suit and the *Times* (London) was prompted to dryly editorialize: "Considering the partiality of the judge's summing up it might be thought surprising that it took even this long."(12)

JOHN PROFUMO

When England's John Profumo, a Cabinet minister in Harold Macmillan's Conservative Government, was caught in an involvement with a call girl, he took the traditional route and denied all charges. Trying to bluff his way out with arrogance and threats of lawsuits, the facts finally did him in. The scandal overwhelmed England, and, as Profumo was flushed out, he managed to pull Macmillan with him.

John Profumo was born on January 15, 1915. In 1954 he married actress Valerie Hobson. As a politician, John was named to the Conservative cabinet in the post of Secretary for War in 1960. He held that job until he resigned in disgrace in 1963. Little is known about Profumo's sex life before the scandal. It was rumored in the press that he was involved with a "widowed member of the Royal Family" - an apparent reference to the then Duchess of Kent. Regarded as something of a "blade", he had a weakness for nightlife. One of his favorite activities was to go to nightclubs where he liked to sit with the hostesses.(1)

On July 8, 1961, Profumo attended a party at the country mansion of a wealthy aristocrat, Lord Astor. Profumo was introduced to nineteen year old Christine Keeler by Stephen Ward, an osteopath and artist who moved in high circles. Ward had met Keeler two years before when she worked as a show girl at a London night club. That same weekend, Christine was introduced to Captain Eugene Ivanov, who was, nominally, a Soviet assistant naval attache at the embassy in London but also thought to be an officer in Soviet Military Intelligence, GRU. Keeler began a sexual affair with both men although they were not aware of each other.

As an osteopath, Ward had treated, among others, Anthony Eden, Winston Churchill, Joseph Kennedy, Elizabeth Taylor, and Frank

Sinatra. As a portrait artist, he had sketched, among others, Peter Sellers, Sophia Loren, and at least eight members of the Royal Family, including Prince Philip. He was fascinated with sex, recruited young women and ingratiated himself socially with powerful and affluent men by introducing them to these women. At Lord Astor's Cliveden estate, he had been given his own cottage where he often held sex parties and provided the women. Prince Philip reportedly attended one of these parties.(2)

Keeler regularly saw, separately, Ivanov and Profumo. John once took her to his place and had sex with her on the marital bed. According to Christine, Profumo suggested he set her up in her own apartment and keep her as his mistress - she then lived in Ward's apartment. Keeler declined the offer. Profumo replied that he couldn't keep on seeing her while she lived with Ward. At the end of 1961, Keeler did move into her own apartment. She was wary that John's plan was to turn her into a call girl on permanent standby to his friends in government. Asked about the attraction to the minister, Christine said, "Profumo exuded power. It was the way other women might feel about fucking Marlon Brando... It was a very, very well-mannered screw of convenience."(3)

Very early, this strange triangle came to the attention of MI5, the British intelligence agency, perhaps by the end of July. They contacted the Cabinet Secretary, Sir Norman Brook, and appraised him of the situation. Brook passed on to his colleague a message from MI5 which warned him to be careful around Ward whom they felt could be loose-lipped. A second part of the message was that Profumo might want to help MI5 in a plan they had to get the Russian to defect. Worried by the fact that MI5 seemed to know everything about his affair, Profumo declined to help. He claimed he broke off with Keeler in August, 1961. Christine claimed the affair didn't end until December, 1961. Other witnesses would later say it went on into 1962.(4)

The scandal moved closer to the surface in 1963 when Christine failed to appear as scheduled at the trial of an ex-boyfriend charged with taking a few shots at her with a gun. The rumor was that she was involved with someone higher up who dissuaded her from appearing lest his name inadvertently come out. Finally, in March,

1963, Labour party MP George Wigg asked a question about the affair in the House of Commons. After a meeting of high ranking Conservatives, the question was answered the next day in the House. Profumo admitted he knew Keeler and had met her at Astor's estate. Since then he had seen her about six times at Ward's apartment but each time it was Stephen Ward he was visiting. The minister made it very clear there was no impropriety - no sex - in his relationship with Keeler. As he made his statement, he was flanked by PM Harold Macmillan and other cabinet ministers. Macmillan knew of the sex triangle by January 28, 1963 at the latest. His Conservative colleagues gave him loud cheers when Profumo warned he would not hesitate to launch libel and slander suits if the "monstrous allegations" he had heard were made or repeated outside the House. There was another show of solidarity the afternoon of his denial when John went to the races with the Queen Mother and was photographed with her. That evening, he took his wife to a dance and told newsmen, "Look, I love my wife, and she loves me, and that's all that matters." Most newspapers published his statement of denial "in full and with sympathy."(5)

The Opposition wasn't satisfied and kept hammering away at the Conservatives. Opposition leader Harold Wilson sent a memorandum to the PM expressing concern over national security. The note suggested that MI5 had known about the triangle almost from the start and that Macmillan knew about it prior to Profumo's denial in the House. It was Ward, who gave Wilson the details. It was also Ward, who saw the PM's Principal Secretary prior to that and thus told Macmillan.

The foreign press took up the story and Profumo made good on his threats. An April 6 issue of the Italian magazine *Il Tempo* contained an article about the minister and Keeler. John issued a writ of libel. All copies of the issue were withdrawn, the distributors, Continental Publishers, issued an apology in the High Court and Profumo was awarded a token 50 pounds in damages, plus his legal costs, which he donated to charity. *Paris Match* also published a story and John got a retraction published. After the truth came out, the tables were turned with Continental suing Profumo for bringing the original action. An out of court settlement was reached.(7)

Under continuous pressure from the Opposition, Macmillan ordered an inquiry into the affair. On June 5, 1963, only four days after the inquiry started, John Profumo tendered his letter of resignation. In the letter to the PM, he admitted he had lied to Parliament about his relations with Keeler. The House of Commons found him guilty of contempt and removed him from his post on the Privy Council. Profumo never returned to national politics and in his later years became active in the social rehabilitation of juvenile offenders. Even though an inquiry had been ordered, the Opposition continued to pound the PM in a no confidence debate on national security. Macmillan resigned as Prime Minister in October, 1963, citing ill health, and then retired from Parliament in September, 1964.

Lord Alfred Denning conducted the inquiry to see if the Profumo case had breached national security. He concluded that it hadn't. Stephen Ward took the brunt of the heat not only from the inquiry but also from a massive police investigation. Ward was the fall guy who took the focus away from the government, Profumo and security. In June, 1963, Ward was arrested and charged with living off the immoral earnings of women and conspiring to keep a brothel. Ward was found guilty but it was a frame-up. The consensus was that, as one writer noted, "The trial... was a mockery of justice."(8)

The osteopath didn't live long enough to hear the verdict for he took a drug overdose on July 30, lingered a few days, and then died on August 5, 1963. Just before he died, he said, "Someone had to be sacrificed, and it was me... when the Establishment want blood they get it." Nor did he live long enough to see the Denning report "which vilified him in death while being hugely polite to the Minister whose folly triggered the trouble, John Profumo."(9) Stephen worked for MI5, and maybe Russia, and maybe even both but he was no pimp. The Denning report cleared all government people of misconduct but was simply a whitewash. It neglected to comment on Macmillan's covering up for his minister and the report claimed that MI5 didn't learn that Profumo and Keeler were lovers until early in 1963. This wasn't true.(10)

Christine Keeler was also a much hated figure. Once when she arrived at Ward's trial, angry women outside the court threatened her with umbrellas and shouted, "Keeler should be burnt." Another time the crowd outside the court hurled both eggs and insults at her as she left the court. Trying to take advantage of Keeler's notoriety, the owner of L'Hirondelle, a nightclub in the West End, offered her 75,000 pounds to appear for twelve weeks at his floor show. Joseph Mourat planned to have Christine act as emcee and introduce the acts. When word got out reaction was immediate and hostile. Hundreds of letters poured in and some even threatened bomb attacks. Labour leader Harold Wilson complained, "There is something utterly nauseating about a system of society which pays a harlot twenty-five times as much as it pays its Prime Minister." Mourat quickly cancelled his offer to Christine, wailing, "I am very sorry I heard of her name."(11)

Keeler later claimed that John Kennedy was one of her lovers. It was so far fetched that it was little noted, or believed. Generally she was considered to be a liar. By the 1980s, Christine lived modestly in obscurity and close to poverty. From time to time she was on social assistance. A fictionalized film of the affair, *Scandal*, was released amid much ballyhoo and publicity in 1989 - which may revive Keeler's fortunes, at least temporarily.

On the day in March, 1963, when John Profumo made his denial in the House, he ended it by saying, "Anyway, who's going to believe the word of this whore against the word of a man who has been in Government for ten years?"(12)

BARNEY FRANK

The scandal that enveloped Congressman Barney Frank (D-Mass) of Boston's 4th District in 1989 was not without parallels to those involving Wayne Hays and Wilbur Mills. Since Frank's scandal was a homosexual one, the outcome might have been expected to be as bleak for Barney as it was for Hays and Mills. Yet it wasn't, as Frank gave a text-book demonstration in using, and manipulating, the media to negate the damage.

Born in 1940, Barney Frank grew up in Bayonne, New Jersey, a bespectled and fat lad who developed a passion for liberal causes. After graduation from Harvard in 1962, Barney entered politics as an aide to then Boston mayor Kevin White. Stints as a Washington congressional staffer and then as a member in the Massachusetts Legislature followed. In 1980 he won a seat in Congress. He has been returned to his seat every two years up to and including 1988.

Frank knew from the time he was 13 that he was homosexual, yet he remained firmly in the closet for decades. His siblings were informed of his sexual orientation only when he was 40 years old. He told his mother in 1984 only because he feared she might learn about it from another source. The people in his district were told in 1987 when Frank went public with regard to his homosexuality. Going public only came after many long and agonizing discussions with aides and advisors about the political risks involved. Frank was then a 47-year-old career politician.

Image was all important to the congressman. Known for a somewhat sloppy wardrobe, he once ran for re-election on the slogan that "neatness isn't everything." To overhaul that image, Frank revamped his wardrobe, took off 70 pounds, got contact lenses and had his hair styled. Frank worried far more about going public than his constituents. Voters ignored his declaration of being gay. They returned him to the House in the 1988 election with 70 percent of the vote. In the House, Barney was known as a man with a quick wit, a high profile, and as the "darling" of the Democratic Party's left wing.

In 1985, Frank picked up a 32-year-old bisexual male prostitute by the name of Stephen L. Gobie. After paying him $80, Barney had sex with Gobie. The congressman found Gobie through a personals ad in a gay newspaper, *The Washington Blade*. The ad read: "Exceptionally good-looking, personable, muscular athlete is available. Hot bottom plus large endowment equals a good time."(1) Next, Barney hired Gobie as his driver and housekeeper at $20,000 a year - paid out of his personal funds. Steve occupied a basement apartment in Frank's town house and turned it into a brothel.

These facts are not in question. Gobie claims Barney knew about the brothel arrangement while the congressman claims he didn't. Parking tickets run up by Gobie were paid for, or fixed, by Frank depending on who you believe. Barney also admitted that Gobie wasn't the only male prostitute he had used. Gobie had sex more than once with Frank, he says, while Frank claims sex only occurred once. The pair split up in 1987, about the time Frank went public about being gay. Cynics felt Frank went public to make himself less vulnerable in case Gobie tried to use their arrangement against him.

Barney said he hired Gobie and let him stay in his house because he wanted to "rehabilitate" him. Stephen's police record included possession of cocaine and taking obscene photos of a 15-year-old girl. The congressman wrote supportive letters to Stephen's parole officer. Gobie alleged the job was concocted as a cover story for his probation officer. According to Barney, once he was alerted to Gobie's brothel activities by his landlady, he immediately got rid of Gobie. Replied Gobie, "He knew exactly what I was doing. It was pretty obvious. If he had to come home early he would call home to be sure the coast was clear."(2)

The story was broken in the summer of 1989 by Gobie, who went shopping around to see if he could get money for his revelations. On the face of it, the story was enough to bring Frank down, just on the points he conceded. A *Newsweek* poll showed 46 percent of those queried felt the incident was reason for him to not be re-elected while

42 percent thought he should be re-elected."(3)   A different poll claimed that his home district voters would return him to office.(4)

When a congressman gets dirt on himself, he gets it on the House as well, and his peers were angry. House Minority Leader Robert H. Michael (R- Ill.) declared that Frank's scandal was becoming "a stain upon the House of Representatives... Quite frankly, if I were to have a woman prostitute in my employ, for my own self-gratification, I'd be run out of town." Democratic Chairman Ron Brown said, "The pressure is building for him to resign." A prominent Massachusetts politician flatly said, "He should get out. Democratic pollster Harrison Hickman stated that, "a lot of Democrats I know are apoplectic. There's just no way to defend him politically, and no one I know will try."(5)

The *Boston Globe*, an influential civil-libertarian newspaper and long a supporter of Frank, contrasted the gap between the congressman's public life ideals and his squalid private life. The paper then editorialized that, "Barney Frank must go." Nationally syndicated columnist, Ellen Goodman, of Boston, expressed some admiration for Barney as a congressman but advised, "Give it up."(6)

Even the gay community was at least partially hostile to what happened, feeling that gays had trouble enough with their image of promiscuity in the community linked with AIDS. Barney had been a frequent visitor in Provincetown, Mass., a gathering place for gay men. Until shortly before the story broke, Barney was often seen there in public with young hustlers whom some gays termed "Provincetown trash."

Publisher of *The Washington Blade*, Donald Michaels, commented, "A lot of people feel that what Barney did was wrong, and that he set back the cause. *Newsweek* commented on the irony of a recent statement by Frank, before the scandal broke, that, in regard to Washington ethics, "the right to privacy ends where hypocrisy begins." It was, thought the magazine, a stern rule that "sounds like his own political epitaph."(7)

Yet, perhaps remarkably, it wasn't. Barney immediately took the offensive by admitting his involvement. The points in dispute remain to be clarified. He even went farther and revealed he had used other prostitutes.   At no time did he lie, at least up to the points in question. It is this novelty, a politician being at least partly truthful, which sets him apart from so many other politicians in scandal plagued circumstances: Mills, Hays, Ted Kennedy and Gary Hart for example. Lying, when the facts are irrefutable, only plunges the subject into greater problems and focuses more attention on him. Then not only must the behavior that provoked the scandal be explained but also the lies.

A House Ethics Committee investigation was a given in this case but Frank gained a public relations advantage by personally calling for one himself before the inevitable one was ordered. His major coup in damage control, and reversal, came with a *Newsweek* cover story. All the negatives were presented of course but they were placed along side a full two page interview with the congressman. To gain such an exclusive interview with any "hot" individual, a magazine usually concedes control to the subject with regard to what is asked and what is printed for the interview. It is not unreasonable to assume that Frank exercised such control in this case.

In the interview, Frank leaned heavily on the psychic burden of growing up gay, his loneliness in the 1980s as a public figure and his difficulty in meeting people. Admitting his error in having a relationship with Gobie, Frank relied 80s buzzwords such as "I was emotionally vulnerable... I was really in a depressive state. I was turning 40... I was lonely,"(8) to turn the tide his way. While his interview is undoubtedly completely truthful if one wanted to construct a couple of pages to manipulate opinion in one's favor, one could not have done better than this interview.

As 1990 began, the scandal was forgotten. Barney Frank escaped unscathed in no small part due to a masterful offensive campaign. The congressman still had his seat. And the people of Massachusetts still had him. Before the scandal broke, Barney was pursuing purported mismanagement in the Department of Housing and Urban Development (HUD). However, as Patrick Buchanan so sarcastically but astutely observed, how can he attack mismanagement at HUD when he himself "couldn't spot a whorehouse in his own basement."(9)

Even though Gobie has appeared on many shows, including that of Boston's Jerry Williams, in telling his part of the story, there seems to be little damage done to Barney's reputation as a politician. In the first of Democratic Party conventions, on being presented to the floor, Barney received standing ovations.

FOOTNOTES

(Full citations in Bibliography)

SEX AND POLITICIANS

1. Shoumatoff. p. 108
2. Sex and the presidency. p.71;   Arnold. Rivers. Sanoff. Griffith. Jones. Lessard. p.10
3. Smith.
4 . Lewis.
5. Alter.
6. Ferraro.
7. Queasiness about sleaziness
8. Hechinger.
9. Griffith. Gary Hart's judgment. Lessard. p.11
10. Sex and the presidency. p.70-72, 74; This is what you thought; Private lives and open politics
11. Sex and the presidency. p.71, 74; Hall.
12. Davis. p.277; Colvin.
13. McConnell. p.304; The political pitfalls...
14. Coburn.
15. Kinsley.
16. Lessard. p.12
17. Bataille. p.111;   Maslow. p.277, 279; Kinsey. p.705; Stoller. p.26
18. Stember. p.145, 150; Millett. p.327
19. Martin. p.478
20. Ibid. p.311; Stember. p.174, 180; Lessard. p.11, 13

ADOLF HITLER

1. Payne. 1973. p.71; Davidson. p.25; Infield. p.36; Manvell, p.31
2. Infield. p.21-22; Bullock. p.392; Manvell. p.31, 225
3. Hanfstaengl. p.51-52, 123

4. Waite. p.224-225
5. Langer. p.88-89
6. Payne. 1973. p.225; Wagener. p.32
7. Infield. p.39
8. Payne. 1973. p.225-26, 254
9. Ibid. p.226; Hanfstaengl. p.162
10. Payne. 1973. p.227, 229; Wagener. p.222
11. Infield. p.51; Toland. p.229; Waite. p.227
12. Infield. p.41, 57; Waite. p.238; Davidson. p.25
13. Infield. p.58-60
14. Waite. p.231-232, 241
15. Ibid. p.241
16. Ibid. p. 229; Infield. p.55,118
17. Infield. p.112; Waite. p.229; Speer. p.92
18. Toland. p.274, 376
19. Manvell. p.81; Toland. p.365, 375
20. Manvell. p.31,117; Waite. p.233; Langer. p.134
21. Infield. p.115

JOSEPH STALIN

1. Hyde. p.39,59
2. Payne. 1966. p.99
3. de Jonge. p.73-74, 221; Delbars. p.53
4. de Jonge. p.92
5. McNeal. p.45; de Jonge. p.144; Hyde. p.169
6. Hyde. p.260
7. McNeal. p.47, 162; Hingley. p.227
8. Hingley. p.227; Romano-Petrova. p.21
9. de Jonge. p.295-296; Grey. p.493; Romano-Petrova. p.23-25; Payne. 1966. p.412
10. Hingley. p.229; Hyde. p.289; Grey. p.493; Delbars. p.223; de Jonge. p.295; Ulam. p.531n
11. McNeal. p.165
12. Romano-Petrova. p.xv-xvi, 27, 28
13. Hingley. p.230

IDI AMIN

1. Martin. p.17
2. Donald. p.31-34; Kyemba. p.146-47
3. Donald. p.35; Kyemba. p.148, 165
4. Donald. p.11-13; Kyemba. p.163
5. Kyemba. p.43, 148; Donald. p.36; Melady. p.144
6. Listowel. p.18; Kyemba. p.149
7. Kyemba. p.150, 159; Melady. p.144
8. Graham. p.160; Melady. p.143-144; Avirgan. p.32; Smith. p.135; Donald. p.30
9. Kyemba. p.55, 161; Kiwanuka. p.7; Donald. p.40
10. Donald. p.43; Kyemba. p.164; Melady. p.169
11. Melady. p.143-44; Donald. p.43
12. Melady. p.169
13. Kyemba. p.165

JOHN F. KENNEDY

1. Collier. 1984. p.65; Blair. p.34
2. Collier. 1984. p 67, 90; David. p.35; Martin. p.50
3. Collier. 1984. p.124; Goodwin. p.634; David. p.39; Davis. p.93, 137; Martin. p.109
4. Blair. p.286, 329, 348-49
5. Goodwin. p723-24; Martin. p.50; Collier. 1984. p.147, 175
6. Lasky. p.107-08
7. Martin. p.399-400
8. Collier. 1984. p.197; Martin. p.51, 127, 313
9. Collier. 1984. p.209; Goodwin. p.724; Steinem. p.127
10. Martin. p.53
11. Longford. p.37; Martin. p.78, 80; Collier 1984. p.177, 197; Birmingham. p.106
12. Birmingham. p.100; Martin. p.128
13. Martin. p.94, 127, 314

14. Ibid. p.315-16; Collier. 1984. p.238, 283; Jack Kennedy's other women. p.12
15. Martin. p.313-15
16. Ibid. p.95, 318, 401; Clarke. p.271
17. von Hoffman. p.260-61; Jack Kennedy's other women; Jack Kennedy's private side; Martin. p.7, 311
18. Collier. 1984. p.283; Martin. p.316
19. Martin. p.314, 398; Davis. p.611
20. Jack Kennedy's other women
21. Martin. p.477
22. Collier. 1984. p.293; David. p.182; Davis. p.618
23. von Hoffman. p.310; Summers. 1987. p.69-70
24. Martin. p.312, 475
25. Wills. p.25; Collier. 1984. p.175; Martin. p. 313
26. Martin. p.475-76
27. Jack Kennedy's private side; Martin. p. 311-12, 401
28. Martin. p.176; Wills. p.23-24, 27, 31
29. Summers. 1987. p.67, 69; Collier. 1984. p.175; Wills. p.31
30. Clarke. p.271
31. Martin. p.199, 397; Davis. p.239, 319
32. Martin. p.398; David. p.183
33. Summers. 1987. p.7, 194-96, 201-03
34. Ibid. p.7, 64-65, 67; Knightley. p.200
35. Summers. 1987. p.67, 69, 79
36. Heymann. p.H12-H13
37. Knightley. p.104, 206; Summers. 1987. p.193
38. Jack Kennedy's other women; Davis. p.610; Martin. p.402
39. Heymann. p.c7
40. David. p.178
41. Rollyson. p.183; Steinem. p.119, 122
42. Heymann. p.H13
43. Summers. 1985. p.217, 223-24; Steinem. p.122
44. Summers. 1985. p.225
45. Martin. p.404
46. Summers. 1987. p192

ROBERT F. KENNEDY

1. David. p.33, 35, 38-9, 43
2. Schlesinger. p.591; David. p.39, 173; Summers. 1985. p.213
3. Summers. 1985. p.214-15; Summers. 1987. p.69
4. David. p.173-74; Martin. p.403
5. Steinem. p.122-23, 126
6. Ibid. p.126-27
7. Steinem. p.123, 127; Martin. p.403; Weatherby. p.201, 213, 217
8. Weatherby. p.223-24; McCann. p.53-55; Martin. p.404
9. Weatherby. p.217, 225; McCann. p.52-55; Summers. 1985. p.335-37
10. Rollyson. p.129, 132
11. David. p.176-77; Summers. 1985. p.350
12. Clarke. p.269
13. Collier. 1984. p.323
14. McCann. p.175; Martin. p.404

EDWARD M. KENNEDY

1. Burner. p.227-228; Collier. 1984. p.216; Davis. p.577; David. p.43
2. Burner. p.230
3. Collier. 1984. p.292n; Martin. p.297
4. Burns. p.335
5. Davis. p.579, 594
6. Collier. 1984. p.369
7. Davis. p.580; Burns. p.164
8. Davis. p.165, 581-82, 612
9. Ibid, p.583, 585; Collier. 1984. p.370
10. Davis. p.586-87; Burner. p.238
11. Burns. p.167; Davis. p.587-88; Sorensen. p.302
12. Davis. p1590-91, 597-98
13. Ibid, p.590, 592, 594; Burns. p.167
14. Burnner. p.238; Davis. p.590; Sherrill. p.1
15. Sherrill. p.1; Davis. p.597; Burns. p. 170
16. Davis. p.162
17. Collier. 1984. p.414, 430-36

18. Burns. p. 337
19. Clarke. p.271

BENITO MUSSOLINI

1. Monelli. p.32
2. Collier. 1971. p.38
3. Hibbert. p.7
4. Smith. p.4
5. Kirkpatrick. p.45
6. Smith. p.89
7. Kirkpatrick. p.175, 244
8. Collier. 1971. p.50
9. Fermi. p.125
10. Hibbert. p.58
11. Kirkpatrick. p.175
12. Smith. p.21
13. Dombroski. p.95-96
14. Kirkpatrick. p.324
15. Smith. p.286
16. Hibbert. p.58
17. Smith. p.160
18. Collier. 1971. p.71
19. Hibbert. p.37
20. Monelli. p.32, 149
21. Hibbert. p.37
22. Collier. 1971. p.146
23. Monelli. p.148
24. Collier. 1971. p.302-04
25. Hibbert. p.155
26. Mussolini. p.73-74

IBN SAUD

1. Howarth, p.36
2. Ibid. p.88

3. Holden. p.101
4. Howarth, p.126
5. Ibid. p.35
6. Ibid. p.36
7. Holden. p.101
8. Howarth. p.126
9. Lacey. p.90
10. Sheean. p.73
11. Lacey. p.90
12. De Caury. p.55

RAFAEL TRUJILLO

1. Ornes. p.41
2. Crassweller. 1969. p.50
3. de Galindez. p.32
4. Crassweller. 1969. p.31
5. Ornes. p.14
6. Ibid. p.215
7. Ibid. p.77
8. Ibid. p.71
9. Ibid. p.77
10. Crassweller. 1969. p.79
11. Ibid. p.80-81
12. Ibid. p.434
13. de Calindez. p.234

SUKARNO

1. Penders. p.7-8
2. Ibid. p.21
3. Adams. 1965. p.57
4. Ibid. p.143
5. Penders. p.54
6. Ibid. p.76

7. Ibid. p77
8. Legge. p.277
9. Ibid
10. Adams. 1965. p.284
11. Penders. p.153-54
12. Adams. 1967. p.79
13. Steinem. p.98-99
14. Dahn. p.188
15. Adams. 1965. p.143
16. Vittachi. p.124
17. Adams. 1965. p.11
18. Vittachi. p135
19. Legge. p.14, 143, 336
20. Adams. 1967. p.160
21. Vittachi. p.21
22. Adams. 1967. p.160

LYNDON JOHNSON

1. Caro. p.161
2. Conkin. p.50
3. Caro. p.155
4. Ibid. p.156
5. Ibid. p.197-98
6. Ibid. p.484
7. Ibid. p.485, 487-88, 491-92
8. Ibid. p.492, 684
9. Brower. p.31
10. Miller. p.31
11. Ibid. p.444-45
12. Ibid. p.445
13. Brower. p.32
14. Ibid. p.33
15. Ibid. p.35
16. LBJ's Mistress. p.42
17. Reedy. p.32

18. Dugger. p.167
19. Reedy. p.32
20. Ibid. p.36
21. Miller. p.445-446
22. Reedy. p.32, 35
23. Caro. p.303-04
24. Mooney. p.255
25. Tuohy. p.24

JEAN-BEDEL BOKASSA

1. Harmon. p.35
2. Ibid. p.36 and Shoumatoff. p.96
3. Shoumatoff. p.98
4. Ibid. p.105-06
5. Ibid. p.109
6. Ibid. p.118-19
7. My Truth. p.22

CHIANG KAI-SHEK

1. Pichon. p.11
2. Crozier. p.4, 37
3. Hahn. p.48
4. Pichon. p.25, 32
5. Ibid. p.61
6. Berkov. p.73
7. Chang. p.73
8. Hahn. p.87
9. Crozier. p.58-59
10. Hsiung. p.285
11. Hahn. p293
12. Ibid. p.77

FERDINAND MARCOS

1. Bonner. p.67
2. Seagrave. p.158
3. Ibid. p.159
4. Romulo. p.96
5. Seagrave. p.160
6. Navarro. p.105
7. Seagrave. p.214
8. Ibid. p.216
9. Ibid. p.224
10. Ibid. p.226
11. Romulo. p.103
12. Seagrave. p.228-29
13. Romulo, p.47
14. Ibid. p.101
15. Seagrave. p.227

BOB HAWKE

1. d'Alpuget. p.39
2. Ibid. p.41
3. Hurst. p.169
4. d'Alpuget. p.93
5. Hurst. p.169
6. d'Alpuget. p.198
7. Pullen. p114, 174
8. d'Alpuget. p.176
9. Ibid. p.198
10. Crawford. p.1

SHAH OF IRAN

1. de Villiers. p.54, 67

2. Hoveyda. p.101
3. Ibid. p.90
4. de Villiers. p.7
5. Laing. p.97
6. Shawcross. p.84
7. Reeves. p.94-95
8. Hoveyda. p.99-100, 102
9. Shawcross. p.339-341
10. Ibid. p.96
11. Ibid. p.339
12. Ibid. p.338
13. Ibid. p.97

WILLY BRANDT

1. Binder. p.27
2. Ibid. p.47, 60, 72-73
3. Ibid. p.88, 93-94
4. Ibid. p.143
5. Ibid. p.333
6. Ibid. p.349, 351

MAO ZEDONG

1. Chou. p.231
2. Pye. p.176
3. Ibid. p.205
4. Chung Hua-min. p.45
5. Terrill. p.230
6. Chou. p.233
7. Ibid. p.146
8. Wilson. p.185
9. Ibid. p.187; Pye. p.211
10. Wilson. p.195
11. Chung Hua-min. p.53

12. Wilson. p.196
13. Chou. p.234
14. Wilson. p.196
15. Ibid. p.436
16. Pye. p.181

ANASTASIO SOMOZA

1. Diederich. 1981. p.36
2. Ibid. p.86
3. Ibid. p.135
4. Ibid. p.211

JUAN PERON

1. Page. p.25, 79
2. Owen. p.9; Crassweller. p.68
3. Page. p.80
4. Crassweller. 1987. p.129, 132
5. Ibid. 134
6. U.S. denounces Argentina Fascism. p.32
7. Cortesi. p.59
8. Page. p.145
9. Crassweller. 1987. p.133
10. Ibid. p.88
11. Page. p.291
12. Crassweller. 1987. p.275
13. Owen. p.250
14. Page. p.339
15. Ibid. p.373
16. Owen. p.181
17. Page. p.293

MUAMMAR QADDAFI

1. Harris. p.53-54
2. Ibid. p.53
3. Cooley. p.151
4. Blundy. p.22
5. Ibid. p.22-23

KING HUSSEIN

1. Snow. p.41-42, 49-50, 66
2. Ibid. p.66-67, 138-140
3. Ibid. p.140-41, 143, 145

JOMO KENYATTA

1. Murray-Brown. p.79, 91, 93
2. Ibid. p.199, 213-214, 216
3. Ibid. p.229, 247, 286

THE DUVALIERS

1. Diedrich. 1969. p.45, 368-369, 378
2. Abbott, p.79
3. Diederich. 1969. p.372-373
4. Abbott. p.163
5. Ibid. p.167
6. Ibid. p.204
7. Ibid. p.221
8. Ibid. p.322
9. Ibid. p.364

DAVID BEN-GURION

1. Bar-Zohar. p.11
2. Ibid. p.20
3. Kurzman. p.98
4. Bar-Zohar. p.36
5. Edelman. p.67
6. Bar-Zohar. p.118
7. Teveth. p.267
8. Kurzman. p.196
9. Teveth. p.476-477
10. Ibid. p.402
11. Kurzman. p.232, 254, 350
12. Bar-Zohar. p.276-279
13. Kurzman. p.229-230
14. Ibid. p.421; Bar-Zohar. p.280
15. Bar-Zohar. p.119
16. Ibid.

ZULFIQAR ALI BHUTTO

1. Burki. p.24
2. Mukerjee. p.28
3. Ibid. p.32-33

ANTHONY EDEN

1. James. p.61, 65, 67, 73
2. Ibid. p.131-32
3. Ibid. p.356-57
4. Carlton. p.318

ROMULO BETANCOURT

1. Alexander. p.650
2. Ibid. p.577-78

SALVADOR ALLENDE

1. Davis. p.49-50

NELSON ROCKEFELLER

1. Desmond. p.32
2. Kramer. p.72
3. Collier. 1976. p.200
4. Persico. p.34-35
5. Collier. 1976. p.346
6. Ibid. p.349
7. Ibid. p.348-49
8. Desmond. p.318
9. Collier. 1976. p.350
10. Ibid. p.353
11. Rodgers. p.67
12. Collier. 1976. p.451
13. Persico. p.288, 292
14. Jackovich. p.20
15. Lipez. p66

CARLOS MENEM

1. Orth. p.196
2. Ibid. p.201
3. Ibid. p.202
4. Ibid. p.200
5. Ibid. p.202
6. de Lama; Orth. p.202
7. Ibid. p.203

PIERRE TRUDEAU

1. Gwyn. p.205-206
2. Ibid. p.205
3. Trudeau. p.48-49
4. Gwyn. p.205
5. Ibid. p.206
6. Ibid. p.205
7. Trudeau. p.53-55
8. Ibid. p.234-35
9. Gwyn. p.202; Trudeau. p.249
10. Gwyn. p.206

KWAME NKRUMAH

1. Timothy. p.161, 187-88
2. Marais. p.79-81
3. Timothy. p.187; Marais. p.98
4. Marais. p.48, 92, 98
5. Ibid. p.88

FIDEL CASTRO

1. Szulc. p.98; Matthews. p.27
2. Bourne. p.73
3. Matthews. p.26-27
4. Szulc. p.240-41; Bourne. p.102
5. Bourne. p.110
6. Ibid. p.128, 131
7. Ibid. p.173-74
8. Ibid. p.180
9. Ibid. p.210
10. Ibid. p.200

HENRY KISSINGER

1. Kamath. p.83-84
2. Ibid. p.85
3. Ephron. p.86
4. Ibid.
5. Kamath. p.182; Ashman. p.131
6. Kalb. p.10; Ephron. p.126
7. Kalb. p.10
8. Hersh. p.115
9. Ashman. p.124, 137-38
10. Ephron. p.129
11. Kalb. p.10; Kamath. p.183
12. Ephron. p.128; Kalb. p.10; Kamath. p.182, 183-84
13. Kamath. p.183
14. Ibid; Ashman. p.131, 183
15. Kamath. p.184

DWIGHT EISENHOWER

1. Miller. p.339-40
2. Morgan. p.15
3. Lyon. p.387-88
4. Morgan. p.23
5. Ambrose. p.190
6. Brendon. p.89
7. Morgan. p.120; Brendon. p.124
8. Brendon. p.90, 105, 125
9. Burk. p.96
10. Ambrose. p.280; Morgan. p.156, 176-77
11. Morgan. p.180
12. Ibid. p.157, 181, 209
13. Brendon. p.192
14. Morgan. p.215
15. Brendon. p.192
16. Ibid.

17. Eisenhower. p.198-99

WILBUR MILLS

1. Mills called occupant...; Crewdson. Oct. 10
2. Crewdson. Oct. 11; Mills says he's still embarrassed
3. Staid image of Mills in Arkansas
4. Reed.
5. Wilbur's Argentine firecracker
6. Tidal Basin Bombshell... and Stripper reports...
7. Mills does a walk-on with stripper
8. Mills derided in Congress; Wilbur in nightgown
9. Mills, back at post...; Mills congressional career...

CECIL PARKINSON

1. Parkinson admits love affair. p.1
2. Bevins. Oct. 7
3. Evans; Parkinson given ovation...
4. Chance of Parkinson survival dwindles
5. Dowden. Oct. 12; Smith
6. The Parkinson affair
7. I'm glad it's ended
8. Dowden. Oct. 14
9. Haviland; Bevins. Oct. 17
10. I'm glad it's ended; Dowden. Oct. 14
11. Hamilton; Kettle
12. The case for Parkinson
13. Dowden. Oct. 12
14. Keays claims... and Inquiry sought...
15. News blackout...; Horsnell; Keays...; Inquiry sought...
16. Inquiry sought...

WAYNE HAYS

1. Paper says an aide...
2. Rep. Hays defers...
3. Horrock
4. Ibid
5. Ibid
6. Franks. May 26
7. Ibid
8. Report in magazine; Horrock
9. House out of order; Madden
10. Crewdson. May 27; Hays terms overdose...
11. Stevens
12. Franks. June 12; Hays terms overdose...
13. Lyons. Aug. 14; Lyons. Spt. 2
14. Lyons. Sept. 3
15. The Hays scandal

FRANKLIN ROOSEVELT

1. Morgan. p.202; Lash. p.146
2. Miller. p.113, 140, 153
3. Roosevelt. p.86, 89
4. Miller. p.153; Lash. p.226
5. Roosevelt. p.95-96; Miller. p.154
6. Lash. p.220, 227; Miller. p.152
7. Miller. p.154
8. Ibid. p.493-94
9. Roosevelt. p.102-03
10. Ibid. p.294
11. Lash. p.22
12. Lash. p.723
13. Morgan. p.203-256

GARY HART

1. Dionne. May 3
2. Ibid. May 4
3. Ibid. May 4, May 5
4. Gary Hart's judgment
5. Toner; Dionne. May 7
6. Toner; Meilsin
7. Dionne. May 8; Washington Post...
8. Miami Herald editorial...
9. Hart photo
10. Hart spent two night...
11. Ibid
12. Dowd
13. Wall, p.555-56

ANDREAS PAPANDREOU

1. Dreifus. p.22
2. Cowell
3. Ibid
4. Dreifus, p.22
5. Anastasi; Hanging it out in public
6. Hanging it out in public; Greek prime minister...
7. McCabe. May 6, May 16

SOUSUKE UNO

1. Horvat
2. Weisman
3. Blustein. p.1
4. Ibid. p.5
5. Weisman
6. Blustein. p.5

7. Horvat; Weisman
8. Sanger. p.1
9. Kunii

JEREMY THORPE

1. Chester. p.31
2. Waugh. p.20
3. Chester. p.40, 45
4. Ibid. p.93
5. Ibid. p.129-51
6. Ibid. p.156, 158, 186
7. Ibid. p.214, 218, 226-27, 236
8. Ibid. p.244-45, 257
9. Ibid. p.310-11, 331
10. Waugh. p.9, 16
11. Ibid. p.11
12. Ibid. p.239
13. Ibid. p.239; Chester. p.10

PIERRE SEVIGNY

1. Inquiry hears...
2. Canadian cited...; Mrs. Munsinger denies...
3. Inquiry on scandal...; Stursberg. p.155-58
4. Stursberg. p.155-58
5. Canada admitted spy...
6. Stursberg. p.143; Pearson. p.181
7. Stursberg. p.145, 147, 152
8. Pearson. p.182
9. Stursberg. p.151-52
10. Ibid. p.153
11. Ibid. p.153-54
12. Ibid. p.159
13. Canadian cited...; Stursberg. p.157

14. Inquiry on scandal...; Inquiry hears...; Canada admitted spy...
15. Scandal report hits Diefenbaker
16. Stursberg. p.157

JEFFREY ARCHER

1. Oakley
2. Archer had sex...
3. Vallely. July 14
4. Oakley
5. Foster; Vallely. Archer Threatened...
6. Oakley
7. Ibid; A risk that failed
8. Vallely. July 14; Archer had sex...
9. Claims of kinky...; Star editor...
10. Vallely. July 9; Vallely. Report of meeting...
11. Did Jeffrey Archer...; Lessons for the press
12. Lessons for the press

JOHN PROFUMO

1. Summers. 1987. p.42
2. Knightley. p.2; Summers. p.4-5
3. Summers. 1987. p.97-98, 110
4. Ibid. p.107-09
5. Holledge. p.10-12
6. Summers. 1987. p.177
7. Holledge. p.15; Knightley. p.158
8. Summers. 1987. p.3
9. Ibid. p.3
10. Ibid. p.6
11. Holledge. p.67, 91, 119
12. Summers. 1987. p.177

BARNEY FRANK

1. Dedman
2. Ibid
3. Homosexuality and politics
4. Kondracke; Morganthau. p.15
5. Fritz; Morganthau. p.15
6. Goodman; Morganthau. p.15-16
7. Morganthau. p.15-16
8. Frank. p.17-18
9. Morganthau. p.16

BIBLIOGRAPHY

Abbott, Elizabeth. Haiti. *The Duvaliers and Their Legacy*. N.Y. McGraw-Hill. 1988

Adams, Cindy. *My Friend the Dictator*. Indianapolis. Bobbs-Merrill. 1967

Adams, Cindy. Sukarno: *An Autobiography as told to Cindy Adams*. Indianapolis. Bobbs-Merrill. 1965

Alexander, Robert J. *Juan Domingo Peron: A History*. Boulder, Colorado. Westview Press. 1979

Alexander, Robert J. *Romulo Betancourt and the Transformation of Venezuela*. New Brunswick. N.J. Transaction Books. 1982

Alter, Jonathan. Sex and the Presidency. *Newsweek*. 109:26 May 4, 1987

Ambrose, Stephen E. *Eisenhower 1890-1952*. N.Y. Simon and Schuster. 1983

Anastasi, Paul. Greek Premier is seeking divorce. *The New York Times*. September 16, 1988, p. 6

Archer had sex and paid for it, says prostitute. *Times* (London). July 11, 1987. p. 1

Arnold, Martin. Reporting the private lives of public men. *The New York Times*. December 8, 1974. Sec. IV. p. 2

Ashman, Charles R. *Kissinger: The Adventures of Super-Kraut*. Secaucus, N.J. Lyle Stuart, 1972

Avirgan, Tony. *War In Uganda The Legacy of Idi Amin*. Westport, CT. Lawrence Hill. 1982

Bar-Zohar, Michael. *Ben-Gurion*. London. Weidenfeld and Nicolson. 1978

Bataille, Georges. *Death and Sensuality*. N.Y. Walker. 1962

Berkov, Robert. *Strong Man of China: The Story of Chiang Kai-Shek*. Boston. Houghton Mifflin. 1938

Bevins, Anthony. Love affair puts Parkinson's future in doubt. *Times* (London). October 7, 1983. p. 1

Bevins, Anthony. Thatcher's key role on Parkinson marriage. *Times* (London). October 17, 1983. p. 1

Binder, David. *The Other German: Willy Brandt's Life and Times.* Washington, D.C. The New Republic Book Co. 1975

Birmingham, Stephen. *Jacqueline Bouvier Kennedy Onasis.* N.Y. Grosset & Dunlap. 1978

Blair, Joan. *The Search for JFK.* N.Y. Berkeley Publishing. 1976

Bluestein, Paul. The Geisha. *Los Angeles Times.* July 23, 1989, Part VI. p. 1,5

Blundy, David; Andrew Lycett. *Qaddafi and the Libyan Revolution.* London. Weidenfeld and Nicolson. 1987

Bonner, Raymond. *Waltzing with a Dictator: The Marcoses and the Making of American Policy.* N.Y. Times Books. 1987

Bourne, Peter. *Castro A Biography of Fidel Castro.* London. Macmillan. 1986

Brendon, Piers. *Ike: The Life and Times of Dwight D. Eisenhower.* London. Secker and Warburg. 1987

Brower, Montgomery. Was LBJ's final secret a son? *People Weekly.* 28:30-35. August 3, 1987

Bullock, Alan. *Hitler: A Study in Tyranny.* London. Odhams Books. 1964. rev. ed.

Burk, Robert F. *Dwight D. Eisenhower: Hero and Politician.* Boston. Twayne. 1986

Burner, David; Thomas R. West. *The Torch Is Passed: The Kennedy Brothers and American Liberalism.* N.Y. Athenaeum. 1984

Burns, James MacGregor. *Edward Kennedy and the Camelot Legacy.* N.Y. Norton. 1976

Canada admitted spy suspect by error. *The New York Times.* April 29, 1966. p. 10

Canadian cited in security case. *The New York Times.* March 13, 1966. p. 17

Carlton, David. *Anthony Eden: A Biography.* London. Allen Lane. 1981

Caro, Robert A. *The Years of Lyndon Johnson: The Path to Power.* N.Y. Alfred A. Knopf. 1983

The case for Parkinson. *Sunday Times*. (London). October 16, 1983. p. 1

Chance of Parkinson survival dwindles. *Times* (London). October 10, 1983. p. 1, 36

Chang, H.H. *Chiang Kai-Shek: Asia's Man of Destiny*. Garden City. N.Y. Doubleday. 1944

Chester, Lewis; Magnus Linklater; David May. *Jeremy Thorpe: A Secret Life*. London. Andre Deutsch. 1979

Chou, Eric. *Mao Tse-Tung: The Man and the Myth*. London. Cassell. 1982

Chung, Hua-Min; Arthur C. Miller. *Madame Mao: A Profile of Chian Ch'ing*. Hong Kong. Union Research Institute. 1968

Claims of kinky sex with prostitute are lies, jury told. *Times*. (London). July 7, 1987. p. 3

Clarke, Gerald. *Capote: A Biography*. London. Hamish Hamilton. 1988

Coburn, Judith. The issue here is whether a Don Juan would make a good president. *Mademoiselle*. 86:64 April, 1980

Collier, Peter; David Horowitz. *The Kennedys*. London. Secker & Warburg. 1984

Collier, Peter; David Horowitz. *The Rockefellers* N.Y. Holt, Rinehart and Winston. 1976

Collier, Richard. *Duce! The Rise and Fall of Benito Mussolini*. London. Collins. 1971

Colvin, Mark. Little brother. *The Age*. (Melbourne). December 10, 1983. Saturday Extra. p. 15

Cooley, John K. *Libyan Sandstorm: The Complete Account of Qaddafi's Revolution*. N.Y. Holt, Rinehart and Winston. 1982

Cortesi, Arnaldo. Portrait of a rabble rouser. *The New York Times Magazine*. February 8, 1946. p. 8+

Cowell, Alan. A hinted love affair becomes an affair of state. *The New York Times*. October 16, 1987. p. 4

Crassweller, Robert D. *Peron and the Enigmas of Argentina*. N.Y. W.W. Norton. 1987

Crassweller, Robert D. *Trujillo: The Life and Times of a Caribbean Dictator*. N.Y. Macmillan. 1969

Crawford, Hugh. Hawke admits: I cheated on Hazel. *Herald* (Melbourne). March 21, 1989. p. 1

Crewdson, John M. Embarrassed Mills acknowledges that he was in limousine stopped by police. *The New York Times*. October 11, 1974. p. 17

Crewdson, John M. Hays asserts woman got $1,000 through threats. *The New York Times*. May 27, 1976. p. 22

Crewdson, John M. Mills in seclusion. *The New York Times*. October 10, 1974. p. 23

Crozier, Brian. *The Man Who Lost China*. N.Y. Charles Scribner's Sons. 1976

Dahn, Bernard. *Sukarno and the Struggle for Indonesian Independence*. Ithaca. N.Y. Cornell University Press. 1969

d'Alpuget, Blanche. *Robert Hawke: A Biography*. East Melbourne. Victoria. Schwartz. 1982

David, Lester. *Bobby Kennedy: The Making of a Folk Hero*. N.Y. Dodd, Mead. 1986

Davidson, Eugene. *The Making of Adolf Hitler*. London. MacDonald and Jane's. 1977

Davis, John H. *The Kennedys: Dynasty and Disaster 1848-1983*. N.Y. McGraw-Hill. 1984

Davis, Nathaniel. *The Last Two Years of Salvador Allende*. Ithaca. N.Y. Cornell University Press. 1985

Dedman, Bill. TV movie led to prostitute's disclosure. *Washington Post*. August 27, 1989. p. A6

de Galindez, Jesus. *The Era of Trujillo* Tucson. Arizona. The University of Arizona Press. 1973

De Gaury, Gerald. *Faisal: King of Saudi Arabia*. London. Arthur Baker. 1966

de Jonge, Alex. *Stalin and the Shaping of the Soviet Union*. London. Collins. 1986

de Lama, George. Argentina's Menem takes fast lane to top. *Chicago Tribune*. May 18, 1989. p. 5

Delbars, Yves. *The Real Stalin*. London. George Allen & Unwin. 1953

Desmond, James. *Nelson Rockefeller: A Political Biography*. N.Y. Macmillan. 1964 de Viliers, Gerard. *The Imperial Shah: An Informal Biography*. London. Weidnefeld and Nicolson. 1975

Did Archer need cold sex with a prostitute. *Times* (London). July 24, 1987. p. 1

Diederich, Bernard; Al Burt. *Papa Doc: Haiti and Its Dictator*. London. the Bodley Head. 1969

Diederich, Bernard. *Somoza and the Legacy of U.S. Involvement in Central America*. N.Y. E.P. Dutton. 1981

Dionne, E.J. Jr. Gary Hart: the elusive front-runner. *The New York Times Magazine*. May 3, 1987. p. 30+

Dionne, E.J. Jr. Hart will reportedly quit race. *The New York Times*. May 8, 1987. p. A1, B6

Dionne, E.J. Jr. Hart's campaign reported in peril over tryst story. *The New York Times*. May 5, 1987. p. 1, B6

Dionne, E.J. Jr. Paper and Hart in dispute over article. *The New York Times*. May 4, 1987. p. A16

Dionne, E.J. Jr. Wife joins Hart in New Hampshire. *The New York Times*. May 7, 1987. p. A1, B16

Dombrowski, Roman. *Mussolini: Twilight and Fall*. London. William Heinemann. 1956

Donald, Trevor. *Idi Amin's Women*. Melbourne. Gazelle Books. 1978

Dowd, Maureen. Hart challenges motives of critics. *The New York Times*. January 29, 1988. p. A12

Dowden, Richard. I implored him to tell Thatcher. *Times* (London). October 14, 1983. p. 1, 28

Dowden, Richard. Miss Keays nearly the Bermondsey candidate. *Times* (London). October 12, 1983. p. 1, 34

Dreifus, Claudia. Margarita Papandreou. *The Progressive*. 51:24 December, 1987

Dugger, Ronnie. *The Politician: The Life and Times of Lyndon Johnson*. N.Y. Norton. 1982

Edelman, Maurice. *Ben Gurion: A Political Biography*. London. Hodder and Stoughton. 1964

Eisenhower, David. *Eisenhower At War, 1943-1945*. London. Collins. 1986

Ephron, Nora. The making of a sex symbol. *McCall's*. 100:86-87+. November, 1972

Evans, Richard. Parkinson affair secretary sues for libel. *Times*. (London). October 7, 1983. p. 28

Fermi, Laura. *Mussolini*. Chicago. The University of Chicago Press. 1961

Ferraro, Geraldine. No celibates, please. *Life*. 10:72 August, 1987

Foster, Howard. Tories' deputy chairman lied and lied, court told. *Times* (London). July 8, 1987. p. 3

Frank, Barney. I was emotionally vulnerable. *Newsweek*. 114:17-18. September 25, 1989

Franks, Lucinda. Hays, in reversal, admits affair with staff member. *The New York Times*. May 26, 1976. p. 1, 16

Franks, Lucinda. Hays pill dose called 10 times usual. *the New York Times*. June 12, 1976. p. 1, 24

Fritz. Sara. Pressure increasing on Frank to resign. *Los Angeles Times*. September 20, 1989. p. 16

Gwyn, Richard. *The Northern Magus: Pierre Trudeau and Canadians*. Toronto. McClelland and Stewart. 1980

Gary Hart's judgment. *The New York Times*. May 5, 1987. p. 34

Goodman, Ellen. Oil slick is starting to cover Barney and it doesn't scrub off. *Los Angeles Times*. September 21, 1989. pt II, p. 7

Goodwin, Doris Kearns. *The Fitzgeralds and the Kennedys*. N.Y. Simon and Schuster. 1987

Graham, Iain. *Amin and Uganda: A Personal Memoir*. London. Granada. 1980

Greek Prime Minister files suit for divorce. *The New York Times*. March 31, 1989. p. A9

Grey, Ian. *Stalin: Man of History*. London. Weidenfled and Nicolson. 1979

Griffith. Thomas. Sex, privacy and journalism. *Time*. 129:90 June 8, 1987

Hahn, Emily. *Chiang Kai-Shek: An Unauthorized Biography*. Garden City. N.Y. Doubleday. 1955

Hall, Trish. Infidelity and women: shifting patterns. *The New York Times*. June 1, 1987. p. B8

Hamilton, Alan. Our man must stay say voters. *Times* (London). October 17, 1983. p. 28

Hanfstaengl, Ernst. *Hitler: the Missing Years*. London. Eyre & Spottiswoode, 1957

Hanging it out in public. *Time*. 132:39 December 19, 1988

Harmon, Jeff B. His former majesty, Bokassa. *Harper's Magazine*. 260:34-39. May, 1980

Harris, Lillian Crain. *Libya: Qaddafi's Revolution and the Modern State*. Boulder. Colorado. Westview Press. 1986

Hart photo. *The New York Times*. May 31, 1987. p. 24

Hart spent 2 nights with Rice, her friend says. *The New York Times*. June 9, 1987. p. 18

Haviland, Julian. Parkinson's affair cost him foreign secretary's post. *Times* (London). October 11, 1983. p. 1

The Hays scandal. *The Nation*. 222:674-676. June 5, 1976

Hays terms overdose of pills a mishap, not suicide. *The New York Times*. July 4, 1976. p. 30

Hechinger, Fred M. The new moralism. *The New York Times*. July 7, 1976. p. 33

Hersh, Seymour M. *The Price of Power: Kissinger in the Nixon White House*. N.Y. Summit Books. 1983

Heymann, David. *A Woman Named Jackie*. 1989. (excerpted in the *Vancouver Sun*. June 9, 1989. p. C6-C7 and June 10, 1989. p. H12-H13)

Hibbert, Christopher. *Benito Mussolini: A Biography*. London. Longmans. 1962

Hingley, Ronald. *Joseph Stalin: Man and Legend*. London. Hutchinson. 1974

Holden, David. *The House of Saud*. London. Sidgwick & Jackson. 1981.

Holledge, James. *Vice On Trial*. London. Horwitz. n.d. 1963?

Homosexuality and politics: A Newsweek poll. *Newsweek*. 114:19. September 25, 1989.

Horrock, Nicholas M. U.S. investigating charges on Hays. *The New York Times*. May 25, 1976. p. 1, 19

Horsnell, Michael. Parkinson to face secrets act inquiry. *Times* (London). October 17, 1985. p. 1

Horvat, Andrew. Uno's sins? *Vancouver Sun*. June 14, 1989. p. A3

House out of order. *The New York Times*. May 29, 1976. p. 22

Hoyeda, Fereydoun. *The Fall of the Shah*. London. Weidenfeld and Nicolson. 1979

Howarth, David. *The Desert King: A Life of Ibn Saud*. London. Collins. 1964

Hesiung, S.I. *The Life of Chiang Kai-Shek*. London. Peter Davies. 1948

Hunger, Marjorie. Mills, back at post, makes a sobriety vow. *The New York Times*. May 6, 1975. p. 10

Hurst, John. *Hawke*. London. Angus & Robertson. 1979

Hyde, H. Montgomery. *Stalin: The History of a Dictator*. N.Y. Farrar, Strauss and Giroux. 1971

I'm glad it's over. *Sunday Times* (London). October 16, 1983. p. 17

Infield, Glenn B. *Eva and Adolf*. London. New English Library. 1975

Inquiry hears woman was spy. *The New York Times*. April 26, 1966. p. 19

Inquiry on scandal ordered by Pearson. *The New York Times*. March 12, 1966. p. 1, 5

Inquiry sought into Keays complaints. *Times* (London). February 5, 1987. p. 3

Jack Kennedy's other women. *Time*. 106:11-12. December 29, 1975

Jack Kennedy's private side. *Newsweek*. 109:22 June 8, 1982

Jackovich, Karen G. Megan Marshack. *People Weekly*. 11:20-21. February 26, 1979

James, Robert Rhodes. *Anthony Eden*. London. Weidenfeld and Nicolson. 1986

Jones, Alex S. Stakeout of Hart seen as fair game. *The New York Times*. May 5, 1987. p. B7

Kalb, Marvin; Bernard Kalb. *Kissinger*. Boston. Little, Brown. 1974

Kamath, M.V. *Kissinger: The Incomplete Diplomat*. Bombay. Jaico Publishing House. 1975

Keays claims by-election chance was blocked. *Times* (London). October 11, 1985

Keays tells of cash wrangle. *Times* (London). October 10, 1985. p.

Kettle, Martin. Sex and politics. *Sunday Times* (London). October 16, 1983. p. 1

Kinsey, Alfred C. *Sexual Behavior in the Human Female.* Philadelphia. W.B. Saunders. 1975

Kinsley, Michael. Yes, we have no bananas. *New Republic.* 181:12+. November 24, 1979

Kirkpatrick, Ivone. *Mussolini: Study of a Demagogue.* London. Odhams Books. 1964

Kiwanuka, Semkula. *Amin and the Tragedy of Uganda.* Munich. Weltforum Verlag. 1979

Knightley, Phillip; Caroline Kennedy. *An Affair of State: The Profumo Case and the Framing of Stephen Ward.* London. Jonathan Cape. 1987

Kondracke, Morton. Lynch mob should quit, not Barney. *Los Angeles Times.* September 25, 1989. pt II, p. 5

Kramer, Michael; Sam Roberts. *I Never Wanted to be Vice-President of Anything! An Investigative Biography of Nelson Rockefeller.* N.Y. Basic Books. 1976

Kunii, Irene. Japan's PM to quit. *Vancouver Sun.* July 24, 1989. p. 1

Kurzman, Dan. *Ben-Gurion: Prophet of Fire.* N.Y. Simon and Schuster. 1983

Kyemba, Henry. *State of Blood: The Inside Story of Idi Amin.* London. Corgi. 1978

Lacey, Robert. *The Kingdom.* London. Hutchinson. 1981

Laing, Margaret. *The Shah.* London. Sidgwick & Jackson. 1977

Langer, Walter C. *The Mind of Adolf Hitler: The Secret Wartime Report.* N.Y. Basic Books. 1972

Lash, Joseph P. *Eleanor and Franklin.* London. Andre Deutsch. 1972

Lash, Joseph P. *Eleanor: The Years alone.* London. Andre Deutsch. 1973

Lasky, Victor. *J.F.K. The Man and the Myth.* New Rochelle. N.Y. Arlington House. 1963

LBJ's mistress signs with Contemporary. *Publishers Weekly.* 232:42-43. October 16, 1987

Legge, J.D. *Sukarno: A Political Biography*. London. Allen Lane The Penguin Press. 1972

Lessard, Suzannah. Kennedy's woman problem: women's Kennedy problem. *Washington Monthly*. 11:10-14. December 1979

Lessons for the press. *Times* (London). July 25, 1987. p. 9

Lewis, Anthony. Degrading the press. *The New York Times*. May 5, 1987. p. 35

Lipez, Richard. Way to go. *The Progressive*. 43:66 April, 1979

Listowell, Judith. *Amin*. Dublin. IUP books. 1973

Longford, Lord. *Kennedy*. London. Weidenfeld and Nicolson. 1976

Lyon, Peter. *Eisenhower: Portrait of the Hero*. Boston. Little, Brown. 1974

Lyons, Richard D. Hays tried for 2 months to end inquiry in House. *The New York Times*. September 3, 1976. p. 6

Lyons, Richard D. Hays under fire, quits House seat. *The New York Times*. September 2, 1976. p. 1, 15

Lyons, Richard D. Hays withdraws from House race. *The New York Times*. August 14, 1976. p. 1, 18

Madden, Richard L. Some in House see irony in Hays plight. *The New York Times*. May 26, 1976. p. 16

Manvell, Roger; Heinrich Fraenkel. *Hitler: The Man and the Myth*. London. Granada. 1978

Marais, Genoveva. *Kwame Nkrumah: As I Knew Him*. Chichester. Eng. Janay. 1972

Martin, David. *General Amin*. London. Faber and Faber. 1974

Martin, Ralph G. *A Hero for Our Time: An Intimate Story of the Kennedy Years*. N.Y. Macmillan. 1983

Matthews, Herbert L. *Castro: A Political Biography*. London. Allen Lane The Penguin Press. 1969

Maslow, A.H. Self-esteem (dominance-feeling) and sexuality in women. *The Journal of Social Psychology*. 1942. 16:259-94

McCabe, Aileen. Greek PM's wedding hits a snag. *Vancouver Sun*. June 16, 1989. p.A7

McCabe, Aileen. The politics of love. *Vancouver Sun*. May 6, 1989. p. B1

McCann, Graham. *Marilyn Monroe*. Oxford. Polity Press. 1988

McConnell, James V. *Understanding Human Behavior*. 5th ed. N.Y. Holt, Rinehart and Winston. 1986

McNeal, Robert H. *Stalin: Man and Ruler*. Washington Square. N.Y. N.Y. University Press, 1988

Meislin, Richard J. Poll finds infidelity a lesser evil. *The New York Times*. May 8, 1987. p. A1, B6

Melady, Thomas; Margaret Melady. *Idi Amin Dada: Hitler in Africa*. Kansas City. Sheed Andrews and McMeel. 1977

Miami Herald editorial asserts that Hart lied. *The New York Times*. May 8, 1987. p. B6

Miller, Merle. *Lyndon: An Oral Biography*. N.Y. Putnam's. 1980

Miller, Merle. *Plain Speaking: An Oral Biography of Harry S. Truman*. London. Victor Gollancz. 1974

Miller, Nathan. *FDR: An Intimate History*. Garden City. N.Y. Doubleday. 1983

Millett, Kate. *Sexual Politics*. N.Y. Doubleday. 1970

Mills called occupant of car police stopped. *The New York Times*. October 9, 1974. p. 13

Mills congressional career coming to a quiet conclusion. *The New York Times*. December 31, 1976. p. A8

Mills derided in congress. *The New York Times*. December 3, 1974. p. 1, 32

Mills does a walk-on with stripper. *The New York Times*. December 2, 1974. p. 42

Mills says he's still embarrassed. *The New York Times*. October 17, 1974. p. 28

Miss Keays denies statement. *Times* (London). November 23, 1985. p. 2

Monelli, Paolo. *Mussolini: An Intimate Life*. London. Thames and Hudson. 1953

Mooney, Booth. *LBJ: An Irreverent Chronicle*. N.Y. Thomas Y. Crowell. 1976

Morgan, Kay Summersby. *Past Forgetting: My Love Affair with Dwight D. Eisenhower*. London. Collins. 1977

Morgan, Ted. *FDR: A Biography*. N.Y. Simon and Schuster. 1985

Morganthau, Tom. Barney Frank's story. *Newsweek*. 114:14-16. September 25, 1989

314--Affairs of State

Mrs. Munsinger denies she was a spy. *The New York Times*. March 16, 1966. p. 14

Mukerjee, Dilip. *Zulfiqar Ali Bhutto: Quest for Power*. India: Vikas Publishing House. 1972

Murray-Brown, Jeremy. *Kenyatta*. 2nd ed. London. George Allen & Unwin. 1979

Mussolini, Rachele. *The Real Mussolini*. Hampshire. Eng.:Saxon House. 1974

My truth: Bokassa on Giscard. *Harper's Magazine*. 271:22, 24-25. October. 1985

News blackout on burglary, Keays alleges. *Times* (London). October 12, 1985. p. 3

Oakley, Robin. Archer resigns over payment offered to girl. *Times* (London). October 27, 1986. p. 1, 20

One scandal after another. *Newsweek*. 112:32. December 12, 1988

Ornes, German E. *Trujillo: Little Caesar of the Caribbean*. N.Y. Thomas Nelson and Sons. 1958

Orth, Maureen. Charisma Argentina. *Vanity Fair*. 52:196-203+. November 1989

Owen, Frank. *Peron: His Rise and Fall*. London. The Cresset Press. 1957

Page, Joseph A. *Peron: A Biography*. N.Y. Random House. 1983

Paper says an aide to House unit calls its head her lover. *The New York Times*. May 23, 1976. p. 33

Parkinson admits love affair. *Times* (London). October 6, 1983, p. 1, 2

The Parkinson affair. *Times* (London). October 7, 1983. p. 15

Parkinson given ovation at dinner. *Times* (London). October 8, 1983. p. 1

Payne, Robert. *The Life and Death of Adolf Hitler*. London. Jonathan Cape. 1973

Payne, Robert. *The Rise and Fall of Stalin*. London. W.H Allen. 1966

Pearson, Lester. *Mike: The Memoirs of the Right Honourable Lester B. Pearson*. vol. 3. 1957-1968. London. Victor Gollancz. 1975

Pedrosa, Carmen Navarro. *Imelda Marcos*. London. Weidenfeld and Nicolson. 1987

Penders, C.L.M. *The Life and Times of Sukarno*. London. Sidgwick & Jackson. 1974

Persico, Joseph E. *The Imperial Rockefeller: A Biography of Nelson A. Rockefeller*. N.Y. Simon and Schuster. 1982

Pichon, P.Y. Loh. *The Early Chiang Kai-Shek: A Study of his Personality and Politics, 1887-1924*. N.Y. Columbia University Press. 1971

The politicial pitfalls of life at the top. *Times* (London). October 27, 1986. p. 2

Private lives and open politics. *Macleans's*. 101:49. January 4, 1988

Pullen, Robert. *Bob Hawke: A Portrait*. Sydney. Methuen of Australia. 1980

Pye, Lucain W. *Mao Tse-Tung: the Man in the Leader*. N.Y. Basic Books. 1976

Queasiness about sleaziness. *New Republic*. 191:4. November 1984

Reed. Roy. Mills forced to campaign hard following Tidal Basin incident. *The New York Times*. October 17, 1974. p. 1, 19

Reedy, George. *Lyndon B. Johnson: A Memoir*. N.Y. Andrews and McMeel. 1982

Reeves, Minou. *Behind the Peacock Throne*. London. Sidgwick & Jackson. 1986

Rep. Hays defers trip, denies aide's accusation. *The New York Times*. May 24, 1976. p. 25

Report in magazine. *The New York Times*. June 14, 1976. p. 23

The return of the 'Butcher of Bangui'. *Newsweek*. 108:45. November 1986

A Risk that failed. *Times* (London). October 27, 1986. p. 17

Rivers, Caryl. Where women are credit. *The New York Times*. June 8, 1976. p. 33

Rodgers, William. *Rockefeller's Follies: An Unauthorized view of Nelson A. Rockefeller*. N.Y. Stein and Day. 1966

Rollyson, Carl E. Jr. *Marilyn Monroe: A Life of the Actress*. Ann Arbor. UMI Research Press. 1986

Romano-Petrova, N. *Stalin's Doctor, Stalin's Nurse*. Princeton. N.J. The Kingston Press. 1984

Romula, Beth Day. *Inside the Palace: The Rise and Fall of Ferdinand and Imelda Marcos*. N.Y. Putnam's. 1987

Roosevelt, Elliott; James Brough. *The Roosevelts of Hyde Park: An Untold Story*. London. W.H. Allen. 1974

Roosevelt, James. *My Parents: A Different View*. London. W.H. Allen. 1977

Sanger, David E. Uno is Japan's no. 1 women's issue. *The New York Times*. July 3, 1989. p. 1, 4

Sanof, Alvin P. Are the sex lives of politicians now fair game? *U.S. News & World Report*. 102:12. June 15, 1987

Scandal report hits Diefenbaker. *The New York Times*. September 24, 1966. p. 1, 4

Schlesinger, Arthur M. Jr. *Robert Kennedy and his Times*. London. Andre Deutsch. 1978

Seagrave, Sterling. *The Marcos Dynasty*. N.Y. Harper & Row. 1988

Sex and the presidency. *Life*. 10:70-72+. August 1987

Shawcross, William. *The Shah's Last Ride: The Fate of an Ally*. N.Y. Simon and schuster. 1988

Sheean, Vincent. *Faisal: the King and his Kingdom*. Tavistock. Eng.:University Press of Arabia. 1975

Sherrill, Robert. *The Last Kennedy*. N.Y. The Dial Press. 1976

Shoumatoff, Alex. *African Madness*. N.Y. Alfred A. Knopf. 1988

Smith, Denis Mack. *Mussolini*. London. Weidenfeld and Nicolson. 1981

Smith, Geoffey. Commentary. *Times'* (London). October 13, 1983. p. 4

Smith, George Ivan. *Ghosts of Kampala*. London. Weidenfeld and Nicolson. 1980

Snow, Peter. *Hussein: A Biography*. London. Barrie & Jenkins. 1972

Sorensen, Theodore. *The Kennedy Legacy*. London. Weidenfeld and Nicolson. 1969

Speer, Albert. *Inside the Third Reich*. London. Weidenfeld and Nicolson, 1970

Staid image of Mills in Arkansas. *The New York Times*. October 11, 1974. p. 17

Star editor sitting in court. *Times* (London). July 11, 1987. p. 3

Steinem, Gloria. *Marilyn*. N.Y. Henry Holt. 1986

Stember, Charles Herbert. *Sexual Racism*. N.Y. Elsevier. 1976

Stevens, William K. Some backers waver as Hays visits home. *The New York Times*. May 29, 1976. p. 21

Stoller, Robert. *Sexual Excitement: The Dynamics of Erotic Life*. N.Y. Pantheon. 1979

Stripper reports Tidal Basin show is opposed by Mills. *The New York Times*. November 19, 1974. p. 15

Stursberg, Peter. *Diefenbaker: Leadership Lost 1962-1967*. Toronto. University of Toronto Press. 1976

Summers, Anthony. *Goddess: The Secret Lives of Marilyn Monroe*. London. Gollancz. 1985

Summers, Anthony; Stephen Dorrill. *Honeytrap: The Secret Worlds of Stephen Ward*. London. Weidenfeld and Nicolson. 1987

Szulc, Tad. *Fidel: A Critical Portrait*. London. Hutchinson. 1986

Taseer, Salmaan. *Bhutto: A Political Biography*. London. Ithaca Press. 1986

Terrill, Ross. *Mao: A Biography*. N.Y. Harper & Row. 1980

Teveth, Shabtai. *Ben-Gurion: The Burning Ground 1886-1948*. Boston. Houghton Mifflin. 1987

This is what you thought. *Glamour*. 85:129. November 1987

Tidal Basin bombshell gets $3,000-a week job. *The New York Times*. December 2, 1974. p.42

Timothy, Bankole. *Kwame Nkrumah - From Cradle to Grave*. Dorchester. Eng.:The Gavin Press. 1981

Toland, John. *Adolf Hitler*. Garden City. N.Y. Doubleday. 1976

Toner, Robin. Hart conceding error, says he did nothing immoral. *The New York Times*. May 6, 1987. p. A1, B8

Trudeau, Margaret. *Beyond Reason*. N.Y. Paddington Press. 1979

Tuohy, William. *Dangerous Company*. N.Y. Morrow. 1987

Ulam, Adam B. *Stalin: The Man and his Era*. N.Y. The Viking Press. 1973

U.S. denounces fascism. *Life*. 20:27-33. February 25, 1946

Vallely, Paul. Archer accused of changing alibi three times. *Times* (London). July 9, 1987. p.3

Vallely, Paul. Archer threatened to use political influence. *Times* (London). July 10, 1987. p. 3

Vallely, Paul. Report of meeting with prostitute was true say journalists. *Times* (London). July 10, 1987. p. 3

Valley, Paul. Sunday paper paid prostitute 6,000 pounds for story on Archer. *Times* (London). July 14, 1987. p. 3

Vittachi, Tarzie. *The Fall of Sukarno*. London. Andre Deutsch. 1967

Von Hoffman, Nicholas. *Citizen Cohn*. N.Y. Doubleday. 1988

Wagener. Otto. *Hitler: Memoirs of a Confidant*. New Haven. Yale University Press. 1985

Waite, Robert G.L. *The Psychopathic God of Adolf Hitler*. N.Y. Basic Books. 1977

Wall, James M. In search of a moral politician. *The Christian Century*. 91:555-56. May 22, 1974

Washington Post reports liaison. *The New York Times*. May 8, 1987. p. B7

Waugh, Auberon. *The Last Word: An Eye Witness Account of the Trial of Jeremy Thorpe*. London. Michael Joseph. 1980

Weatherby, W.J. *Conversations with Marilyn*. London. Robson Books. 1976

Weisman, Steven R. Ex-geisha accuses Premier. *The New York Times*. June 10, 1989. p. A7

Wilbur in nighttown. *Newsweek*. 84:21-23. December 16, 1974

Wilbur's Argentine firecracker. *Time*. 104:21-22. October 21, 1974

Wills, Gary. *The Kennedy Imprisonment: A Meditation on Power*. Boston. Little, Brown. 1981

Wilson, Dick. *Mao: The People's Emperor*. London. Hutchinson. 1979

INDEX